So You W

So You Want to Be a Politician

edited by Shane Greer

First published in Great Britain in 2010 by
Biteback Publishing Ltd
Heal House
375 Kennington Lane
London
SE11 5QY

ISBN 978-1-84954-025-4

10 9 8 7 6 5 4 3 2 1

A CIP catalogue record for this book is available from the British Library.
Set in Sabon
Printed and bound in Great Britain by TJ International Ltd

Contents

Acknowledgements

Putting this book together has been a labour of love. But without the incredible generosity of the many authors who joined me in this endeavour, it would quite simply never have taken form. With that in mind, I would like to extend my heartfelt thanks to Luke Akehurst, Jessica Asato, Robert Ashman, Elaine Bagshaw, Melanie Batley, Shirley Biggs, Eleanor Burnham AM, David Canzini, Douglas Carswell MP, Nick Cuff, Katy Diggory, Simon Hamilton MLA, Tom Harris MP, Phil Hendren, James Hibbert, Tom Hirons, Mary Honeyball MEP, Bethan Jenkins AM, Syed Kamall MEP, John Lamont MSP, John McCallister MLA, James McGrath, Andrew MacKinlay MP, Sarah MacKinlay, Charlie Mansell, Mark Pack, Gil Paterson MSP, Paul Richards, Hopi Sen, Jonathan Sheppard, John Shosky, Jag Singh, Janice Small, Ed Staite, Louisa Thomson, Shelley Tidmore, Stephen Twigg, Andy Wasley and Chris Younce. And although he is not one of the authors, it would be remiss of me not to thank Rodney Corrigan, whose assistance in identifying authors from the Northern Ireland Assembly was much needed.

I would also like to thank my good friend Iain Dale for agreeing to publish this book and for his constructive criticism throughout. As ever, his advice and guidance has been invaluable.

I owe incredible thanks to my wife, Brittany, who had to put up with so much of our time together being dominated by this book. Rarely did an evening or weekend go by where I wasn't either editing those chapters submitted by other authors or writing chapters of my own. Her patience speaks volumes, and I can't thank her enough.

Finally, I'd like to thank my parents for constantly reminding me when growing up that you can only achieve what you want if you work to make it happen. This book, as with so many other endeavours in my life thus far, is testament to that philosophy.

Part I

So you want to be a politician

I

In defence of politics

Shane Greer

It's always been easy to bash politics and politicians. But, at the moment, it's fashionable. It's the new black. It's vogue. One need only flick on the television or open a newspaper to experience the vitriol being directed at our elected representatives and our democratic system as a whole. 'They're all in it for what they can get', we're told. 'They're completely removed from reality', we hear. 'They're all as bad as each other', we're led to believe. And believe it we do, in tremendous numbers. An ICM poll for the BBC News Channel back in 2005 found that eight out of ten voters didn't trust politicians to tell the truth, 87 per cent felt that politicians did not keep the promises they made in advance of general elections, and an incredible 92 per cent said that politicians never gave a straight answer. Fast forward to 2009 and the situation hadn't got any better; in fact it had got worse. According to an Ipsos MORI poll for the *Observer* newspaper only 13 per cent of people trusted politicians to tell the truth. What's more, politicians were seen as the least trustworthy of all professions (including lawyers, who so often are the butt of jokes pertaining to dishonesty).

To say that politics is in crisis is an understatement on a par with saying that Muhammad Ali was a pretty decent boxer. Public confidence in the British political system could barely be lower, and trust of politicians has been all but destroyed. Indeed, if politics were a business and voters were its customers, it's almost certain that, by now, it would either be bankrupt or propped up with a government bailout.

That we find ourselves in this calamitous situation is hardly surprising, though. We live in the age of 24-hour media. An age in which negative stories sell and positive stories get cast aside. Why talk about the politicians diligently working on behalf of their constituents when there's another politician who's abused their position for personal gain or enjoyed the company of some rent boys?

But to blame the media would be wrong. To do so would be to ignore the fact that the media ultimately succeeds or fails (even the BBC) on its ability to satisfy its audience. And if the audience is excited more by negative stories than positive ones, what media outlet in its right mind wouldn't give them what they want?

But let's be clear about something. While it might be tempting to blame the audience, to bemoan their obsession with negativity, the simple fact is that we politicos are no different. Can any of us honestly say that we didn't enjoy the last story about a member of another party running into difficulty? Can we honestly say we haven't navigated to the BBC News website and found ourselves drawn immediately to the story about natural disaster in a far off land? After all, who doesn't like a juicy story they can get their teeth into? And let's not forget one of the most fundamental rules of democratic politics; you, the aspirant candidate, don't get to decide what the voters are interested in. They hold the power.

However much we might like voters to look up to their elected representatives, to hold them in high regard, and to view them as generally honest and decent people, it simply isn't going to happen. If you want to become a politician you have to accept that.

But never forget, for all its detractors, politics remains a noble endeavour. Perhaps ironically, given the effect his decision to go into Iraq had on the public's trust in politicians, it is Tony Blair who best reminded us of the inherent value and virtue of our parliamentary democracy when concluding his final Prime Minister's Questions:

Some may belittle politics. But we know, who are engaged in it, that it is where people stand tall. And, although I know it has its many harsh contentions, it is still the arena that sets the heart beating a little faster. And if it is, on occasions, the place of low skulduggery, it is more often the place for the pursuit of noble causes.

Those who rail against our political system forget that without politics, and specifically democratic politics, decisions would be taken by force. The Melian principle would come to characterise our way of life; with the strong doing what they can and the weak suffering what they must.

All too readily history teaches us the lessons of dictatorship; peoples enslaved, rights curtailed where they are not obliterated, the rule of law replaced by the rule of force, the persecution of minorities, the invasion and subjugation of sovereign nations, the extermination of entire social, religious, ethnic and national groups, the imprisonment of political opponents, the presumption of guilt rather than innocence, and the sacrifice of liberty at the altar of conformity.

As citizens of a liberal democracy it's all too easy for us to forget how rare and hard won the freedoms we enjoy really are. Stories of genocide and totalitarianism exist in the abstract. Far from being tales of individual tragedy, they become little more than matters of statistics; involving numbers so high as to remove utterly any hope that their real meaning will penetrate our relatively privileged existence. But it is ultimately the individual human stories behind the statistics that serve as a stark reminder of how privileged we really are. One such example found expression in an article by Professor Mahmoud Bassiouni, who chaired the Commission of Experts to Investigate the War Crimes and Other Violations of International Humanitarian Law in the Former Yugoslavia:

A man on crutches whose legs seemed to have been broken came over to see us yesterday . . . When the war broke out, his neighbourhood became Serb controlled . . . One day, a group of about half a dozen young thugs . . . came over and hauled the man away from his café to the police station. They tied him up on the floor . . . they then proceeded to take their rifle butts and break both his legs . . . While he was lying there on the floor with two broken legs, the thugs went and got his wife and two daughters. They told the wife in the presence of her husband and her two daughters that unless she did everything they wanted, they would rape the two girls. The mother, in order to protect her daughters, complied and submitted to degrading and humiliating sexual acts. Then when they were finished with her, they slit her throat. While she was withering on the floor dying, they raped the two girls in the presence of their stepfather. Then . . . they slit the throats of the two girls. Next, in perhaps the worst possible cruelty, they took the man and dumped him out in the streets . . . This morning I discovered that he had committed suicide during the night, leaving only the message: 'I lived long enough to tell my story to someone in the hope that it will be told in the future.'

That we as citizens of a Western liberal democracy find such brutality incomprehensible speaks volumes of the virtue of the political system we have come to take for granted.

Is our system perfect? Of course not. Are all our politicians paragons of virtue? Hardly. But for all our system's flaws and our politicians' shortcomings, we still wake up in the morning and find that the battle to get to No. 10 is fought with words rather than weapons. That alone is something we should be proud and fiercely protective of.

And let's not forget that it was our ever evolving system of democracy which over the years abolished the slave trade, made suffrage universal, stood firm against dictatorship when it threatened the freedom of Europe, granted rights to workers, delivered a universal healthcare system based on an individual's need rather than their ability to pay, made education free and compulsory for all children, ensured habeas corpus, recognised homosexual relationships through civil partnerships, embraced religious freedom and protected freedom of speech. The list goes on.

Ours is a political system which should be celebrated, both for its achievements in the past and its acknowledgement that it must constantly improve if it is to make greater achievements in the future. For sure, there will always be an abundance of individuals ready to throw mud at politics and politicians, but let's not forget that they have yet to propose an alternative system of government which promises to be better.

Winston Churchill said it best: 'Democracy is the worst form of government, except for all those other forms that have been tried from time to time.'

Shane Greer is the executive editor of Total Politics

2

What it's like to be a politician

Andrew MacKinlay

Many years ago while an aspiring candidate in a pretty hopeless seat, someone advised me that there was no point going into public life and also being a shrinking violet. This was sound advice.

Consequently, both in making speeches and at dinners, coffee mornings and other social occasions, much energy and mental preparation has to be expended in order to fulfil the expectations of your supporters.

It is essential to overcome (or, perhaps more accurately, disguise) the insecurity and lack of self confidence that so many of us suffer from. This can of course lead to embarrassing over-compensation. We have all met the very loud, over the top, gladhanding personality. The skill is to try and improve one's game on each new occasion.

If you are shy or lacking in self confidence, your task is to overcome this, and with the help of your supporters build an 'image' of what their chosen candidate or MP should portray.

One will draw strength from what, in my opinion, is normally an overwhelming amount of goodwill and in some cases considerable deference. However, there will always be one who shakes his head or doesn't laugh and who asks a spiteful loaded question or makes a remark about MPs' expenses. They are like an Exocet missile racing into your side, destroying and crumpling the fragile hull of your newly acquired confidence.

The thing to do is to focus on the fact that overwhelmingly your audience appreciates what you have to say and that they have had a 'chat' with you and had an opportunity to have their say. The politician's nightmare is remembering people's names and also those to whom you have written in response to a query. The volume of those you meet and those who write is enormous and is never ever understood by journalists or those who are charged with assessing the 'worth' of MPs when it comes to expenses.

A bishop gave me a tip one day. When you don't know who is speaking to you – say 'Please remind me of your name?' If the reply comes back 'Margaret' you then, clasping the lady by the hand, swiftly rejoin by saying: 'I know you're Margaret! It was your last name I just couldn't remember!'

Clement Freud, who was the Liberal MP for Ely, recalled the formula for those who come up to you and about whose identity you haven't the foggiest idea. You simply say: 'I got your letter', obviously reassuring them that you immediately recall and identify the subject matter, and that you will be keen and able to converse and enlarge on what was in their letter. Maybe it was a wrong that needed to be righted; maybe you were tipped off to send condolences following a bereavement or a disappointing failure; or maybe it was to congratulate the person on some great success. You have no idea!!

The microseconds flash past. You hope that you will be rescued by another who wants and is competing for your attention or that the first person will give you a clue about the subject matter to which they are referring.

Your face muscles will work overtime as you 'work the tables' at a social. You will laugh at the joke, the critical punch line lost as the teller doubles up with laughter at his own story. Your face will lift and your eyes light up when a proud lady tells you about her grandson who is going to university, only for the mask to change as if a switch was flicked on hearing from a widower of the recent loss of his wife of sixty years.

You desperately hope too that when picking the raffle tickets as the principal guest at a function, you avoid picking out one of the many tickets you paid for. . . and most certainly that if you have already won the big box of chocolates, you don't win again. If you do, and the 'choice' is between the bottle of Famous Grouse and bath salts. . . well there really is no choice. You'll enjoy your bath!

In the final weeks of my time as an MP I got one of those letters from a very pompous man (who was not a constituent) in which he boasted how hard he worked, unlike so many others, and how he was paying for others while he maintained himself and his family by private schooling and private health insurance.

He then posed a series of 'questions' in which he challenged me to proffer my views and/or defend my party's position. He continued in his letter to ask: ' Is there anybody in Parliament today that fairly represents British people like me?'

Hopefully not!

I replied that if he thought he could do a better job as a Member of Parliament, and do it more cheaply, then not only could he stand at the next election but arguably he had a duty to do so!

I think this is an important point. Those most vociferous critics of either your individual style and stewardship of public office, or of the government, must be asked why they have not the courage to stand for election.

The Friday surgery can never be shown on TV. At the end of a long, hard week it can be emotionally draining but also most rewarding.

There are the 'regulars', including those being spied on by the CIA, and those who get messages from space through their TV sets. However, by far the greater numbers are those whose problems are numerous: victims of a heartless bureaucracy, or those who are starving because of the appalling and gross incompetence of the UK Border Agency to determine their status, or to find their papers lost in a Home Office tower block in Croydon – not for months but years. Then there are the parents who have bought their council home but cannot understand that there is a shortage of municipal properties for their daughter and son-in-law and infant grandchild. These are good people but one wonders if on occasion they expect the good Lord to come down from heaven each night and replenish the housing stock in green pastures. You try! You try to explain the shortage and the demand and every time you send a letter to the housing office you try to muster and craft new arguments which always end up as variants on the same point. Nevertheless you explain why this young family is 'a special case'.

A weekend will be filled with many pleasing duties, when invariably one is welcomed to a variety of different functions. Friday may include a veterans' dinner and Saturday might be the presentation at the under-12 soccer tournament. Saturday afternoon could be a non-league football match – to be welcomed by the quip 'Eh!. . . haven't seen you lately. . . must be an election in the offing' – and in the evening it could be the scout gang show, choral society or the male voice choir.

Sunday might include a civic service, an ordination or induction of a new rector, or the Apostolic Church of God from 10 a.m. to 2 p.m. – always exciting, with sermons delivered with great fire and passion interspersed with some of the great sounds and anthems from west Africa.

Sunday evening – where has the weekend gone?

I went to the gang show every year for ten years. I enjoyed it every time and it allowed me to reinforce my regard and commitment for the Scouts, an organisation of which I was such a beneficiary in my childhood and adolescence. However, after ten years one really does know every gag, every line and every dance step.

One year I could not attend the show and was somewhat taken aback when I faced a mild rebuke from an old scout who said: 'We never see you these days.'

When you're out campaigning, in the run-up to an election for example, that's often the kind of response you get on the doorstep. When you ask for someone's support you need to do so confidently and boldly. They will often say 'Well, they [the council] never come and cut our grass' or 'It's a secret ballot, isn't it? Well, then, it's between me and the ballot box'. Your response must always be scrupulously polite but you can gently point out where and how you are available in between elections.

Of course, it must be stressed that there are also those who are supportive and you obviously devote time and spend a few minutes talking to those who encourage you, telling you they've 'never voted anything else'.

So now you've arrived! Your first day is daunting there are no two ways about it. You're like the new kid arriving at secondary school. Certainly when I arrived back in 1992 there wasn't any guidance. It is very much down to you how you organise your day, your time and your staff. You will have to orientate yourself around the maze of rooms within the Palace. This is an exciting time and these early days might be the only opportunity you have to explore the building and learn about its great history.

Foremost among your many tasks is to get yourself an office, either in the main building within the Palace itself or in one of the many surrounding buildings on the parliamentary estate. It is important to consider where you want to place yourself strategically. If you want to be 'in the thick of it' you will have to make do with a small stuffy, possibly windowless office. But there are advantages to this, such as being close by when the Division bell starts to ring.

There is no overarching way to behave as a politician other than the obvious things: honesty, integrity, humility. Part of the problem has been that there is very little guidance but hopefully when you get to the other end – as I am now – you will look back at your time as a politician with some pride and with fantastic memories of all the people you have been able to help: the achievements, the opportunities to travel and visit many countries and also to make contact with some incredible people which will often lead to lasting friendships.

For me it has been a long and fascinating journey and one which I would not have missed for all the world.

Andrew MacKinlay is the Labour MP for Thurrock

3

What it takes to be a politician

What it takes to be a councillor

Nick Cuff

I didn't really plan to be a councillor, it just happened. Before I got selected, my knowledge of local politics was hazy. If you had asked me what a councillor did, I would probably have muttered something about social work.

I remember things moved quickly. I had recently relocated to Wandsworth and signed up with the local party association. However, I hadn't been to a single local event and I didn't know any political activists.

One day while at work I received an association wide e-mail. A candidate had dropped out and they were asking for people to come forward. I thought it was worth a shot and filled in an application while sipping my coffee.

That night I told my girlfriend what I had done. She looked on in horror. 'Do you realise how much additional work being a local councillor actually involves?' I remember her asking.

I promised her with usual bravado that as a virtual stranger there was no chance I was going to get selected. It wasn't the first time I had been wrong and it certainly won't be the last.

I don't remember too much about the night of the interview. I remember being very nervous but thinking things had gone quite smoothly. I joined a few friends in the pub afterwards and happily forgot the experience.

The next day around 8 a.m. I received a call. I have come to learn that agents don't do small talk on the phone and this was no exception.

My girlfriend was in the kitchen and I remember her hovering within earshot. After one or two pleasantries the agent told me I was being put into a safe seat, and I would be a councillor in three months. She must have heard because within seconds there were floods of tears and accusations of broken promises.

The agent also must have heard. He stopped in his tracks and asked who was crying. I replied it was my girlfriend and was about to explain when he cut me off: 'Crying with delight! It's great to have someone supportive behind you.' A second later, I had my instructions and he was gone leaving me to manage expectations on the home front.

I've been a councillor for nearly four years now and have been selected to stand again. My life hasn't been radically altered by the experience but I find I sleep less and organise myself more.

One of the great things about being a councillor is that you can combine a day job with being a local politician – something unfortunately increasingly frowned upon at a national level. This keeps you in touch with the real world.

I find there is a cross over between the skills you learn in business and the skills you learn as a local politician. I talk from experience here. I have had two different careers since I became a councillor – first in public affairs before retraining and joining a City surveying practice. My experience and knowledge as a councillor has benefited both and vice versa.

There are certain character traits common in all aspiring local council candidates and councillors: the skin of a rhino and a steely determination to keep you going. Both traits don't necessarily need to be inherent; the longer you're in this game, the more you find they naturally come about.

The most effective councillors also pick their battles. There is a mountain of paper and the tentacles of a local council seem to stretch out for ever. Rather than trying to master everything, it's far better to specialise in one or two areas.

And one final thing: being a councillor doesn't destroy relationships. I've even managed to convince my girlfriend to come out and deliver leaflets.

Nick Cuff is a Conservative councillor in the London Borough of Wandsworth

What it takes to be an MLA

Simon Hamilton

When considering the question 'What does it take to be an MLA?' it is tempting to say if anyone else has an idea could they please let me know.

Being a member of the Northern Ireland Assembly – like holding any public office – doesn't exactly come with a job description.

There are characteristics and qualities that an MLA should have that are common to any elected position.

It almost goes without saying that you should have a desire to make a difference however you might define it. Astute political antennae, an ability to argue one's point and the patience to sit for hours scrutinising the detail of legislation or a policy proposal are essential.

When I entered the Assembly in spring 2007, I believed I possessed at least something of each of these traits. Or at least I thought I did.

Take for example, the absolutely key requirement of speaking in public. While some MLAs seem to have become trappist monks, taking vows of silence, if you want to get noticed and get votes, speaking in public – whether that be on radio or on TV or in the Assembly chamber – is imperative.

Having your homework mentally marked by the big beasts of the NI political jungle like Paisley and Adams doesn't make for an easy environment to come across as cool, calm and collected. It was a big step up for me from having been a local councillor. After a year on Ards Borough Council I was prognosticating and pontificating on all sorts of subjects. It doesn't matter where you get your grounding – Council, the courtroom or in a community group. The common refrain we hear on radio phone in programmes, 'that even I can do better than that shower in Stormont', may be true in the odd case but generally you need time to settle in, to start to understand the system and simply to find your feet.

Perhaps the one big difference to being an MLA in NI as opposed to being a legislator elsewhere is that NI politics is much more 'retail', much more constituent focused than I have experienced elsewhere. If you think you can just sit in Stormont burying your head in policy work and talking endlessly in debates, then you shouldn't be surprised when the votes are counted and your pile isn't as big as others. Voters expect you to open a full time advice centre and operate surgeries and they demand to see you personally and aren't afraid to stop you in the street and ask you about their problems.

Maybe the one thing that is forgotten when weighing up embarking upon a career as an MLA is the impact it will undoubtedly have on your life. An understanding family is critical as any semblance of a normal working life disappears on day one. As much, though, as you will have to devote your time to helping perfect strangers, you must never lose sight of the needs of your own family and indeed yourself. I have observed too many politicians miss seeing their own children grow up and watched as their own health has deteriorated as they pursue every possible vote to know that balance is what you should aim for even if you don't always achieve it.

But above all, this is something you must want to do. It isn't good enough to think you'll just give it a go. It has to spark something in your core. I do this job because I absolutely love what I'm doing. This was something I always knew that I wanted to do at some stage in my life so there was always a passion for politics burning deep inside me that made it an easy choice for me to abandon a fledgling career in accountancy. I have worked in jobs where I haven't wanted to get out of bed in the morning and face what a day in the office or the shop holds. In being an MLA, the problem I find isn't getting up in the morning, it's getting to bed at a respectable time at night.

I know that this is one of the best jobs I'll ever do. It is certainly challenging, but the sense of having done something positive that you feel when you help a pensioner get their windows fixed or win a DLA appeal is worth everything you have to go through.

Confident but not cocky. Interested and engaged but not appearing overly intellectual. Accessible and involved but not to the detriment of your own life. This is what I think it takes to be an MLA. I will find out if I am right when I ask the people to renew my contract.

Simon Hamilton is the Democratic Unionist MLA for Strangford

What it takes to be an AM

Bethan Jenkins

Politics is in the blood of the Jenkins family. My parents were heavily involved in the anti-apartheid movement in the 1970s and 1980s as well as anti-open-cast mining campaigns in my home town of Merthyr Tydfil. My father, Mike Jenkins, an Anglo-Welsh poet, writes for the Red Poets, so socialism runs in the veins.

I studied at the University of Wales, Aberystwyth. Here, I became heavily involved in student politics, becoming president of Aberystwyth Guild of Students in 2004. The town is steeped in the history of the struggle for Welsh independence, and I became actively involved in Plaid Cymru at this time.

This led on to work with Plaid MEP Jill Evans after university, before joining Leanne Wood AM's team and setting up the new youth movement for Plaid Cymru, Cymru X. It was a job I loved doing, and it inspired me to put my name forward as a Plaid list member for the National Assembly. I achieved this in 2007, becoming an

Assembly Member for South Wales West and, in the process, the youngest member of the house at the time.

The past three years have provided the steepest of learning curves, but I am privileged to be an elected representative, with Plaid Cymru in government for the very first time.

I deal with a range of individual cases and campaigns as an Assembly Member, from dealing with matters pertaining to the health service, the environment, asylum cases, to housing and transport. These issues might not sound as ambitious as the pursuit of independence for Wales, but they are enormously important to the people affected. Sometimes it is frustrating if cases cannot be progressed as swiftly as constituents envisage due to processes and bureaucracy, but I hope that most people appreciate the effort I put in to helping them manoeuvre their way forward to progress.

I don't wait for constituents to come to me. I always make sure I have a busy programme of visits and meetings with local organisations and businesses. This contact is essential as it allows people and bodies to see how they can communicate with me as their Assembly Member in ways that they perhaps hadn't thought of previously. Many of them will have dealt directly with civil servants or local authorities, who often don't have the latitude to find solutions in the ways that AMs can. I can, for example, go straight to a minister if the matter is urgent enough. I can initiate a committee inquiry, as I did with a casework matter concerning prejudice against AIDS patients in the NHS, and when I initiated a cross-party committee on eating disorders having received letter bags full of casework from people who could not be treated in Wales for their condition.

Often, you will find that there are groups of people rather than just individuals that need assistance. Think, for example, of opposition to housing developments or wind farms. Not all such cases are negative. I'm currently working with a group that want rail services returned to their area.

The democratic development I am most proud to be involved with at the National Assembly for Wales is the petitions committee – a dedicated committee of AMs who scrutinise and meet with petitioners. This is the gateway to the Assembly for local communities, allowing them to effect change through legislation. For example, an end to the provision of plastic bags in supermarkets in Wales began life as a petition. Now there is a law for a levy on plastic bags.

As a committee, we'll consider petitions signed by as few as ten people. It is a chance for Welsh citizens to take part in politics, and to practise their rights in a new, creative way – aided by the development of an e-petitions system. We feel we have led the way, and now Westminster is hoping to follow suit.

Anybody considering entering politics should understand that it is very hard work, sometimes frustratingly so. However, if you believe in politics as a force for change it can be incredibly rewarding. I never thought that I would be a politician as a child growing up in the south Wales valleys, but anything is possible if you are passionate, dedicated and proactive.

Bethan Jenkins is a Plaid Cymru MLA for South Wales West

What it takes to be an MSP

Gil Paterson

I don't know a single MSP who regrets in any way being an MSP. Yes, we have our moans – not enough time in the day, frustration when constituents have what we believe is a legitimate concern that the system does not sort, the time away from families and so on. Would any of us walk away? I don't think so.

It is handy if you have the ability to run an issue-based campaign. Even if, like me, you're a member of the governing party, running a campaign gives you the satisfaction of being involved with the grass roots and keeping in touch with the public. It very much keeps you focused on the real issues affecting your constituents.

The system that surrounds being an MSP could easily disconnect you from real people.

First, there is the committee work, lots of reading and evidence taking. Being the convener of the Standards, Procedures and Public Appointments Committee brings additional work load.

The chamber work takes up a fair amount of a member's time: not only the time you spend in the chamber but the time to research in advance of speaking and the actual writing of our speeches. However, by and large the chamber is the place for me to broaden my knowledge over a wide variety of subjects and issues where people with specialist knowledge frequently surprise me with their particular work.

Most MSPs are members of cross-party groups, of which there is a substantial number in the Scottish Parliament. I am a vice-convener of three cross-party groups – Men's Violence against Women and Children, China and Chronic Pain. In each case, the convener is of another party but when it comes to the policies of the groups we are as one, which seems to be typical within the Parliament.

I would say half of your time, that is 9–5, is spent on constituency work, which may be dealing with a constituent's complaint or visiting a local establishment to hear their concerns and plans for the future. Most requests for assistance with a complaint come via the phone and increasingly by email, although I do hold a regular surgery every Friday evening.

One of the frustrations in dealing with the public is when a complaint is on a reserved power which is retained by the British Parliament. Informing the constituent that you are unable to help them can be very difficult to get across, especially if they have a legitimate complaint that needs to be addressed. However, passing it to the appropriate Westminster department normally does not cause any ruptures.

Meetings, public or otherwise, of course continue into the evenings and the weekend. A meeting could be with an individual, a local group or an organisation in a house, hall or office, and on any day or evening the meeting may be to inform or be informed, but it is sure to generate work of one kind or another. Engaging in this way is the part of the job I like the best; it is where in most cases you can make a difference.

It should be appreciated that most politicians also pay attention and give time to their own political party, attending local party meetings or campaigning. For me, I normally attend two different branch meetings per month along with meetings with local SNP councillors or SNP council groups.

It can be a difficult job but one filled with great rewards, most important of all helping an individual constituent overcome a particular problem. I wouldn't give it up for the world.

Gil Paterson is an SNP MSP for West of Scotland

What it takes to be an MEP

Syed Kamall

MEPs were once seen as having less power than MPs in Westminster. No longer. Successive European treaties granting ever more powers to Brussels – and the power of co-decision to the European Parliament – means MEPs are now as powerful as national ministers in making the law. Whereas having power at Westminster depends upon the patronage of the party and Prime Minister, those who wield power in the European Parliament rely on their own ability to construct coalitions of interest on a particular issue. Our votes in amending European Commission proposals are subject to the checks and balances of the decisions of the Council of Ministers but there is no denying that the European Parliament is the most powerful parliament of any, across the twenty-seven EU member states.

That in itself makes becoming an MEP an attractive job to someone who has a vision about how he or she wants to change the world, even if – like me – you want to see a world where the European Union and government interfere less in our lives. One of my proudest moments in the European Parliament was the publication of the International Trade Committee's Report on Trade in Services (known as the Kamall Report), which was described by one Socialist MEP in the chamber as 'the most free market report ever to go through this parliament'. Achievements such as this bob up only rarely in a sea of soul-destroying legislative and regulatory measures which are rammed through the Parliament on a monthly basis.

One of the things we have to live with as politicians is the enmity of people who do not agree with us. They sometimes do not realise that most politicians care deeply about making the world a better place, and fail to recognise that we simply have different ideas as to how to solve the world's problems.

Some of the biggest highs that come from this job arise from using my influence to put right the little things that can go wrong with public administration, which can nonetheless mean a great deal to the people affected. Some cases are cross-border, such as when a constituent who also owned a property in France came to me after being chased for a €3,000 water bill which had arisen when a tenant or builder had left a tap on in the property. I wrote to the CEO of the company and managed to persuade him to drop the charge. Others involve public authorities closer to home, as in the case of a disabled lady who contacted me after she was issued a parking ticket unfairly and couldn't get through to the council bureaucracy dealing with her case. I asked the council leader to look into it personally, who discovered that the ticket had in fact been issued in error.

Elective public service has been very rewarding but at times can be frustrating, especially with a young family. I miss being able to drop our children at school when I am away in Brussels, and it is challenging for my wife to look after them alone during the week and sometimes at weekends. We all struggle with finding the right balance between family and work life. And within my work life, I have to be conscious of balancing my time between Europe, my constituency and my party.

During the week, we sit in committee rooms or debating chambers rubbing shoulders with some of the most preeminent statesmen of our time. But we are not masters of the universe. Politicians need grounding and coming home to normal family life every week reminds us why we make the effort.

Syed Kamall is a Conservative MEP for London

What it takes to be an MP

Tom Harris

Politicians are strange people.

Think about it: they spend year after year attending boring meetings on wet, cold Thursday evenings in draughty community centres, listening to other strange people discussing the most esoteric and obscure of issues. They undertake the most menial tasks as office holders of their local political party branch or constituency association, the only reward for which is a lot more work and a lot more criticism from those who reckon they could be doing the same job, and doing it better.

Then, if they're lucky, they might be selected as a candidate for the local authority, or even for Parliament, giving them the opportunity to receive even more criticism – much of it personal – from their prospective electorate during the election campaign.

And if they're actually elected? Oh, dear, oh, dear. . .

Few of us at Westminster even stop to think about whether or not we've got what it takes to be an MP, or to consider what those qualities actually are. We're already here, after all, so someone, somewhere, must surely have decided we have 'the Right Stuff', yes?

Well, possibly.

As a new MP in 2001, I would have listed determination, integrity and principle as the essential prerequisites to becoming a tribune of the people.

Nearly nine years on I would add: a thick skin, an understanding and tolerant spouse and a great deal of patience.

But I would suggest that the qualities needed to perform the job of MP are subtly and crucially different from those required to achieve the ambition in the first place. An incredible and reality-defying self-belief, for example, has propelled many a jobsworth party activist onto the green benches of the House of Commons, only for them to find, after their election, that their talent and ability remain apparent only to themselves.

Similarly, while an ability to connect with ordinary voters is undoubtedly crucial in an election campaign, there are plenty of colleagues whose minds seem to have been wiped of all such interpersonal skills the very moment the returning officer announces the name of the winning candidate.

But of all the many qualities needed in order to pursue a relatively successful career in parliament, I would list 'sense of perspective' pretty near the top of the list. MPs need to know their place in the scheme of things. They have to understand that, as one of 646 legislators, they are not about to play a pivotal role in the life of the nation. At least, not right away.

That sense of perspective is invaluable, both at Westminster and in the constituency. When inundated with requests for help from constituents, it's vital to know how much help you can actually provide – and how much you can't.

In the Commons itself, in its debates and arcane procedures which govern the conduct of standing committees and secondary legislation committees, in its select committee structures, that sense of perspective can help prevent the onset of insanity, or at least can help convince you that the Herculean efforts you expended on achieving your position have not been entirely for nothing.

But life for the British MP post the expenses scandal will be entirely different from that experienced before it, and I suppose I should consider myself privileged to be one of those who will be able to draw a comparison. In that context, perspective is required to understand that MPs, while still retaining a residual level of influence, respect and prestige within their communities, will have to show a degree of patience as they wait for the public to recognise their finer attributes.

Tom Harris is the Labour MP for Glasgow South

Part II

Getting selected

4

The process

Getting selected for the Labour Party

Charlie Mansell

So, you want to be selected as a Labour candidate?

The Labour Party has a very detailed set of rules which have evolved as a result of a number of factors:

> › The demand for accountability of representatives to members in the early 1980s, which reflected the tradition of Labour as a party that started outside Parliament;
> › The need to tackle issues around the political acceptability of candidates and media controversy in the late 1980s;
> › The requirement to ensure diversity of candidates, particularly more women, but also more ethnic minorities from the mid-1990s.

Therefore Labour has a lot of rules, constantly reviewed over the last thirty years, and a high level of centralisation, with a lot of power exercised by its full-time regional directors on behalf of the General Secretary. This is backed up by a lot of case law, established in this area over the years as a result of a number of legal challenges. Indeed this has even led to legislation that formally allows all-women shortlists.

The other key difference is that, unlike the other parties, Labour has external affiliated organisations, such as trade unions, the Co-op Party and socialist societies, who have certain rights for establishing panels of candidates. The larger affiliates will go out of their way to promote favoured people for some selections – certainly at parliamentary and at devolved assembly level.

If an election is called, the Labour Party National Executive Committee (NEC) is likely to draw up panels of candidates for local members to choose from. Thus panel membership and local connection are likely to count. Probably the best position to be in is that of a strong local candidate, but one not perceived as the 'official candidate'. Party members are likely to select people not necessarily by their politics, but more by whether they are seen as committed to the locality and with a track record that is not just 'House of Commons researcher'. Community experience and 'hinterland' are likely to count much more in this election.

Diversity

This is seen as an important issue. Labour has had all-women shortlists for candidates since the mid-1990s and the NEC is aiming for a Parliamentary Labour Party which is at least 40 per cent women in the next parliament. And it is clear this has made a difference. Unlike the other parties, Labour has made a lot of use of the anti-discrimination legislation on gender that it has introduced. As the legislation allows political parties to voluntarily operate rules to promote women candidates, it is assumed that this will not now be repealed if there is a change of government, so this is likely to remain a key difference between Labour and the other parties.

At a local government level the party strives in three member wards to have a minimum of one woman candidate selected in every ward, though there has been some flexibility around the issue of sitting councillors.

Rules and application forms

Chapter 5 of the Party Rules – 'Selections for Elected Party Office' – along with the Selections Procedures Guide and the Code of

Conduct for candidates issued by the NEC are important for you
to read and understand. Key points to remember at this stage are:

> Continuous membership of the party of at least twelve months
  (Rule 5A1Bi)
> Membership of a union affiliated to the TUC (5A1Bi)
> There will be a minimum standard of candidate quality set out
  by the NEC.

The application forms are not there to catch you out. They are
designed to bring out all the skills and experience you have. Don't
just focus on a long list of party committees, but also reference
community activity. Think of things you have done where you
have taken the lead in something. This makes it easier to talk about
during any panel interviews. A useful point is to list all the various
connections you have to places you might apply to stand in as well
as all the organisations that might make a nomination. You can
secure easy votes by reference to membership of a trade union and
the Co-op Party.

Read all the conditions listed at the back of the form. These
set out undertakings you give to the party to comply with party
rules and standing orders and with standards legislation. This is
important as some will be very relevant when we come to panel
interviews.

Interview by panel of candidates

This is mandatory for all selections except parliamentary selections.
However, failure to be on a panel can mean a selected parliamentary
candidate still has to go through an interview after selection. The
problem is that the party will then keep a non-panelled candidate
waiting for endorsement. When a general election is imminently
due, this may not be an issue; however, the NEC could decree that
only panelled candidates can take part in any selections that occur
after any election has been called.

Generally parliamentary panels contain Labour Party NEC
members. Much of the panelling at other levels is done by regional

board members. These people are elected by the regional conferences and tend to be long-standing activists.

The sort of questions a panel will ask include:

› *Why do you want to be a representative?* It's remarkable how many candidates fall apart at this point. They either have no idea, or come across as far too careerist. Talk about what inspired you and how you can make a difference working with others, perhaps illustrating it with an area of policy where you have knowledge or interest.

› *What is your understanding of the work of the body you are seeking selection to?*

› *Give examples of where you have a made a difference in some part of party or community activity.* This is not a list of committees but what you have actually done.

› *What is your understanding of how the whip system works and your commitment to it?* It is always amazing how many people fall down at this point and try to qualify their commitment to the party whip as if this is some sort of political test or a form of ultimate authority they cannot commit to. The question is fundamentally designed to find out whether you are a team player and will engage with members and other elected colleagues to secure the best possible negotiated solution, in often difficult circumstances, prior to any final decision. However, if you are a team player, at the end of that process you do need to state you will accept the whip. For a party strongly committed to public services, this has probably not really been much of an issue in the last decade, as services have expanded. However, in a future era of cuts, this could be an area where even more potential candidates get themselves into difficulty by qualifying their commitment to adhere to the whip. From long experience I can say that panels do not look favourably on those who spend their time qualifying and do not demonstrate they are prepared to be part of a team with their elected colleagues.

› *Do you have any issues that could cause the party embarrassment?* This often causes candidates problems. For example, at local government level, the application form may in some circumstances give permission for the party to seek information on relationships with the local council in terms of arrears of council tax and rent. The best thing is to be honest and get things in the open. The issue here is to take action to regularise the issue. If you were arrested on a demonstration twenty years ago, or been to court for a civil debt, which you resolved, the party is very unlikely to want to stop you. What they want to know is that this happened, so that if there is a media query it is not unexpected.

Selections

So, you have got through the panel with flying colours. What happens next? Panel members tend to be notified by email on what selections are available and can apply by sending the standard CV to the procedures secretary of the constituency they are applying to.

Selection process

At parliamentary level, the basic process is that:

> You apply for advertised seats and seek to secure nominations from local branches and affiliates.
> There are likely to be 'meet the members' events as well as possibly voter ID events where the more active Constituency Labour Parties (CLP) get potential candidates to go out and do some work for them. Show your face and make sure you talk to everybody, not just the key players. Every vote counts.
> The CLP General Committee (GC) will draw up a shortlist of candidates. This is done through a single-round secret preferential ballot (so securing some core support early is important to get you through the rounds as votes are transferred). For open selections, 50 per cent of those shortlisted must be women.
> There will be a selection meeting, though many members will apply to vote by post.
> Only those members who reside in the area with six months' continuous membership are entitled to participate in the selection and a freeze date will be agreed to confirm eligibility (Rule

5A1Ai). Thus if you are starting at the beginning of a selection process, you cannot simply sign up all your friends, relatives and neighbours!

Campaign funding

You can of course use your own money, but you can also receive donations from certain organisations of individuals. For example, if you are active in your trade union or the Co-op Party and have got on their panel of candidates, you may well get financial support from them. The crucial thing to remember is to record all donations remembering that all those over £200 have to comply with PPERA legislation.

Nominations and shortlisting

For a parliamentary selection, there are likely to be a number of branches, trade unions, Co-op Party and socialist societies making nominations. People make expressions of interest for a seat and their CVs are circulated around the CLP.

Branches and affiliates will generally nominate up to three people, at least one has to be a female candidate as well as one ethnic minority candidate where at least one has shown an interest in applying. Where there is an all-women shortlist, branches and affiliates will need to nominate two women, one of whom would be an ethnic minority candidate where at least one has shown an interest in applying.

Active branches might invite you to address their nomination, but often this is done as a paper exercise by the nominating organisation. It is useful to clarify this early, so you know how much effort to commit at this stage. The CLP will draw up a shortlist. It is likely to be balanced between men and women, unless it is a prior-agreed all-women shortlist. There needs to be at least one ethnic minority nominee on the panel.

Targeting the larger branches makes a lot of sense. If you get nominations from branches that comprise over 50 per cent of the membership, you are automatically shortlisted.

Campaigning
The NEC issues guidelines here which do change from time to time. However, core elements are:

> Utilising the local party membership list, which you can purchase, to send out a two-sided leaflet and a covering letter
> Phone or doorstep contact of each member; do not come across as hectoring or disparage other candidates
> A significant number of members will apply for a postal vote, so make sure you target those first.

Talking to members, where the rules allow it, does make a vast difference. Phone calls with a relaxed flexible script are a good starting point. There is debate on how best to do this, but getting a commitment for support is useful if you are already well known. However, if you are not known, it might be better to start by just introducing yourself, drawing attention to your leaflet and offering to answer questions. A follow-up contact can then obtain a support commitment.

Speeches
An important part of the selection will be the hustings meeting. This will be where all those who have not yet voted cast their vote. For most selections these tend to last 5–10 minutes, with 10–15 minutes for questions.

Other selections
Devolved assembly selections for constituency seats are very similar to parliamentary selections. However, selection to the relevant list of candidates will operate (in London the order of candidates for the GLA list is determined by the Regional Board, for example).

For Members of the European Parliament, the Regional Parties selection panel draw up a shortlist of candidates from those who have applied to that region. The order of the list is determined by members in the region through a postal ballot, with 'zipping' of candidates by gender – in other words alternate men and women candidates.

For council candidates, getting on the panel is essential. In recent years, Labour has not stood a full slate of candidates outside core urban areas, so you are likely to be welcomed and should get some candidate experience even if it is initially in an unwinnable ward.

Labour has probably reached a low point in local government representation, so over the next few years there is a good chance you could win in a marginal seat narrowly held by one of the other parties.

The crucial thing here is to be seen to be active. Go to as many of the voter ID sessions as you can. Get elected to the local government committee (LGC) of the party to indicate you are interested. Get appointed as a Labour school governor and attend committee and council meetings. Members do tend to like to see commitment from candidates.

Summary
The whole process is designed to bring out the best in you and to ensure a wide range of candidates. It can be a bit bureaucratic at times, but it is less daunting than you might think. It's a great experience and the sheer diversity of Labour's membership in comparison to the other parties means you are likely to meet very interesting people and learn a lot.

Charlie Mansell is the research and development officer at the Campaign Company

Getting selected for the Conservative Party

Andy Wasley

As a political tribe, we Conservatives tend to believe in putting people before process, and beliefs before bureaucracy. If you want to stand for office as a Conservative candidate, then, you'll be pleased to hear that that party's core principles extend well into its selection procedures. Not for Tories the Supreme Soviet-style morass of sub-committees, affiliated partnerships and regional policy forum executive co-operatives of the Labour Party – nor, indeed, the quasi-formal semi-regulated federal decision-making whatnots of the Liberal Democrats. Just simple, accessible democracy, open to anyone – regardless of gender, age, religion, sexuality, race or educational background – who shares the party's basic values and a passion for public service.

To stand for the as a Conservative candidate in England or Wales for the UK Parliament, the European Parliament or the Welsh Assembly, the selection process starts with an email or phone call to Conservative Campaign Headquarters (CCHQ), addressed to the Candidates' Team (candidateenquiries@conservatives.com or call 020 7222 9000), stating your interest in becoming a candidate and asking for an application form. Local government candidates follow a slightly different process, which I will detail later. If you're looking for a seat in Scotland, you can find an application form online at http://bit.ly/scots_candidate, or call 0131 247 6890; helpfully, the Scottish form covers constituencies in Scotland for Westminster, Holyrood, Europe and local government.

At this point, you should be aware that you cannot attend a Parliamentary Assessment Board until you have been a member of the party for at least three months. If you are not already a member, you can join via http://bit.ly/join-party. On joining, you will be put in touch with your local Conservative Association, who will be able to get you going with some campaign experience (you can also find your association online via http://bit.ly/local-association). From joining the campaign trail and canvassing constituents to organising fundraising events or using the party's call centre facilities to canvas people by telephone, there is a lot you can do to build a good political background.

Like any other application form, the candidate application form aims to get key information out of you (employment history, address and so on), as well as some more abstract information about you as a person. Don't be daunted; the party is giving you a chance to explain why you think you'd be a great public servant, so don't hold back on listing your achievements. Think hard about what you've done to demonstrate your public spirit and commitment to your local community or the nation. This could be anything, from raising funds for a local or national charity, to being a magistrate, school governor or TA soldier. If you can't think of anything, there's nothing to stop you getting involved in volunteering or public service now. The excellent site www.volunteering.org.uk is a good place to start.

Part of the application form concerns your political activities. Don't be worried if you are completely new to politics; as outlined above, the Conservative Party believes you should have the freedom to stand for public office even if you're not a dyed-in-the-wool policy wonk who has attended every fundraising coffee morning since the invention of hot water. Political experience is a definite advantage, but what really matters is your wider life experience and your belief in basic conservative values – and that's exactly what the selection process is there to assess.

Perhaps the trickiest part of the application form is explaining why you want to be an MP, MSP, AM, MEP or local councillor. I'm going to assume you've thought long and hard about that already, but make sure you take the time to learn what the different roles entail and what sort of work is involved. Helpfully, the Conservative Women's Organisation has an Amazon book store (http://bit.ly/tory-books) with some excellent reading material about Parliament and politics in general. Be honest about what you would hope to achieve, and why you think your chosen level of government is the right place to achieve it. If in doubt, get in touch with a local Conservative councillor, MP or prospective parliamentary candidate. They or their offices should be able to provide you with useful information about their jobs.

If your application is successful, you'll be invited to attend a Parliamentary Assessment Board (for a flat fee of £250). This is where you have a chance to meet the Candidates' Team and to prove to them, in person, that you would make a good Conservative candidate. The exact details of the selection procedure are kept confidential to ensure that all candidates have an equal opportunity to pass, but there are some key elements to prepare for. Expect to be put through practical scenarios of what you might have to do as an MP, such as basic case work and public speaking. You will also need to be prepared to write a short, timed essay about a public issue, and to be interviewed by a senior member of the party. Be prepared to defend your political convictions, and be honest about what you hope to achieve.

Those who pass the Parliamentary Assessment Board will be contacted by CCHQ or Scottish Conservative Headquarters (I'll refer to both as CCHQ from now on) and asked to join the Conservative Candidates' Association, which aims to ensure that all candidates receive the best, most up-to-date information about party policy and vacant seats. If you haven't passed, don't be too dispirited. Competition to become an approved candidate is fierce and you can always try again at a later date. At the time of writing, the list of approved candidates had closed ahead of the general election. The list will be opened again shortly after the election has been held (and, hopefully, a Conservative government returned to office!).

Assuming you've made it through the Assessment Board, it is time for you to find a vacant seat. Parliamentary and devolved assembly constituency vacancies are advertised by CCHQ in tranches via email. You will need to consider your options carefully at this stage; competition for the very safest seats will be extremely strong, and CCHQ will be insistent upon the very highest standards for candidates in marginal seats. Do not discount seats that look as though they will never elect a Conservative: stranger things have happened, and there is, in any case, absolutely nothing wrong with gaining valuable campaign experience. Margaret Thatcher, after all, stood in the safe Labour seat of Dartford twice in the early 1950s; fighting a losing battle at the start of her career certainly did her no harm in later years.

CCHQ will sift applications for vacancies so that each constituency's local association has a manageable number of candidates. There are, basically, two ways in which the selection process for the seat will proceed: a local association vote and local primaries. The main difference is that under the traditional system you'll be meeting with local Conservative party members, whereas in an open primary everyone on the electoral roll for the constituency will be invited to attend the hustings and vote on their preferred candidate. In either case, you will be asked to give a speech about why you want to be the local MP/AM/MSP and to answer questions from the audience about your stance on local issues. Questioning is likely to be extremely detailed, so you will need to make sure you have done your research. Although nerve-racking, these events tend to be quite friendly and straightforward, so try to relax and enjoy the experience – and, of course, to make contacts with your competitors, who could end up being your colleagues in the future.

Following the hustings a vote will be taken to decide who to adopt as the official candidate. Don't be dispirited if you don't succeed at this point: Michael Howard, the former Home Secretary and Conservative party leader, fought thirty hustings competitions before being selected for Folkestone & Hythe. With enough effort, research, determination and patience, approved candidates stand a good chance of finding a constituency.

The process for becoming a local councillor in England or Wales is a little less formal than that outlined above. Simply enough, nominations for local government candidates are handled by constituency associations, so get in touch with your local chairman and tell him or her that you are interested in standing for council. Your local association will maintain a list of approved candidates; to be added to the list, you will need to sign an agreement to stand as a candidate. All campaign management will be co-ordinated through your constituency association, who will provide you with all the support you need to fight to represent your community at council level. To find out more about becoming a candidate for local government, visit the Conservative Councillors' Association website at https://www.conservativecouncillors.com, which has a section explaining the nomination process and the basic duties of a councillor. You can also obtain a document about the process from the association by emailing cca@conservatives.com.

Hopefully, all of that will put you on track. It may seem to be intense and exhausting, but the Conservative Party is determined to make sure that its candidates are excellent, honest and capable public servants. As long as you have the drive, commitment and desire to stand for office, you are already halfway there. Get campaigning – and good luck.

Andy Wasley is the editor of ToryRascal.com

Getting selected for the Liberal Democrats

Elaine Bagshaw

The selection process for becoming a Liberal Democrat candidate was revamped and relaunched in 2008. As a party, we recognised that we wanted to see a greater diversity in the candidates we had, and that our application and selection process would need to change to help us achieve this.

Our application form was made substantially shorter, and the onus is for the applicant to perform on their assessment day – the application form predominantly collects information from the applicant on things such as their employment history.

There are still a number of seats that are due to select a candidate before the general election; however, it's highly unlikely that any further assessment days will be run before then, so these seats will select from our list of already approved candidates. It's worth submitting an application now, though, so that you can get an assessment day soon after the election. After all, you never know when the next by-election will be called!

The application form and rules
If you want to apply to attend an assessment day, you have to have been a party member for at least one year, and your three referees on the application form must not be:

› blood relatives or those with whom you are in a 'spousal' partnership
› your employees
› anyone who has a financial or contractual obligation to you, or who is in your debt.

And at least one of them must be an office holder of a local, regional or state party within the Liberal Democrats. Anyone who hasn't been a member for a year yet is encouraged to attend events and training at Party Conference, and to get as much campaigning experience as possible from their local party, or from one of our specified associated organisations, for example the Women Liberal Democrats.

The application is mainly so that the Candidates' Office can gather information about the person applying. This can then be used should they be successful in getting approved and later selected. For example, all applicants are asked for a short biography about themselves that can be used should they get selected.

Assessment day

For the English party, assessment days are split into five sections, with a mixture of written and spoken exercises. The aim of the assessment day is to measure the following competencies:

> Communication skills
> Leadership
> Strategic thinking and judgement
> Representing people
> Resilience
> Values in action.

You are scored against each of the competencies during each assessment. At the end of the day the panel of assessors will review how you have scored against each competency and let you know the result a few days later.

For the Scottish party, the assessment day is similar. The day consists of an interview and then a media spot role play. This is followed by a group role play and a policy questionnaire. Again, candidates are assessed by a panel and informed of the assessment result a few days later. The process is similar for those applying to the Welsh party for approval.

Getting selected

Once you're approved, you can then start applying to be selected for seats. Seats requiring candidates will be advertised by local parties in internal party publications, on the Internet, and some parties will approach people directly to ask them to apply. It is also useful for candidates to be proactive and to contact local and regional parties to find out about available seats. Once applications have been submitted to the local party's returning officer, a shortlist of candidates will be drawn up. Before hustings take place, candidates will often take the opportunity to meet members of the local party at events, meetings, and sometimes by contacting members individually. People who have been members of the local party for a minimum of six months are eligible to vote at selection hustings, and can either do this in person or by requesting a postal ballot.

Other elections

People who wish to become candidates for the European Parliament will complete the same form and assessment day as those who are applying to become Parliamentary candidates. The selection process is similar, and results in candidates being placed on a list for the election. This is because of the voting system used in European elections.

Council candidates will need to complete an application form and go through an interview with their local party. They will then go through a selection process which includes a hustings event to select the council candidates for a particular ward.

Selections and approval for Welsh Assembly members and members of the Scottish Parliament are run by the Welsh and Scottish arms of the Liberal Democrats. You can contact them through their websites at the following addresses:

http://www.scotlibdems.org.uk/contact
http://welshlibdems.org.uk/e-contact.php

Diversity

To help ensure our candidates are diverse and reflect the make-up of the population, a number of organisations offer support to people considering becoming approved, and will maintain that support through to them being selected and campaigning. This includes the Campaign for Gender Balance (www.genderbalance.org.uk), which was set up to support women who want to become candidates, rather than enforcing all-women shortlists. The following organisations also offer assistance:

PCA – Parliamentary Candidates' Association
www.parliamentary.org.uk
LDDA – Liberal Democrat Disability Association
www.disabilitylibdems.org.uk
EMLD – Ethnic Minority Liberal Democrats
www.ethnic-minority.libdems.org
DELGA – Liberal Democrats for Lesbian, Gay, Bisexual and Transgender Equality
www.delga.org.uk

Summary

We've revised our process so that it has minimal bureaucracy, and applicants are assessed on how competent they are to be a candidate. A lot of support is offered to those who are going through the process, so it doesn't have to be daunting. You'll learn a lot by going through the process and meet a great range of people at the same time. Good luck!

Elaine Bagshaw was the chair of Liberal Youth from 2008 to 2010

5

Knowledge is power

Janice Small

Getting selected

Research, research, research and research again. This cannot be emphasised enough. Then you have to sell yourself and know the local politics as well as our policies; you must have an overview on the EU and our relationship with the US, UN and the Commonwealth.

The research is no different whether you are seeking a safe target or a 'no hoper'. Knowledge is impressive and powerful.

The electorate are only interested in their seat and some will be looking to trip you up on your local knowledge; they don't necessarily mean to do this, but you will get the question 'What's your view on hunting?' even if you are standing for Peckham or 'What is your view on the local drug crime statistics?' You have to have that knowledge.

When I was interviewed for Dover I was told that the electorate were really impressed with my local knowledge and I told them things that even they didn't know. You can get this across in your speech and Q&As. It is time consuming but worth it. You will feel more comfortable and, if you don't win, at least you put in the ground work and this will be appreciated.

Any candidate researching Dover would see that the local MP's majority did not change at the 2005 election. They would assume he was popular / the previous PPC had run an awful campaign /

Dover wasn't ready for the Tories. All wrong. The local guy was the leader of the district council (and would inevitably come with local baggage) but he was good on the streets and down to earth, had excellent media coverage and was a good performer. However, the crux of the problem was that we had decided to privatise the Dover Harbour Board, the major, unionised employer. The opposition seized upon this and won the argument with scares about deep cuts and unemployment. In-depth research worked and more candidates should have applied and not just looked at the 'majority'.

Research areas

These include transport, education, economy, employment, NEETs, major employers, local authority (particularly if it is an opposition council), the NHS, three local issues (crime, housing, local quangos), rural issues (if applicable), demographics, wider county issues, what your opposition is up to, local sports issues – is there a famous rugby/cricket/football team/player?

Example 1: NEETS and unemployment
You need three key facts:

›   Number of 16–24-year-olds out of work
›   Current total unemployment rates
›   Where the jobs have been lost.

You then weave this information on how you would tackle it, linking into education, training, and into local industry. You can get this information from the ONS.

Example 2: What is your opposition up to?
How many times has he or she spoken in Parliament? What are his or her interests? What committees does he or she sit on? Does he or she vote against or with the government? What are the areas of contention?

Put him or her on a TheyWorkforYou.com alert. Read his or her blog and website, see what local campaigning he or she is doing.

What is the situation on the minor parties (BNP, UKIP, Green etc.)? You have to know what they are doing and saying.

Where to get the information

› Person to person: make an appointment to speak to the chief executive of the local council, speak to the local journalists and find out the year's major issues and anything that has happened that week, read the local blogs, interview a policeman / nurse / farmer / victim of crime / pensioner, read the local BBC website and tune into the regional news programmes.
› On the web: Parish/district council websites, county council website, Dr Foster for NHS information (www. drfosterintelligence.co.uk), NFU, crime statistics from the police, Office for National Statistics, government websites, opposition websites, TheyWorkforYou.com, UKPolling Report – you can also get 2001 census demographic information from there.
› On the ground: if the police will not speak to you, stop an officer in the street. Go to your local supermarket – everyone shops there. Interview the mum with a baby and shopping, the pensioner, the till operator. Ask them what their three main issues are. A young lad on the checkout at Tesco in Colchester told me that his main issues were the NHS, transport and the economy, in that order. A pensioner told me how she was afraid to go out after dark and had been for ten years, I mentioned her name and where I spoke to her. Try interviewing the local headteachers.
› From the party: speak to the area campaign director, campaign director, MEPs and local MPs, previous PPC (unless disgraced!), councillors, leader of council or leader of your party's group.

When I was interviewed for the safe seat of Hexham I visited the local NFU, the local livestock market and two farmers. I brushed up my knowledge of the Common Agricultural Policy and how it affected the local area and the useless Rural Farm Payments Agency. Hunting was an issue as the active local hunt was very much part of the Conservative Association. However, the seat was one of two halves. One half was very rural and wild with farming communities, isolated villages and high pockets of deprivation linked with rural living. The other was an upmarket suburb just by Newcastle airport that had a 'footballers' wives' feel about it and which, in contrast, was anti-hunting. The skill lay in bringing those two communities together and how you would deal with them as the future MP. I interviewed the chief executive of the council, which was about to change from a county council where my party had a majority, to a unitary authority where it was predicted we wouldn't. The major employer was a manufacturer looking to expand its business and premises. There were going to be issues around planning and the environment, balanced against jobs. I had to know the issues and what the opposition were saying. I tried speaking to the owners of the business but they were part of the selection process. So, I went to journalists, councillors, local people and the council chief executive.

Selling yourself

You have to sell yourself. Research your unique selling point. Why me? Who are you? What is it in your background and current life and work that sets you apart and makes you what you are; something they can buy into. Why do you want to be their MP?

Find a quirky fact about the constituency and make them laugh or ponder it. I was interviewed for Calder Valley, a West Yorkshire target seat. The local man Craig was best placed to win. Research found that one of the villages, Hebden Bridge, is the lesbian capital of the UK. I wound this interesting fact into the Q&As and the audience found it hilarious – most of them didn't know that it was.

You have to distil this mass of information onto an A4 sheet of bullet points with headings. Learn the facts and get friends and family to fire questions at you; you will learn to weave the information in with national policies.

Your speech. Yes, have a standard speech but always weave in your local knowledge – how you are going to help them win the council seats, how well they did last time, how you are going to win the hearts and minds of the electorate, etc. Above all, praise them.

The pitfalls of the deluded, neurotic and infighting of associations – what to avoid

I was up for a Liberal Democrat-controlled seat (6,000 majority), where they also ran the council. The local Tories had been fighting for years, all hated each other and had no chance of winning the seat nor the council seats; in fact we had dwindled to three aged councillors. They had lost all strategy, it was a fractured association and there were no ground troops to help. It was a classic former Tory seat, a garrison town, we controlled the county council and most of the district councils, yet this lot believed their PPC could do everything that they had failed to do. I felt like Boudicca. One of the questions was, 'what have you heard about us?' This was a loaded question as they were all clearly certifiable but the local knowledge carried me through and I was able to praise them. I couldn't wait to get out of that interview room.

Understand the possible in-fighting because there will be pitfalls. Also, research the relationship with the neighbouring Tory seats. This is a minefield too. I was interviewed for one seat, which will remain nameless, whose incumbent had a number of expenses issues, was elderly and his majority had dwindled over the years with the Lib Dems hot on his heels. In contrast, the neighbouring seat had a young, dynamic, former army officer who had revitalised the local association, had made a name for himself since winning in 2005 but was disliked by the next-door MP and his association. Therefore, suggesting collaboration with the councillors to ward off the Lib Dems was futile.

Should you work with the local association if there is a council by-election before the selection or court the media?

Again, a minefield. To my knowledge there are few PPCs that got selected because they delivered leaflets and canvassed. You will have local rivals and prejudices will form. If you take a team in with you (as I did) this is seen as 'buying the seat'(!). I was approached to do the local PR for the councillors in the same safe seat (again nameless) as we had to win back the town council (it ping-ponged between us and the Lib Dems). It was a very safe seat with an interfering, retiring, high-profile MP. The councillors were more interested in fighting each other than getting a press release with local pictures and I was caught in the crossfire of the association chairman, who was also a councillor, and the rest of the association and the MP. It did me no favours and I was put on the 'reserve list'. To crown it all I received a text while watching a Harlequins match from a friend, a high-profile candidate, to say we were both on the front page of the regional newspaper as 'top Tories go head to head for safe seat'. Again, the death knell sounded for both of us. I never sought the media coverage but was well known in the county. However, the message is also not to court the media and to keep a low profile if you do help in a by-election.

In complete contrast, when the Medway seat was up for interview the local association put on a briefing day and tour of the constituency. Only those candidates that went on that briefing day were interviewed.

Your CV

Do have a standard CV but half of it should be about your knowledge of their constituency. Check, check and check again for spelling, grammatical and political errors. The obvious one is not replacing the constituency name if you have cut and pasted it from a previous selection! I know someone who would have made an excellent MP but he failed to replace one town in Kent for another in Essex.

*

Two of the best final questions I have been asked:

'Do you think Margaret Thatcher will always be the best prime minister in living memory or do you think PM David Cameron will be better?'

'Which do you prefer: *The X Factor* or *Strictly*?'

What they were asking was: do you understand popular culture and can you have a normal conversation with people on the street who are not interested in politics? Basically, have you got the X Factor?

Janice Small is the Conservative prospective parliamentary candidate for Batley & Spen

6

Surviving selection panels

Robert Ashman

Selecting candidates today is a very different process than ten years ago. The process is much more professional and really does test the competencies that an MP needs. Gone are polite and very predictable interview panels where you give a set presentation followed by a series of set questions that had little to do with your role as a candidate or Member of Parliament. Although I can only give my experience on the process run by the Conservatives, all parties had comparable processes and followed similar programmes, as detailed below.

Candidates submitted a CV and were invited to speak for ten minutes on 'Why I want to be the MP for. . .'. They then faced a series of similarly predictable set questions on issues. There would be some reference to a local issue, how you would involve younger people in the campaign and a few questions on party policy and some local issues. This format was replicated for the rest of the selection process: the selection committee, followed by the Executive Council, culminating in the Special General Meeting (SGM), each with a ten-minute speech followed by a set of questions. At the SGM there would be questions from the floor, which were sometimes quite tricky, but on the whole the process favoured those who were good presenters.

Occasionally some constituencies would throw in a social event where members of the selection committee could meet with the candidates informally – this became affectionately known as 'Trial by Sausage Roll', or 'Vol-au-Vent' in the more affluent constituencies.

This all benefited candidates who could learn a brief, present and perform well under cross-examination. So it was no surprise that there were so many lawyers and career politicians in Parliament. The process did little to test the real competencies required by an MP and disadvantaged those who had little background in politics and political parties.

All parties wanted to get a better cross-section of people into Parliament. This is even more important now that trust in politics and politicians is at such a low ebb.

So the process has changed and been modernised. However, occasionally some of the old methods still seem to persist.

Right from the start – getting on the candidates list – things have changed. Like most modern companies do, parties have hired occupational psychologists to produce modern assessment tools. Potential candidates are assessed on the necessary skills used by MPs on a day-to-day basis. These are much tougher and are designed to elicit the correct skills and to be as objective as possible. The result has been a much more representative cross-section of candidates, with a variety of experiences and from a variety of backgrounds.

Similarly the whole selection process is much tougher and has developed to test candidates on the skills that they will need to make them a suitable candidate for a particular seat. Candidates are expected to have thoroughly researched the seat and to make this clear in their presentations and questions.

The old format has gone and more and more new ideas have been tried out. Primaries/caucuses are popular now, where any voter can sign up and vote at the selection meeting. Usually presided over by a moderator, often a journalist, they select questions from the audience and then probe candidates on their responses. In many cases now candidates are given only 2–3 minutes to make a formal presentation with the rest of the process being questions and probing from the moderator.

Candidates are encouraged to canvass around the constituency to encourage voters to sign up and turn up at the primary. Expenses for the production of leaflets and website are limited by national party rules. It is amazing in some situations how many leaflets you can produce for a limited amount!

And the questioning has changed a lot as well. No longer are people interested in their views on Europe. Now you are more likely to be asked about what experience and qualities you have that would make you a good MP. You are also expected to be able to show from your life experience that you have the necessary skills to be a successful candidate.

Many seats will now invite candidates to undertake tasks to test their abilities in campaigning and communication. So applicants can expect to be invited to join members canvassing or running a street stall. They will be observed and marked according to their performance. Are they dressed appropriately, do they stand around waiting for direction or try to take over? Are they able to chat easily to voters, listen to their concerns and respond appropriately?

Candidates are expected to have an understanding of popular culture. So they can expect to be asked about comments from the judges on *The X Factor* or *Strictly Come Dancing* as they are on local and national politics. Those who think this is low brow are reminded that more voters in their constituency watch these programmes than *Newsnight* and Andrew Marr! In fact news about these programmes are often reported on *Newsnight* and Andrew Marr!

There are also those questions that are designed to see if candidates have done their research. These often focus on local issues that will have required more than a glance at the local papers or the internet.

Then there's the 'they think it's all over' question! Just when a candidate has got to the end of the session the moderator throws in that tricky question. Sometimes these are designed to be unanswerable. They want to see if the candidate can think on their feet. Often these are simple questions but it's amazing how many are completely thrown – staring like a rabbit in the headlights. Think of Gordon Brown being stumped by choosing his favourite biscuit. And this was reported for days!

Remember, it's easy to try and plan for the topical questions that may be asked and then think of a good answer and how these can be linked to the constituency and/or candidate.

So what are the party members looking for?

Too often candidates make the mistake of delivering a political speech based on party policy making no reference to local issues and, even worse, no mention of what makes them want to be and MP. People want to know what experience they have that would make them a good candidate and MP. They want to know what motivates them, what has shaped their lives to make them want to become a legislator? Anyone can produce a speech on policy or even the local issues, just by looking on the internet. What the members want to know is 'Who is this person and what makes them special enough to be our MP?'

So what are the tips for surviving the selection process?

1. Research, research and research

Thoroughly research the seat. Find out the issues and then delve into them in as much detail as you can. With the internet it's very easy to get access to a lot of information. But remember that the information may not be accurate and may be out of date. The local media organisations are usually the best way to find the main issues and point you in the right direction. (For more on this, see Chapter 5, Knowledge Is Power.)

2. Visit the seat and speak to real people

This is essential and if it becomes clear you have not visited, expect to be given a tough time at the selection interviews. The local media are an excellent place to start and a good source of what the real local issues are. There will be many local organisations – the chamber of commerce, residents' groups, National Farmers Union and other local associations. Then there are head teachers, doctors, religious leaders and other professionals. And don't forget about taxi drivers, shopkeepers and market stallholders. Remember, however, that they will give their personal views so you need to balance what they say with proper research.

3. Understand the issues

The more you research and the more people you speak to the more you will really understand the issues that matter. What can sometimes seem a brilliant issue on the surface can, on more investigation, turn out to be a poison chalice. For example, everyone wants affordable housing, but not necessarily where it's planned. Remember that you may be grilled by a local journalist during the selection meetings whose job it is to test every argument. So if you don't know the pros and cons on the local issues you could well be digging yourself into a hole. Identify the pitfalls and prepare for these.

4. Address their concerns

There are some issues that the selection panel are going to want to know and you have to address these. Will you move to the constituency and, if so, when? Will you move your home here or simply 'establish a base'? How often will you be available for campaigning? If you have a demanding job, how will this allow you to devote time to the campaign? If you're a councillor elsewhere, are you going to continue and, if so, how will you balance your time and will you stand down before the election? You must address these concerns in your speech rather than wait for them to be brought up.

5. Perfect preparation

People who make speaking look easy will have done a lot of preparation. The ease of their presentation hides many hours of preparation and practice. Once you have accumulated your research and decided what you want to say you will need to write down what you are going to say. It will always be longer than you thought so you will need to edit and re-edit to get it down to the correct length. It's essential that you do this so you know that you can cover the areas and issues you must within the limited time available.

6. Keep it simple

Avoid long and complicated words. Keep it simple and keep to the point. Look at how newspapers and the media communicate. They make no assumptions on the level of understanding of their audience. Use vivid language. It helps illustrate what you're saying using fewer words. Keep paragraphs short and sentences shorter. If you fail to communicate your message *you* have failed, not the audience!

7. *Visualise*

Illustrate the important issues with stories. These should be about things that have happened to you or that have showed you the importance of an issue. This helps show you have done the real research around the constituency and is a much more effective way of getting across your point in an entertaining and memorable way. You will find it easier to remember the points visually – as will your audience.

8. *Plan for the questions*

Think about what you are likely to be asked. Your research will have given you a lot of information that you can use in the local questions. But read the national and local papers. Look at the stories that are in the news and think about how you can best answer these. It's even better if you can add a personal link in your answer. Remember, if *The X Factor* or *Dancing on Ice* are in the main papers then you need to know about this. Run through a selection of questions and think about your answers. If you only think of the right answer after the interview, it's too late!

9. *Practice makes perfect*

Actually it's practice of good practice that makes perfect. Read through your speech aloud and edit and amend accordingly. Video yourself, it makes a real difference. Practice as many times as you need so that you feel comfortable that you can deliver your presentation with passion and personality. Try not to use notes as they distract and stilt your performance. That said, you should take up some prompt cards to keep you on track. Always look to improve. If the top sports stars and professional performers have to practice for hours to keep at the top of their game then so do you!

10. Be honest

Always be honest and always be yourself. There's no easy way, there are no tricks. It's about putting in the hard work, researching thoroughly, preparing and practising. This will allow your personality to come through and for people to see the real you.

Robert Ashman is a deputy director of the Conservative Party

7

Open primaries?

Jessica Asato

Recent history

Usually associated with politics over the pond, primaries came of age in the UK in 2009. Though the Conservative Party had used caucuses to select around 100 candidates in previous years, it was only in 2009 when open primaries were trialled for real. The two biggies were held in seats where the expenses scandal had taken its toll – on Sir Anthony Steen in Totnes and Sir Peter Viggers in Gosport.

Where the Conservatives had opened up selections to ordinary voters before – for the selection of Annunziata Rees-Mogg in Somerton & Frome in 2006, for example – the fact that citizens had to attend a meeting to be able to vote meant that only around 250 turned up. In the cases of Totnes and Gosport, however, voters were offered postal ballots and the novelty and convenience, plus the national focus, meant there was a much larger turnout. Totnes witnessed a turnout of around 24 per cent with 16,000 voters participating, while in Gosport, 12,659 votes were cast. *The Times* called the Totnes experiment 'the best political news for months'.

Until last year, parliamentary selections were mainly the preserve of signed-up party members. The right to select a candidate who reflected grassroots opinion and could be held accountable to members was sacrosanct and mainly went unquestioned. Declining party membership, however, has led some to question the legitimacy of selection processes. Research undertaken by Will Straw for Progress in 2009 found that in the Labour Party, a median of forty party members vote in the final round of parliamentary selection contests – a tiny proportion of the average electorate of 70,000. When a party could boast over a million members, there was a stronger likelihood that the final candidate chosen by members represented a significant part of the community. That is less likely to be the case when the vast majority of the public don't join political parties.

Moreover, the worry that politicians of all hues have lost touch with the electorate has convinced people such as Douglas Carswell MP that new selection methods must be embraced to reconnect with the electorate. As he said when introducing a Bill in 2009 to legislate for primaries: 'As long as we retain the right to stand under the colours of our parties, we have tenure. Our incentives are thus twisted. Instead of answering outwards to their voters, MPs in safe seats are encouraged by the system to answer upwards to their whips.' The argument goes that if the public feel they have voted for a candidate they are more likely to want to hold that person accountable than if they were selected by a committee of members. Since the expenses debacle, politicians and activists in all parties are searching for ways to give the public more control over politics and primaries look like one method gaining favour.

Outside the Conservative Party, primaries do not look set to be immediately picked up by other political parties, but there have been some signs that there is some appetite for it in the Labour Party. Senior party figures such as David Miliband, Tessa Jowell and Andrew Adonis are on record as being in favour. Interestingly, the potential two frontrunners for Labour's London mayoral candidate – Ken Livingstone and David Lammy – are also supportive of primaries. The Liberal Democrats are strongly committed to their members having a say over candidate selection and are likely to find it harder to raise the necessary money to run a primary, which suggests Lib Dem selections will stay as they are unless there is legislative change.

Whether political parties other than the Conservatives follow suit remains to be seen, but just in case they do, or Douglas Carswell wins his way in Parliament, here are a few thoughts about how to get selected.

Different types of primaries and their impact on selection

Many people use the phrase 'open primaries' as a catch-all term for primaries, but technically, open primaries are one specific type of primary. There are broadly three different types: open, caucus and closed. Open primaries give all voters in a particular electoral area the opportunity to participate even if they are affiliated to a party which they then don't vote for. This selection method was used in Totnes and Gosport, where anyone could apply for a postal ballot. Caucus primaries may be open to all to attend, but limit participation by holding the vote at a specific venue on one day. This happened in the Bracknell primary, for example. Closed primaries tend to only be open to pre-registered supporters of one political party.

Obviously, your selection strategy will change depending on which type of selection method is being used. Open primaries require the biggest shift in selection technique. Instead of working with small numbers of members who can be individually canvassed, potentially lots of times, you have the whole electorate to convince. The selection would be similar in some ways, therefore, to the actual election. The focus should be less on how many campaigning hours you have under your belt, how many positions you hold in the Party or how many senior party figures you can wheel out to support you, and more on your life experience, your political views and policy positions, and how you come across to a politically immature audience.

Without restrictions on spending, open primaries will likely benefit candidates who have access to personal resources or are backed by big organisations such as trade unions. It wouldn't be impossible to win on a shoe-string – after all the British like an underdog – but even Barack Obama with all his charisma and vision had to pull in the biggest campaign spending of all time to secure the Democrat nomination. Open primaries will benefit those candidates who can build a good media presence and can perform to a high standard throughout the campaign. Given the size of the electorate, it is unlikely that the contest will be won on the final hustings speech, so consistency of message will be important.

Caucus primaries are more likely to benefit candidates who are able to get their vote out on the day and who perform well in the hustings and any question and answer session. While many voters may have already made their mind up, a strong performance may convince swing voters. This would suggest that speech-writing training and public speaking experience are a must for this type of selection. Time should be spent on convincing party members who are most likely to come to the hustings, voters who regularly vote for your party and who might take part in volunteering activities, and key influencers in the area.

Closed primaries are in some senses easier than the other two because you will be working with a defined electorate – those who have decided to register as party supporters. The electorate, however, is likely to be bigger than during conventional selections so if the time period is short candidates would be best advised to hold meetings for bigger groups of voters rather than trying to get round everyone individually. Targeted mail will probably play a big part, and since voters have already identified their support for your party, you won't have to spend time trying to woo people from other political persuasions.

Who will benefit from primaries?
Since primaries are such a new phenomenon in British politics, it's hard to know what the effect on candidate selection will be. From the two open primaries we've seen we can speculate about a number of things. The first is that women do not appear to be at a disadvantage – in Totnes voters selected Sarah Woollaston and in Gosport they selected Caroline Dinenage. Research conducted by the Centre for Women and Democracy found that 27 per cent of all Conservative candidates selected through primaries are women, which is not far off the number of women applying for selection.

Certainly evidence from the US seems to suggest that there isn't a gender disadvantage.

The second potential impact of primaries on candidate selection is that the more local connection you have with an area, the more likely you are to be selected. Caroline Dinenage was a local councillor and had lived in Gosport all her life. Sarah Woollaston was a local GP in Devon. It is a myth that in the past parliamentary candidates were local born and bred, but post-expenses, it is to be expected that voters might choose someone they feel knows their area and understands the people living there. If primaries are introduced wholesale, however, and the feeling of detachment from Westminster wanes, perhaps the local factor might be less important.

Finally, there was some suggestion that Sarah Woollaston, in particular, won Totnes because she represented a 'different style of politics' as was conceded by her main rival Nick Bye, in an article for *The Times*. In particular he highlighted that 'party political point-scoring was just not what this audience wanted to hear'. Bye admitted that he 'made the mistake of using one of my favourite lines of attack. "The biggest myth in British politics is that Liberal Democrats are such nice people" went down a storm in front of the party executive. But in front of a wider audience, it fell as flat as a pancake.' Barack Obama recognised this in his primary selection too, sticking by the strategy that 'the same old Washington textbook campaigns just won't do'.

If primaries represent a form of selection designed to change politics for the better, then wannabe politicians may have to change their behaviour for the better too, if they want to be rewarded by the newly enfranchised electors.

Jessica Asato is the acting director of Progress

Part III

On the campaign trail

8

Developing a campaign plan

David Canzini

So now you have been selected. But the euphoria will be short lived as you settle down and realise the task ahead of you. Not only have you just got yourself an unpaid job but that job means you are now a figurehead, executive chairman, head of resources, agony aunt, motivator, organiser, strategist and decision maker all rolled into one nervous wreck.

Within the professional campaigner ranks the candidate is sometimes, but wrongly, referred to as 'only the legal necessity'. This is a view based in the post-war years and is no longer relevant – although with all the roles you will have to undertake perhaps you will hanker for those days.

For the purposes of this chapter it is assumed that you have twelve months to polling day; whether your actual time is shorter or longer doesn't matter as the key elements remain the same.

Why do you need a campaign plan?
The only way you are going to pull everything together to culminate in a massive effort on polling day is to create a campaign plan. The plan should have all the necessary elements to ensure that when the formal election campaign commences you have an organisation and profile that will give you a fighting chance to run an effective election campaign which, to repeat, will culminate in a massive

effort on polling day. When developing a campaign plan there's something you need to keep in mind: *Pace and flexibility*.

The overall structure of the plan should not change but the detail and tactics will. Don't be afraid to change things that need changing, whether it's personnel or tactics, as long as it's to improve your chance of winning. Your plan will also help bring you back to reality when you get the urge (or are urged) to completely change direction to cope with an opponent's strategy or tactics (if you do make a massive change for that reason, you have acknowledged you are going to lose).

What is your campaign plan going to look like?

Each election is different and you have to take into account how big or small your organisation is. You need to end up with a plan that is easy to explain so your team know what they have to do and when. Some candidates will create a war book that is broken up into sections on each ward with the plan for each area and a set of messages. Others will create a wall planner of activity with a separate record of the messages/issues that will be raised as and when necessary. The key to creating a successful campaign will be ensuring as many of your activists as possible know what the overall plan is so they are bought into it and feel ownership.

Research

You may or may not have conducted much research into how your constituency/ward ticks to prepare for your selection. Either way it doesn't matter because you have to start again with fresh eyes as you now have to deliver!

How many votes do you need to win?

This may seem to have an obvious answer but it does not. The reason you need to do this is that it will be the target you have to break down ward by ward (street by street) which will help you marshal your resources to best effect. This exercise will help identify the demographics of where you can get the votes from, which in turn will inform your strategy and dictate your tactics.

How should you work this out?

Look back over three to five elections (depending on boundary changes) and look at share of votes and turnout – after all, if you are a long way behind but there is traditionally only a 20 per cent turnout, perhaps if you increase turnout then you will be in with a chance. Break your research down to each ward / polling district. Assume your campaign will increase turnout and add 5 per cent to the average turnout of the past elections you looked at and that will give you the total of votes that could be cast at your election. Then average the share for third parties and others to give you the number of votes they will take and subtract that figure from the total; then you need a 50.1 per cent share of the rest, and that will be your total vote target.

Where are you going to get your votes from?

Again go back to recent elections to see what your party 'normally gets'. This will help you prioritise where you will get your votes and more importantly identify where you will need to maximise turnout of your supporters or increase your share of the vote.

Local intelligence

'Time spent in reconnaissance is seldom wasted'. When preparing your campaign plan it is worth spending time with local activists and others who are involved in your party's local organisation to 'download' from them local political information. The best source for this information will inevitably come from councillors or council candidates (don't forget parish or town councillors). These people will give you real-time intelligence on what is happening in their area such as:

> › demographic changes
> › new residents / recent housing developments
> › ward issues
> › and most importantly – war stories from the campaign trail.

This will help you formulate your strategy ward by ward / polling district by polling district.

Issues/messages matrix

You will already have some idea on what issues your campaign will focus on as they will be clear from the national picture. You need to prioritise these issues and localise them to show practical examples across your whole electorate or on a ward by ward basis. You will then be creating your message matrix, which can be slotted into your campaign plan.

When starting out your campaign you have the time to have a broad and all-encompassing set of messages. Over the year running up to your election you will need to refine and then reduce this set so you end up with your election campaign messages, which will be then honed to short and sharp motivational Get Out the Vote (GOTV) messages for the final ten days.

At whatever level you are fighting your election (ward/constituency/region) your campaign issues will be defined by the national or council issues. Most election campaigns are focused on 'the national debate' on issues such as:

> Law and order
> Economy/tax
> Health
> Education
> Transport
> National leadership.

So for your local campaign you need to formulate and then lock down messages on these issues that can be localised. Each of your key messages should relate back to what the national campaign will be – don't forget no matter how much you do locally your electorate will receive most of their political information from the national media and therefore from the national party. Your key messages should also relate to local issues by using examples to illustrate your message from the local constituency.

In an ideal world you will have an issue per ward but more likely you will have generic issues that will impact across your area. Don't be afraid to stray onto issues that are not necessarily the purview of the level of administration you are looking to be elected to. Most of your electorate will not differentiate between what is a local council or parliamentary matter; what they will look for is whether you relate to their hopes, fears or desires.

A mistake some candidates make is to assume their electorate is selfish and only concerned about themselves as individuals. Although that emotion may be the first criterion on which your campaign will be judged, many people will vote on the policies that improve or solve problems in their local community or the country and benefit them in the long run.

Together with your set of generic messages on the big issues you then need to formulate some key messages to headline the targeting (see below) that you will undertake during the course of your campaign. The key to communication with target groups is to grab their attention with messages that they feel are for them (thus demonstrating that you have an interest in them) which then flow into the generic messages. Don't assume a group (young, elderly teachers etc.) is only interested in their issues to the exclusion of everything else.

Strategy and tactics
When looking at setting out your strategy and tactics, consider what your constituency is made up of. A typical constituency is made up of these groups of voters:

› The opposition (will undermine and disrupt)
› Non-voters (will waste your time but never vote)
› The cynical (fire cheap shots to test your resolve)
› Undecided (not engaged; waiting to see how it goes)
› Core vote (vote for your party at every election)
› Champions (active supporters who take responsibility for ensuring success).

The campaign strategy and tactics should:

› isolate the opposition and non-voters

› move the cynics to undecided;
› move the undecided to core vote;
› convert the core vote to champions.

A definition of a campaign strategy is 'an alternative platform chosen to make happen a desired future, such as achievement of a win', or 'the art and science of planning and marshalling resources for their most efficient and effective use'. A definition of campaign tactics is 'the means by which a strategy is carried out; planned and ad hoc activities meant to deal with the demands of the moment, and to move from one milestone to another in pursuit of the overall goal(s)'.

Decision making
In a campaign, strategy is decided by the candidate and senior staff/ activists, and tactics by the campaign team for implementation by activists.

Strategy
A campaign strategy is ultimately designed for you to motivate enough electors to vote for you on polling day. The strategy is your broad-brush template for the campaign and every speech, press release, leaflet and direct mail piece should fulfil one or all the elements of your strategy.
    Motivate the voters by:

› showing you are a credible alternative;
› finding an issue or issues to make your own;
› attacking the record of your opponents – link national failures to local communities;
› providing regular and relevant communication with electors;
› building a coalition of third-party advocates;
› building an effective and well-resourced fighting force.

Tactics
A political campaign is all about communicating your messages using methods that your electorate can relate to. When drawing up

your campaign plan it is best to map out your activity to ensure that you can spread your communication out on a regular basis, building up the campaign activity to the election. Mapping out your activity will help identify key activity periods and it will help you get commitment from your activists to take part. The tactics you will plan for should include:

> Voter ID – door-to-door / telephone canvassing
> Regular communication – literature (generic / locally targeted)
> Media – local media
> Third-party groups
> New media
> Direct mail.

Some of the tactics can include a specific mini-campaign where you focus for, say, a month on one issue or area. For example you could identify third-party groups and get them in for meetings, or the campaign could be based around an issue such as education, where you get around the constituency to talk to teachers, parents and pupils about what is going on and laying out your plans to them.

When setting out your plan don't forget to take account of public/ bank holiday periods as these can be an opportunity to interact with electors who are at home or out and about. Also understand that sometimes people don't want to see or hear from politicians so use this to recharge your campaigns' batteries.

Targeting
Failing to plan is planning to fail
Targeting is seen as the 'Holy Grail' by campaign professionals and at every level of the campaign you will be urged to target, so when preparing your campaign plan you will have to consider the following statements that will be thrown at you.

'Just target your voters.' This may seem obvious unless of course there are not enough of 'your voters' to win. Also if you spend your whole campaign amongst this group then during the election campaign you may well only have motivated your core vote and that will rarely be enough to win a seat.

Solution: there are several ways to build a target voter campaign including making sure that previous campaigns' canvass records are up to date. Also you can access the marked register from previous elections – these two combined databases will indicate which of your party's voters actually turned out (therefore likely to again) and more importantly they will highlight those of your party supporters who did not bother to turn out and should be a 'target group' for you as the candidate to motivate.

That data, overlaid on your target areas and broken down by polling districts (see above), could well indicate where you will have to work the hardest to reach out to non-voters, soft opposition supporters, lazy supporters and the important swing voters (who give their vote to a different party at each election).

'Demographic groups'. Again this is seen as a sensible idea until you realise that the 'groups' people talk about do not live in one area and cannot be assumed to all have the same views. Therefore any meaningful targeting will be very difficult unless you have the resources to purchase or obtain lists of demographic breakdowns of your constituency (Mosaic data). Some candidates will be lucky enough that their party HQ has this information.

Solution: Clearly it is desirable to target tailored messages at specific groups within your constituency but with limited resources you may have to be more general. Here are some suggestions:

Elderly: worth targeting as this demographic tends to be good at turning out on polling day. You can identify sheltered accommodation or nursing homes as a start; perhaps you can obtain the 'non-jury list' from the council as this actually identifies those over the age of seventy-five who are no longer required for jury service. Ask your activists to identify an age group (e.g. 55+) of the people they interact with.

Young / young families: As with the elderly, your canvassers should mark up a younger group (e.g. 18–25) of people they meet. The electoral register indicates those who will turn eighteen in the year and if you are lucky enough to have the registers for several years you can use the info to find those who are 18, 19, 20, 21 and so on.

New housing developments: These are often fertile ground for targeting new families. City centre apartments can be a good place to start for young professionals. If you have a college or university, it will have student accommodation or, even better, a club or society that could be aligned to your party who then can reach out on your behalf.

Ethnic groups: As with every other group, don't assume their demographic means they have the same set of views. In some areas ethnic communities will reside together but this is less common than it used to be. The electoral register will give you a clue with ethnic names. Ethnic communities tend to have organisations/societies/clubs which may welcome you to introduce yourself to the community.

'Areas/wards'. This is the easiest targeting to undertake as previous election results (see above) will indicate if an area or ward should be the focus of your campaign, i.e. targeted. However, before committing resources to a target area, be sure you are going to get some return.

Solution: Be clear as to what the objective is. Is the reason to target the area to deliver your campaign extra votes? Will you have to target the area so as not to lose votes to another party? Is there a big personal vote for a local councillor that you need to harness or neutralise?

Also, if you are targeting a ward, do the electorate appreciate that they live in a ward or is it actually made up of a number of communities and therefore should you reflect this in your campaign communications to them?

Budgets

Your campaign plan will help you set your budget and fundraising timetable. Elections at every level have strict legal maximums that can spent on the campaign during the election period. Prior to this period there are (currently) fewer restrictions, but as the candidate you should be absolutely clear what your legal limits are as your campaign has to pay its bills. Your budget should be in two parts:

1. Pre-election campaign – up to nomination period (in parliamentary elections this will include the five months before the last possible date of dissolution and is called the long campaign)
2. Election – the period from nomination to close of poll.

How much will the pre campaign cost?

This is a difficult question to answer as it really depends what you want to do and whether you can raise the money. Clearly you should set out your campaign plan to achieve victory and then set your budget accordingly. Then amend your activity (increase or decrease depending on how you are doing with fundraising).

You cannot fatten a pig on market day or *Early money works harder.* The reality is that literature and activity will have more impact in the run-up to the election campaign than it will during the campaign. The reason for this is because during the campaign you will be one of many candidates and inevitably you will all be fighting hard amongst some of the same voters so they will be swamped in literature and have several calls either to the door or by telephone. However, in the run-up to the election campaign you will be more likely to be running your campaign in isolation from your opponents so what you do will be more memorable and have greater impact upon the voters. Your spending in the pre-election campaign should reach a crescendo just before the actual election campaign commences.

Election campaign spending limits

For a parliamentary campaign the legal maximum for the election campaign would be around £11,000. For a local government election campaign the figure will be between £2,000 and £5,000 depending on the type of local authority and size of electorate.

As a rough guide your election campaign spending should be broken down as follows:

Staff /HQ/admin   30%
Campaign material (literature/
direct mail/ new media/ advertising)   65%
Contingency   5%

Summary

A year-long campaign can be distilled into three phases:

› Research phase (Month 1). The research phase should take a matter of weeks and will identify the 'likely route' and therefore the communities that should be targeted for maximum political impact.
› Ground war phase (Months 2–10). Identifying possible supporters using traditional campaign methods such as door to door, local 'push polling', literature drops, petition gathering, planted letters in the local media and making use of new media. Creating an effective election organisation and raising the funds for the campaign.
› GOTV phase (Months 11 & 12). Ensuring supporters are motivated to cast their vote and opponents are demoralised so stay at home (for more on this, see Chapter 17, Getting Out the Vote).

Likewise, a successful five-week election campaign has three phases:

› Phase 1 – Fast start (Week 1). As soon as the election is called then your campaign needs to explode into action by delivering leaflets and first direct mail piece (raising extra funds) and getting posters up. The candidate should be 'out and about' in areas where there are swing voters. This is about getting momentum and demoralising opponents.
› Phase 2 – Delivering the message (Weeks 2 & 3). Ensuring your voters are bombarded by the campaign with high-visibility events, regular literature and communication. This is also the machine phase of the campaign, which ensures no potential supporter is missed.

› Phase 3 – Get Out the Vote (Weeks 4 & 5). Every supporter and swing voter still in play has to be targeted relentlessly with key motivational messages to ensure that by close of poll they have cast a vote for you.

Conclusion

A campaign plan is a candidate's guide which will help them see clearly what they have to do to whom and what they will say. It will help focus the activity of the campaign team to ensure the prize of victory on polling day is always the aim.

David Canzini is a political and campaign strategist

9

How to choose a campaign manager

Tom Hirons

As a bright new candidate for public office you will have in your own mind the sort of campaign you'd like to run. You're probably dreamily imagining running for election in Camelot & South Camelotshire – all white knights and shining armour, great battles of ideas and intellect – but that way disaster lies. Ideas and policies will play an important part in your election, but so will strategy, manpower, money and sheer bloody hard work. Politics can be a messy business, and never more so than in a closely contested election. The key to success is in striking the right balance; a politician without the resources to deliver victory is just as vulnerable as one bereft of ideas and policies.

Whatever the level of your election, from parish council to Parliament, you will need to campaign. Campaigns come in all shapes and sizes, from hundreds of thousands of pounds for parliamentary by-elections and Euro-elections, to just hundreds for local government elections. The person responsible for planning and enacting that campaign, for budgeting the expenditure and running the organisation will be your campaign manager. He or she may or may not be the same person as your agent, but your agent will have to take ultimate legal responsibility.

Your campaign organisation may already exist, a local party branch perhaps, or you may have to build it yourself. But there is a sure way to identify a campaign organisation that is working well: the candidate will only ever be doing one of two things, winning votes or raising money. Everything else will be someone else's job. Even though you won't be running your campaign from day to day, it is still vital that it reflects you and acts according to your wishes. The campaign is about you, the public will see it as your campaign, and it will ultimately be you who answers for it at the ballot box.

So, choosing a campaign manager can seem a daunting task; it is necessarily a matter of compromise. Every candidate would like to employ some Rove-esque genius, grizzled and scarred by years of combat in the political bear pit, but UK election law, mercifully, makes it impossible in all but the glitziest of races – the London Mayoralty perhaps?

The work of a campaign manager varies enormously from high politics to lowly errands. You will need your campaign manager to hold the attention of a room and disappear in a crowd with equal ease. You will want to recruit a campaign manager with Margaret Thatcher's tenacity and assertiveness, David Attenborough's trustworthy smile, George Washington's strategic brilliance and the patience of St Francis. In this, as in all things, you are going to have to compromise. . .

So, if a compromise must be reached between what you would like and what you can afford, you should begin with the immovable: trust.

The facts are simple: in the course of discharging his or her duties your campaign manager will routinely make decisions that affect the outcome of your election. You will not have time to make those decisions yourself. There will be times when your campaign manager will speak with your voice, to volunteers, to voters, even to the press. And, in the course of doing the job your campaign manager will likely become privy to personal information about you and your family.

Those important decisions may not be glamorous, may not even seem important. They might include choosing the words on a flyer, or the recipients of a mass mailing. They might include something bigger, like choosing where to focus big resources and where to use a lighter touch. If they go wrong all these things could have a damaging effect on your campaign; if the mistakes are repeated the consequences could be very serious.

Your campaign manager will inevitably be addressing volunteers in your absence, perhaps to offer training or words of encouragement. They will most certainly, if they're worth their salt, be speaking to voters on the doorstep and will probably be training and monitoring others who do. They may field a phone call from the press at a busy time or have a casual conversation with a local journo at the back of some crowded room. In all these scenarios the listeners will assume that your campaign manager is speaking with your voice. Saying the wrong thing or worse, misrepresenting you and your views, could prove disastrous. Letting slip some of your campaign's weaknesses to the wrong people could clearly land you and the campaign in some pretty hot water.

You may choose not confide your deepest secrets to your campaign manager, but after a tense meeting you might let off steam in the car and say a few things that you'd rather stayed in the car. The secrets need not be big to have the potential to do damage; indeed it would be unwise to enter politics at all if you have too many skeletons in the closet. But small everyday things, like your mood swings, private details about your family, or the inner workings of your home life could still be a problem if they fall into mischievous hands. Perhaps none of these things would damage your credibility, but at the very least they will distract people from your policy message.

It will be a huge weight lifted from your shoulders if your campaign manager is someone with whom you can share private details in confidence, someone around whom you can relax and let off steam. It is vital that you are able to trust your campaign manager to make the right decisions, to direct your campaign in the manner you would wish and to understand and respect the difference between personal and public information. That bond of trust will, at times, be the single frayed thread from which your entire campaign hangs.

In a small campaign, especially one with a low budget, it may be sensible to ask a friend or relative to be your campaign manager.

Someone who already knows you and what you stand for; crucially, someone you know you can trust. If the task is bigger than that, you will need a more serious commitment.

There are some simple rules to follow when recruiting your campaign manager. Firstly, bear in mind that the person you are looking for may already be involved, in the local party for instance. A keen volunteer you know well or a reliable local councillor might be the perfect fit. Their knowledge of the constituency and experience of the local party organisation might prove an invaluable asset to your campaign. If you know of nobody locally who could fill the role to your satisfaction you will need to bring in new blood. There are numerous places to advertise such a post to eager potential applicants; for example, www.w4mp.org is a fantastic resource, and your party will probably have an internal system for the same purpose.

You will obviously want to bring in the best talent that your war chest can afford but remember, if you're looking for a professional, whether full time or on a consultancy basis, if you are only prepared to pay peanuts you will only get monkeys. A good campaign manager will be working seven days a week in preparation for an election. They will begin to forget what their friends and relatives look like and start pulling out their own hair in lumps with the stress. You are asking someone to make a very serious commitment, so be sure to reward it well. And remember that money is not the only incentive in your gift. Invitations to exciting events, access to high-ranking politicians and a varied diet of little things to say thank you will ensure that frayed thread stays just strong enough.

Always try to find a professional recruiter to help you read job applications. The understanding that such professionals bring to the language of CVs and personal statements is close to clairvoyance. More than likely your local contacts will know of someone with such skills who is prepared to help.

Always seek strong personal references and take real time to follow up and interrogate referees. Time spent here could save months of anguish later should you recruit the wrong person. Focus on trustworthiness and look for evidence from impartial sources.

Ideally seek out other candidates or elected officials who know the applicant. They will understand the pressures the job entails and will be well placed to judge the suitability of the applicant.

If trust is immovable, then experience is an opportunity to compromise. But consider carefully the scale of your campaign. Clearly, it would be unwise to entrust a campaign of national importance to a complete novice, but you may have time for your campaign manager to grow into the role – provided he or she has the basic skills. You should have no worries about recruiting someone with a successful history in smaller campaigns, provided your own election is not imminent. Even Karl Rove had to start somewhere!

If your campaign is small, for the local council, say, the Campaign Manager's role will likely be simple: largely organising canvassing and leafleting. Any local supporter with a dash of campaign experience could do it. For such elections you may even be your own campaign manager, though you will need to manage your time very carefully. In larger, more complicated campaigns, for Parliament or a national assembly for instance, you should obviously look for someone more experienced. Someone who has successfully run a local government campaign would be ideal, as such a person will have already grasped the basics and should be ready to move on to the next level.

As well as experience there are some key skills to look for, regardless at what level your campaign is being fought. Your campaign will be broken up into a series of projects: a leaflet to be delivered, a mail shot to be sent out and so on. Each project will involve several operations and with each will come a deadline. Your campaign manager must be able to prepare and maintain plans for each of these projects, ensuring that deadlines aren't missed. Managing a constant and overlapping stream of projects like this isn't easy. Anyone applying should be able to demonstrate that they have a proven record. Do bear in mind that this is an interdisciplinary skill; examples from outside politics are equally valid.

Self-discipline is also important. Nothing will be more irritating than a campaign manager who is always late and under-prepared.

The surest way to judge an applicant's self-discipline is their employment history. No employer will long tolerate someone who can't get out of bed in the morning. So, have they held down a job for any length of time? Follow up references from previous employers and ask about punctuality, preparedness and turnout.

You should also look for someone with 'people skills', not a woolly 'character attribute' but a real demonstrable ability to work within and manage teams of people. Perhaps they have run clubs or societies, or undertaken team assignments at university or college? There will be times when your campaign manager will be the one calling the shots and also times when they will have to fit into teams that already exist. It is very likely that your local party organisation already has an established hierarchy, with chairmen, presidents and agents. Your campaign manager must work well with all of them to secure the outcome you need. That will take patience, tenacity and assertiveness too. These structures will all need to be subtly driven in the right direction by you and your campaign manager.

Bear in mind also that your campaign manager will have a considerable degree of influence over your work–life balance. The Terminator's work ethic might be admirable, but over the years of long campaigning you will need to pace yourself. It will be much easier for you if your campaign manager has an understanding of the balance you need to strike between work and home life. Nothing will pile on the stress as quickly as feeling that you are neglecting your nearest and dearest.

In all things, as in politics, when looking for someone to work with be honest with yourself about your own weaknesses and recruit a team that fills the gaps in your ability. If you have no experience of political campaigning, an experienced hand would be useful. If you are bursting with ideas and not good at seeing things through, find a campaign manager who is an expert at driving tasks to completion but maybe not such a creative thinker. This will ensure that your teamwork adds value to the campaign, putting you in a far stronger position on the battlefield.

Other qualities to add to the wish list will be a strong knowledge of IT and in particular the technologies used in e-campaigns, email,

Web 2.0, websites and so on. Some knowledge of graphic design and print processes will come in handy too, as will a working knowledge of any proprietary systems your party uses, such as Merlin, Ears or Excalibur. All these skills could be farmed out to professionals or taught in house, and none of them should stop you choosing a campaign manager; think of them as a way to choose between the best applicants.

So choosing the right person to lead your campaign is not easy. There are a great many factors to take into account. You need to find someone you can trust. You need to get the balance of experience right for you and your campaign. And you need to find someone with the temperament and skills to make your campaign work. But if you find the right person, a true believer in your cause, you will share all the high and low points of the election roller-coaster. You will become brothers in arms. And once the dust of your election has settled, one way or the other, you will have recruited not just a colleague, but a firm friend as well.

Good luck!

Tom Hirons is the campaign manager for Jesse Norman, the Conservative prospective parliamentary candidate for Hereford & South Herefordshire.

10

Building an army

Katy Diggory

Building a team of volunteers sounds easy enough from the outset. However, that the recruitment of volunteers has become something of a science in itself over the last ten years is no accident with political candidates, community and voluntary organisations, statutory agencies and even private companies all recognising that the work volunteers do is crucial to their campaign or organisational survival.

This chapter is intended as a practical guide in the art of recruiting, managing and getting the best from volunteers in a political context. Guidance will be offered on how to identify your volunteers, how to best match them to different tasks, the need to assess their motivations, the need to set clear direction and boundaries and how to retain volunteers by making the experience sociable and fun.

Identifying your volunteers
Identifying volunteers is relatively straightforward, so long as some background research is done first. It sounds like an obvious place to start, but the most important thing you can do from the outset is to actually see what tasks your campaign requires and recruit a volunteer base most appropriate to help you fulfil these tasks. For example, it would hardly be worthwhile in recruiting a group of elderly pensioners if your campaign plan consists of weekly leafleting sessions of the local tower blocks.

By and large, your most faithful volunteer base will consist of the following:

> Friends and family (anyone with whom you have a personal connection)
> Party activists
> Students or those seeking work and looking to gain new skills.

Start by making a list of people who you think might help, but be realistic. Only include those people who have similar political values as you and those who might have some time to spare. Depending on how big your campaign is and the size of the area you are seeking to represent, aim for a long list of around 30–40 people (once you start contacting people this will obviously reduce).

For the first two groups listed above, it is a good idea to introduce the idea of volunteering by paying these people the courtesy of an initial phone call or a visit, rather than asking a member of your campaign team to do it. On first approaching a new volunteer, whether you know them well or not, you will need answers to the following questions.

Would you like to help in my campaign?
Sounds basic, but we are too often guilty of assuming everyone is interested in political campaigning. Even if they are related or befriended to a political animal (you), this should not be a given. Never assume people will help out. However, the most important single thing you can do is ask and more often than not they will offer you at least a few hours of their time. Getting their initial agreement to help will give you permission in the future to ask them to undertake various tasks.

What would you like to do?
Have a ready list of jobs at your disposal and get a sense of what they like doing. And remember, it is their spare time they are giving up for you, so people generally prefer doing things they like and things they feel they are good at (more on this later).

How much time do you have?
This might not be something you have to clarify straightaway but is a useful indicator of the level of commitment the person can offer. For example, students might be able to give a whole month to the campaign over their summer holidays, whereas those in full-time work might be able to do a couple of hours every week for an indefinite period. Ensure you thank each person for every offer of help, no matter how small.

Finding students and those seeking work who might help in your campaign and will appreciate the opportunity to learn new skills is also relatively easy. If you live in an area with a university or college campus, it is worth posting adverts on noticeboards and websites asking for help (note that often institutions like this will need to show political balance). Befriend the head of the politics department at the university and offer to talk to students about your experiences. All too often the university politics course focuses on international politics and institutions rather than the nuts and bolts of being elected (which is the whole point of politics surely?). These people should be biting your hand off for first-hand tales from the campaign trail. Sites like w4mp.org are regularly visited by students from across the country looking for volunteering opportunities with candidates.

The most important thing to remember in these cases is to be absolutely upfront from the outset about the opportunity you are offering (in terms of tasks and voluntary time commitment). It is also worth being unequivocally clear about the political nature of the opportunity you are offering. Unless you are a political animal, the combative nature of politics can be offputting. If you are running on a party ticket, be clear that while being a party member is not a prerequisite for the role, the nature of the tasks will require sympathy with your values (this is as much for their benefit as for yours). It is good practice to draw up a task description for this type of volunteer. Often the work they do for you will be conditional on you (as the co-ordinator) satisfying a number of protocols for their host organisation, such as filling out a final evaluation form or providing a reference.

Ensure you keep a record of all of the above (on a BlackBerry, a laptop, a bit of paper in your pocket) as a constant companion which will help when reviewing your campaign plan and making urgent calls for replacement helpers when people drop out. Use this record and set yourself a target of calling all volunteers once a month (or whatever timescale you view appropriate) to ask them how they think the campaign is going. They will appreciate that you have taken the time to do so and talking to those helping on the ground always helps in gathering useful campaign intelligence. It also offers an opportunity for you to ask for further commitments from them.

What does your volunteer want from the experience?
Volunteers are not a homogeneous group of people with the same motivations. Once you have identified your pool of volunteers, the key to retaining volunteers is to get a sense of *why* people want to volunteer for you and what they want to get from their experience.

You will find volunteers who are passionate about one or more causes you represent and want to see you elected because of this. You will find volunteers who are passionate about the party you represent, and want to see that party form the next government. A family member or friend might be less attracted to the political side and might want nothing more than to see you do well. A student looking to get work experience will simply be looking for the broadest range of tasks possible so that they can go on to talk about this experience in interviews and on their UCAS form and job applications. Some volunteers will be happy to simply work behind the scenes and some will want more responsibility and direction over the campaign. Each of these motivations is useful in your campaign, but each should be viewed quite differently.

When it comes to matching volunteers to tasks, keeping a focus on this information will assist you in ensuring volunteers get the best from their experience and, most importantly, continue working hard for your campaign.

Match jobs to what that person can and wants to do
There is little worth in extolling the virtues of leaflet delivery to

someone who works full time and needs to be at home the rest of the time to look after children. This does not mean, however, that they cannot contribute usefully. Think smart about the jobs available to volunteers. Do they have a PC at home and could they update the website? Do they have free minutes to use up at the end of the month on their mobile and could they do some telephone canvassing from home? Could they take 500 letters and envelopes and do some stuffing from home?

Maximise volunteer skills. Perhaps they have good written skills and could design and pen a leaflet. (As long they have a good understanding of the local issues, students are particularly good at this.) Perhaps they are good with equipment and could use a Risograph and folding machine. Perhaps they manage a team at work, they like being the boss and would be happy to organise a weekly phone bank for volunteers (involving sending out emails and letters to other volunteers of course!) or organise a weekly canvassing session around their local area?

Again, it is vital to keep records. Once you have done this, your campaign plan will indicate where the gaps lie and at this stage it might be time to embark on some gentle persuasion or even training for keener volunteers.

Set clear direction and milestones for delivery

So your volunteers have volunteered and the campaign is up and running. The hard work is over and done with, right?

Wrong. Frequently throughout this chapter I have emphasised the need to be absolutely clear with volunteers from the outset what your expectation of them is. This is fairly straightforward for more formal relationships (e.g. students and interns) but when you have friends and party activists offering to deliver leaflets for a few hours each week, setting boundaries becomes more complicated within a centralised campaign and can easily be forgotten in the urgency of an election.

It is absolutely vital to brief volunteers effectively, whatever work they do for you. Not doing so will create a tension that did not need to exist, and might lead to the volunteer walking away.

Taking canvassing as an example, at the start of a session someone should always give a brief explanation of the doors to be knocked on, the questions to be asked and how to mark the sheets properly (so that the volunteer entering the data afterwards can do so quickly and accurately). There is no harm in doing this even if you have experienced canvassers. If volunteers take on any responsibility, ensure that their work is checked. This will not be necessary for your more reliable volunteers, but if for example a new volunteer takes away some leaflets to deliver, ensure they are aware of the time scale in which you would like the leaflets delivered. Give them a 'get out of jail free card' by offering them the opportunity to return the leaflets to you (in good time) if they are concerned they will not be able to do them. Check with anyone you know living in the relevant areas that the leaflet was distributed. If not, then have a quiet inward grumble and be aware for the next time that a different task will better suit this volunteer.

But it is not just about the logistics of the work. You should also take time to explain the strategy underpinning the campaign to volunteers. Sometimes they might even disagree with the strategy, but they should be given an opportunity to put their views forward.

Beware the volunteer who becomes a full-time job to manage. At times a volunteer might become disillusioned with the tasks they are being asked to do and the strategy of the campaign. They might even begin to take matters into their own hands, and go beyond what they have been asked to do. One example of this might be if your campaign strategy involves targeting your resources at smaller sub-areas in your ward or constituency where your support is strongest. This is generally accepted wisdom among campaign managers, and is inevitable, as the resources of all parties and particularly of independents are finite. Volunteers may feel disincentivised if the areas where they live are not made a priority and they feel their efforts go unrewarded. So they might go ahead and leaflet their area, even if to do so would mean that their time and leaflets could have had a greater impact elsewhere.

The volunteer should ultimately relieve your burden, not exacerbate it. Personal egos can only be indulged for so long, even if volunteers are generously giving up their time. Everyone helping in your campaign should be signed up to your strategy and their number one priority should be getting you elected.

In conclusion, people need clear direction in order to do a job properly. They need to know what they can and should do, and – equally importantly – what they should not do. Do not be afraid of setting boundaries. What you should get in return is a team of motivated, well-briefed volunteers who are equipped to deliver your message on the ground.

Make it fun and social

For some, getting a good candidate elected is reward enough for their efforts. But for many, the social side of political volunteering and meeting like-minded people is one of the major sells of joining in an election effort.

You might want to take people out for a few drinks after meetings, or you might even hold your meetings in social venues – pubs often have upstairs rooms and sometimes they offer these rooms for free if there are going to be people buying drinks. You could ask volunteers to hold coffee mornings in their homes for other volunteers. Leading personalities in your party will often be willing to come down and address events, and generally either you can advertise these as purely political events (where volunteers get the chance to ask questions) or often volunteers will be willing to pay a small amount for a ticket to attend a fundraiser with a good speaker and dinner and drinks included. Even if you are running as an independent, charities and other worthy causes will often make speakers available to address meetings if their values correspond with your own. As the candidate you should try and attend as many of these occasions as possible, as the volunteers will actively want to spend time with you and get your thoughts on the progress of the campaign, and it is vital that you show commitment to the volunteers if they are to continue working for you towards the election and beyond.

Pitch social events to the profile of your volunteer base and involve them in deciding what to do and where. It might be worth investing in some hot drinks and bottles of wine at these events, just by way of thank you. Most importantly, enjoy yourself, be positive about the forthcoming election and your enthusiasm will rub off on others.

And finally. . .

As a candidate, you are not just representing yourself but a whole range of different ideas, proposals and values. There are voters to mobilise, phone calls to be made and leaflets to deliver. It stands to reason that the help of others will be absolutely essential in delivering your campaign.

Building your campaign army should consist of the following elements:

› Identifying your volunteers and asking for help
› Assessing what your volunteers want from the experience
› Matching task to volunteer appropriately
› Setting clear direction and milestones for delivery
› Making it a fun and sociable experience.

Throughout the chapter, I have tried to make clear the need to strike a balance between listening to, rewarding and involving your volunteers and taking ownership and driving through your strategy, even if this goes against the views of some.

If you follow these simple steps, you will have a well-motivated volunteer base which will work on your behalf up until the forthcoming election and beyond.

Katy Diggory is the campaign manager for Bill Rammell MP

11

Dress for success

Women

Shirley Biggs

To dress for success is a challenging double-edged sword. You either adopt a style chosen for you by the image makers or develop a style that has real affinity with your own personality, thus demonstrating the effectiveness of yourself.

I believe it was Coco Chanel who remarked: 'To disguise oneself is charming: to have oneself disguised is sad.' Women in all walks of life, but particularly in politics, face an almost impossible task. They may be captains of industry or specialists in the fields of medicine or law. These high flyers are confident in their abilities to achieve, but falter before the altar of fashion. Frequently they fail to realise that – while fashion goes out of fashion – style never does. These women often fall into the hands of the so-called 'make-over artists' who take account only of the outward and visible, but rarely the character and personality beneath.

If we look at some of the well-known figures of our time we see that Margaret Thatcher, for example, had a definite style of her own. A statuesque lady, she wore her broad-shouldered, double-breasted two-pieces with panache. She felt powerful; she was powerful; and everything reflected that. This was her style and the essence of her personality. This effect is what we most remember of her.

Let us look at others. Take Edwina Currie for instance, or Margaret Beckett, Harriet Harman and Tessa Jowell. Generally, they have no effective fashion style. Their personalities are subsumed into the general drabness of the dress and have no individual impact. By way of contrast, however, Sarah Brown has over a period of years softened her dress sense, while Samantha Cameron now epitomises today's young, stylish, go-ahead woman. Each in her own way has found a style to flatter and support their menfolk.

The outstanding fashion exemplars of our time could be said to be Carla Bruni and Michelle Obama. They differ physically and are highly successful and intelligent in their own fields. But both exhibit pleasing and attractive personalities by the adoption of their own individual choice of style of dress.

I have mentioned at length the need to develop one's own style. If you can do this with confidence, you will be 'dressed for success'.

Let's now cut to the chase and examine how we can achieve this. The essential elements are a combination of colour, shape and personality.

Let's take the first element, colour. It is important to choose colours that have affinity with you. These will be determined by your skin, hair and eyes. For example, if you are blonde, blue eyed and fair skinned you would be termed as 'cool and light'. Colours such as soft blues, silver greys, rose and lilac are going to enhance you. By contrast, if you are black, have a polished ebony skin and dark brown eyes you would be 'deep and warm'. Hues such as terracotta, gold, tomato, khaki and olive would add that *je ne sais quoi* to any outfit or accessory you wear. A typical porcelain Irish skin with green eyes and red hair would indicate a light, warm-coloured personality complemented by turquoise, sea-green, apple, yellow and ivory.

You will have noticed that I have not mentioned the ubiquitous white or black. These can be worn by any colour group provided that there is a hint of your own 'colour personality' by way of scarf, shirt, jewellery or other accessory.

Before discussing shape, let us take a moment to look at hair, makeup and – where necessary – spectacles.

Your hair should be styled to suit your face – and also take account of the body structure. Hair is nature's biggest potential compliment (unless you are a bald headed man!) and the treatment of this potential compliment lies in our own hands. The cut is the most important element – something easy to care for and shaping which is adaptable for the busy and successful woman without the time or inclination to pay constant visits to the hairdresser.

In makeup, less is always best. Over-indulgence suggests a lack of confidence, or perhaps a hint that you are hiding behind the mask which you present to the world. A base coat will complement one's natural colouring; a touch of blusher to highlight the cheekbones and a shade and shape of lipstick that flatters, rather than the post box effect adopted by Cherie Blair.

For the wearer of spectacles a hint of colour on the eyes with a touch of mascara could benefit. The shape of spectacles should always, of course, take account of the shape of the face.

Turning to body shape, this can be divided into three rough categories:

1. Angular and tall
2. Slightly curvaceous
3. Rounded.

Tall, angular figures are lucky. Like many fashion models they are perfect clothes horses and able to wear almost anything. However, patterns to avoid include narrow pinstripe, herringbone or chalk stripe. Any of these tend to over-emphasise the height and leanness of the body.

But this shape can advantageously wear wraps or belted dressing-gown-style coats or sharp, figure-hugging jackets with streamlined or wide-legged trousers with turn-ups. They can also wear wide belts on the waist or at hip level, and belted tunics; they can carry oversized handbags and sport a single extravagant piece of jewellery. If one is over 6 feet tall, stylish loafers or Cuban heels help to minimise height – unless one is seeking to create a more adventurous appearance! The look which this shape should seek to achieve is understated elegance with a hint of drama.

For the curvaceous figure – of whatever proportions – you should go straight to sexiness! Such figures are generally between 5 feet 4 inches and 5 feet 8 inches tall. Make the most of yourself. Short, cropped one- or two-buttoned jackets and pencil skirts hovering on or just above the knee with a sexy slit at the back are the order of the day.

Really, the world is your oyster with the right colour, makeup, stilettos and designer tights as part of your armoury. Plunging necklines on shirts or blouses will suit, as will trousers – either narrow or with plain bottoms.

In fabrics try startling plains or tone stripes. Try not to overload the jewellery. Simple is best. The look you are trying to achieve is one of presence with a hint of sexiness.

The majority of rounded women spend much time and effort attempting to hide themselves under loose layers of material. A big mistake. Even the more elegant dressers tend to resemble an upmarket bag lady. A very strong personality may get away with it – but why try to hide some of the attributes of which you have every reason to be proud? Ample bosoms are often accompanied by good legs!

By all means wear a loose-fitting – possibly slightly long-length – jacket. Try it over a low-cut draped blouse or top, being sure that the sleeves are three-quarter length. Short sleeves need to be in line with the bosom – and emphasise it. Long sleeves tend to look shapeless.

Slight A-line skirts flatter more than hip-hugging pencilled styles, but ideally should fall just over the knee.

Trousers need to be straight, but should be slightly tapered and visually balance the top in the same way as your angular friends. You can afford to wear one oversized piece of jewellery.

Avoid fabrics with too much design detail – checks or pinstripes – and choose instead plain, draping fabrics in colours that flatter skin, hair and eyes. As the fashion designer Jean Muir once said: 'When you have found something that suits you and never lets you down, why change it?'

For the rounded figure you are trying for the look that suggests regal elegance with a touch of femininity.

Shirley Biggs is a director of Dress2Kill

Men

James Hibbert

Take a good look at yourself naked, preferably in a full-length mirror, and remember mirrors don't lie.

Be honest with yourself. Are you tall or short, fat or thin or somewhere in the middle, do you have long legs, do you have a fat face, is your torso out of proportion, do you look older than your age or do you look too young – are you a spotty youth, have you got a belly, are you going bald or is there a bird's nest being created up top?

Ok, well, having beaten yourself up and answered some honest, probably quite hurtful, questions, it's now time to do something about it. Remember we can all but improve and that's the idea. Improve in body and you'll improve in mind; improve in mind and you'll improve in politics.

There is no hard and fast rule in how to look good; the key is that you feel comfortable. Think back in your mind to an occasion where you felt the monkey's nuts, not literally but in how you appeared. It might have been at a party or when you'd purchased a new suit or when you chatted up your first lover – she must have liked something about you! Ask yourself why you exuded that self-confidence and why you felt smart, and more importantly think about the positive outcome that came out of it. Looking back is a great way of reinventing your own success and it works very well with your attire. I am not suggesting that you pop out and buy some winkle pickers and stay press trousers, but just that the overall look or fit needs to be reinvigorated.

Now, let's look at what we are and what we stand for. This is key in addressing the image we want to portray. We are in the public arena, we are looked up to by society and we are pillars of wisdom, therefore it is important to give that impression. With this must come confidence and an aura of 100 per cent belief in what we stand for.

What we are trying to do is build a jigsaw puzzle of all the elements that contribute to our image and look. What we now need to do is begin to piece together all these different facets.

It is important to remember that we are all different – just like a bespoke suit we are all different shapes and sizes, we all have different personalities and we all represent different things. We are not living in a communist state – well, not yet, anyway – and therefore it's important to remember that everyone's jigsaw will be different – thank God!

With regards to suiting here are a few guidelines. If you are short or round you need to look taller and slimmer so try a striped cloth – don't go over the top or before you know it you'll be seen as a banker (spelt with a w)! If you're a tall lanky beanpole of a shape then you need to look more in proportion – try a check and avoid stripes as they will only make you look taller and even skinnier. Short people should avoid double-breasted suits as they tend to suit the taller, slimmer figures. Granted, double-breasted suits aren't massively in at the moment but that might change. Single-breasted two-button is the safest option all round – timeless, classic, Bond-like and easy to wear either with a tie or without.

Be individual – with bespoke tailoring becoming more affordable, why not give yourself a subtle signature? A small attention to detail like a buttonhole stitched in a different colour on the sleeve or the lapel hole stitched in the same colour as the lining. These subtle style options will allow you to stand out from your peers without having to dye your hair a different colour.

Ties and shirts should compliment each other – the rule of thumb is that a patterned tie should be worn with a plain shirt and vice versa. Ties are a great way of bringing out one's personality – look at Jon Snow!

For shoes, there is one rule and one rule only. You may not think people look down that way, but they do and one's shoe hygiene says a lot about the person. Always wear clean and polished shoes and make sure you regularly change your socks – you'd be surprised how the smell of cheese can waft upwards. While we are at it, your underpants may not be on show, but you know if they are clean and it comes back to that inner confidence – change them daily please!

As for personal hygiene, if you get up in the morning thinking you stink and that you have smelly breath, then do something about it. We don't smell ourselves so what you may think is fresh air could in fact be a mixture of BO, garlic breath and cheesy-smelling grot. Shower, bath, wash, deodorise, shave, moisturise, put some aftershave on, clean your teeth and always carry some breath freshener. Can you imagine going to all the effort of looking the monkey's nuts only to get stabbed in the back because your breath stinks? It happens more than you might think.

So in summary, be honest with yourself – see it as a challenge and make it fun. Reinvent yourself. Dress yourself in things that make you feel and look better. Bring out your personality and don't be afraid. Ask for advice – metamorphose and enjoy the outcome. Politics needs a facelift.

James Hibbert is the founder of Dress2Kill

12

The art of engaging with voters

Melanie Batley

What's the point?

Why do you need to interact with voters? We're living in an age of mass communications. One email can offer exposure to thousands of people instantaneously. Plodding the streets for eight hours on a Saturday certainly seems like a less efficient use of your time.

Plus, let's be honest, the public isn't exactly smitten with politicians these days. There's a widely held feeling that politics is just empty spin by people seeking privilege and power, and the recent expenses scandal has only compounded that perception.

However, it is precisely these developments that make individual voter contact more important than ever. For one, people are bombarded with so much electronic and media communications that they have become quite skilled at tuning it out.

Meanwhile, the overall distrust of politicians makes differentiating oneself crucial – a face and a name puts you into a personal and direct relationship with the voter that transcends general perceptions about the value of politicians.

Like it or not, your fate is decided by voters. A successful campaign requires a robust programme of voter interaction, with a campaign schedule that ensures you are getting out there, meeting people and conveying your messages directly.

Meeting voters – a practical guide

Till now you may have focused on becoming a candidate: developing your agenda and messages, refining your image, getting selected and assembling a campaign team. Surely the worst is behind you?

But now, uninvited, you're standing on the doorstep of someone whose supper you've interrupted. You've gone from being a celebrity among admiring friends and family to an unknown, or possibly loathed, member of the political class. Are you sure you want this job?

Three golden rules

1. Be genuine. No one likes a phoney and most people can scent it a mile away. You can't be everything to everyone, so just be yourself.
2. Speak simply. Long-drawn-out explanations of policy may be riveting to you, but most normal people don't have the time and couldn't care less. Learn how to summarise your position on any issue within ten seconds. (More detail can be offered on paper.)
3. Never tell a lie. Your mother told you never to do it, and mothers are always right. History is littered with plenty of budding politicians that were brought down by their own lies.

Suppose you follow this advice. Still, we're left with the question: what are the nuts and bolts of a successful voter interaction? How should you start a conversation or conduct yourself among voters?

There are a number of practical tips that will make this (perhaps intimidating) aspect of the job a lot easier.

Meeting one-on-one

So let's get back to that withering look of the stranger on their doorstep. What should you say now?

Introduce yourself

Tell them who you are and what you're doing. 'Hi, my name is

John Smith. I'm standing to be your council member. I wanted to introduce myself and get your thoughts about the local parking charges. Do you have a few minutes to talk?'

Believe it or not, people will usually get over the annoyance of being bothered and feel flattered that a candidate is at their door asking their opinion.

The key here is to listen more than you talk. Show that you are receptive to their thoughts, listen to what they are saying and demonstrate you care.

This exercise is valuable, not just from the standpoint of trying to add another voter to your ranks, but it also enables you to understand what is on their mind and how you will respond to these concerns.

Listen instead of talk

Once you get them talking, respond with questions rather than your own opinions. 'I'm not surprised to hear you think the parking levies are too high. Do you think the problem is the way the fees are structured or that the overall rates are too high?'

The key is to validate a voter's concern and encourage them to talk. The more someone talks, the more they think they like you.

Take notes

Sounds corny and maybe you would feel ridiculous writing something down – a clipboard isn't the sexiest accessory. But it is a very powerful way to give someone the message that you really are listening.

If your campaign is well run, these notes will go straight into a database so that the next time you visit this house, you can refer to your last conversation. 'Hi, Mr Sinclair, I'm John Smith. You and I met a few months ago and you expressed some concerns about the parking rates in town. I just wanted to stop by and talk with you again to see how you think things are progressing in that area. Do you have a few minutes?'

Leave a leaflet with your key messages

The leaflet should elaborate on all of your policy proposals and positions, which you will not be able to do when you are meeting people briefly.

You can say, 'Here's a leaflet that outlines my position on the issues, which you can read when you have time. Please don't hesitate to contact me if you have any questions or concerns.'

Don't go through the leaflet or read it. Just leave it with them.

Ask for their vote

In the race to finish a conversation, don't forget to ask for their vote. For example, say, 'Thanks for your time. Would you consider voting for me on 6 May?'

Yes, it is putting someone on the spot, but it's important to do this to make them conscious of the election date as well as their own intentions regarding their vote.

It may feel unnatural or embarrassing the first few times you say it, but let's face it, this is the entire point of why you are there. Most socially adjusted people would 'consider' voting for someone (and if you meet someone that says 'no' and slams the door, console yourself with the thought that he probably lacks the clarity of mind to get himself to a polling booth anyway.)

Follow-up

Set aside time to write to every person you visited. A personalised letter would be very impressive, but if you simply don't have the time, a generic letter will do the trick as well.

A general follow-up letter could say, 'I really appreciated the chance to talk to you and get your thoughts about the big issues in this campaign. Please don't hesitate to contact me about any concerns you have. The election is on 6 May and I would really appreciate your vote so that I can work to represent your concerns in the council.' It is also an opportunity to list the top issues that are on your agenda.

If possible, sign it by hand. Try to get envelopes addressed by hand as well. They are more likely to be opened. The personal touch is very powerful.

Attending events

An event is an opportunity to meet and influence many voters at once. It also has its pitfalls. If it goes badly, many people witness it. Your job, in addition to showing up and putting on a good show, is to make sure you protect yourself against the possibility that things will go wrong. Though one cannot plan for every eventuality, by thinking through the logistics in advance, you have the opportunity to increase the odds that the event will be a successful one for you.

The best events are the ones you organise yourself. A strong campaign will host numerous events throughout the campaign season, inviting potential voters to participate, but on its own terms, within its own format.

But events cost money and there are plenty of gatherings (special interest events and debates, for example) that offer you a platform to convey your ideas and reach more voters that you might not otherwise reach. Take advantage of these events and build them into your calendar.

This section outlines how you can get the best result from any event you attend, and protect yourself against potentially negative outcomes.

Choose your events carefully

You are not obliged to attend every event, least of all those hosted by people that may be interested in attacking you. If you do not immediately know the organisers, investigate. If the vast majority of the people in attendance are unlikely to vote for you or your party, is it worth attending?

It may sound obvious, but you must measure an event based on whether it is an efficient use of your time, and this is based on whether it will help you build support for your campaign.

Consider, and negotiate, the format of every event you attend

In politics, as in life, everything's negotiable. If you're invited to an event to give a 45-minute speech, but public speaking is not your strength, you don't have to agree to a major speech.

Speak to the organisers and arrange a format that will help you showcase your strengths. Perhaps you are better at a question-and-answer session. Are you concerned about potentially over-hostile questions? Find out if you can do a speech but take questions at an informal reception. Don't put yourself in any situation that you think could spin out of control and damage your reputation.

If you have the resources, it's also worth scoping out the venue in advance to ensure you are comfortable with the setting. This also affords you the opportunity to make any adjustments beforehand (microphone or no microphone? Lectern too high? Perhaps you don't want a podium at all. Poor background or dubious signage? Get rid of it).

Details can make or break the success of the event for you. Don't be afraid to ask for the things you want, but also be sure to arrange it beforehand.

Think about your audience

Once you agree to attend an event and have decided on the format, consider very carefully what you will talk about and why. The best way to do this is to start by thinking about who your audience is. Do they share a demographic commonality? What are they interested in? Are there any big policy issues that will resonate?

Sure, if you have developed a solid set of messages, they should resonate with 90 per cent of your audiences. But the opportunity is often there to tailor your messages more specifically to the audience so that you maximise your reception.

Your remarks should emphasise areas of commonality so that you can develop a rapport with the audience and generate support. Target your messages appropriately and you will maximise 'return' for your campaign on the event.

Facing the fire

There are times you will face hostility, sometimes publicly. In these cases, preparation is the key to weathering the storm.

Invest time at the beginning of your campaign to prepare a general set of questions and answers that will cover a range of subjects you could be challenged on. Additionally, do this for every event you attend, tailored to the special interest being covered.

Beyond that, there are a few guidelines you should always keep in mind:

> Don't lose your cool in public. . . EVER.
> Don't take it personally even when the attack is personal.
> Use any attack as an opportunity to talk about the issues *you* care about. (You don't have to answer any question on the terms on which it is asked. Answer the way you want to.)
> Agree to disagree.
> Humour can diffuse tense situations – use it when you can!

You may feel immense pressure when facing potential voters. You want to win and every vote counts. You've poured your heart into your campaign and it's easy to get disheartened when you hit a stumbling block.

Nevertheless, it is important to remember, that while you are proposing to represent people, you are not required to be God. There will be questions you don't know the answer to and topics that are out of your depth. Acknowledge that early and realise that these are opportunities to develop rather than an indictment on your suitability to serve.

Keep it real. Voters can be fickle, but you cannot afford to be. Be true to your principles and conduct yourself in an upstanding way at all times. At the end of the campaign, regardless of the result, the one thing you won't want to have sacrificed is your integrity. Not only is it the right thing to do, but in an age when people crave authenticity, you are more likely to win.

Melanie Batley is a journalist and former US campaign advisor

13

Going negative

James McGrath

> *Your tax dollars are being used to pay for grade school classes that teach our children that CANNIBALISM, WIFE-SWAPPING and the MURDER of infants and the elderly are acceptable behaviour.*

Jesse Helms, the pugnacious American Senator, knew a thing or two about negative campaigning. The above extract was taken from a fund-raising letter sent out by his campaign and worked a treat. In a Senate career of thirty years, the North Carolinian Senator *and* his opponents set the benchmark for negative campaigns. A lot of it wasn't pretty. Negative campaigning can be ugly. And I am not a fan of it, but it is and has always been an essential element of campaigning in a democracy.

Bluntly, if you wish to run campaign for public office, there are three tactical approaches. You can run a positive, cuddly, open and forward-looking campaign. Or you can campaign by comparing and contrasting yourself with your opponents (a form of negative campaigning). Or perhaps, you can run a negative campaign that focuses on the deficiencies of your opponent and how their election will ensure Armageddon. Or if your brain cell count is above an amoeba and you want to win, you will run a combination of the first two yet prepare yourself to deploy a negative campaign should the circumstances arise.

In this chapter, the concept of negative campaigning will be defined along with an explanation of why it works, certain campaign tactics and if you are so minded, when you should use such tactics.

How long has negative campaigning been around?

Claims that negative campaigning is a recent or modern development are piffle. As Mark David points out in *The Art of Negative Campaigning*, the American Declaration of Independence is actually a work of negative campaigning aimed at King George III. The declaration not only claims the monarch's unfitness to rule but substantiates his wrongs against the colonists. It is a classic negative piece of propaganda that, after listing numerous faults, fails to mention specific solutions and instead plumps for something called 'Independence'.

The first properly 'competitive' American Presidential election, in 1796, was hardly a byword for old-fashioned civility in the contest between John Adams and Thomas Jefferson. One contender, according to his opponent, was an 'atheist', 'anarchist', 'demagogue', 'coward' and 'trickster' while the other was either 'pro-French' or 'pro-British'.

And it didn't get better for Jefferson in the contest of 1800. In probably the first 'modern' case of opposition research, Jefferson's opponents found out about rumours concerning the birth of child to a slave, and after 'investigating', ran the allegations.

Before we fall for the classic mistake of decrying all things American, our own negative campaigning history reaches back much further. The Tories are living victims of centuries-old negative campaigning. The seventeenth century saw one of the Court factions brand the supporters of the Catholic Duke of York, heir presumptive to the throne, as 'Tories', the common name for Irish brigands. Charming. But wait, there's more. The newly branded Tories started calling their opponents after the Scottish Gaelic word for horse drovers. Or 'Whigs', as we know them. Equally charming.

What is negative campaigning?

There is a fair bit of confusion as to what is meant by negative campaigning and, let's face it, the actual name 'negative campaigning' could do with a rebrand.

Negative campaigning is more than petty name calling. It is a serious and substantive approach to holding your opponent and their views, record and policies to account. And, to be candid with you, reader, it is about maximising your chances of winning. To help you, though, in a study of the 1997 British general election, 'negative material' was defined as that which 'explicitly apportioned blame or criticised the policies, record, competence or credibility of a named rival party or politician'.

When you think about it, negative campaigning is the most honest form of campaigning as it focuses on the available facts and figures and is therefore more believable, unlike positive campaigning, which tends to be a series of nebulous motherhood statements. Such fluff is then combined with a plethora of promises in a feeble attempt to disguise the bribing of certain socio-demographic voting bases.

Negative campaigning is telling the truth. If you are running for your local council and your incumbent opponents have run the organisation into the ground, you have a choice. You can ignore the record of the incumbents and focus on your experience and skills. That could work. . .

Or you can highlight the failures of the current administration and call for change. You can focus on residents facing not only increased council tax but failing local services. In the most basic definition, such an approach would be called negative campaigning. So are you still opposed to negative campaigning? I didn't think so – comparing and contrasting your record with that of your opponent is classic negative campaigning. Everyone does it.

However, when negative campaigning extends beyond the broad definitions above to descend beyond reasonable discourse, then no British politician or campaigner would support it. And at this point I would like to say a big cheery 'hello' to Damien McBride. Last year, Downing Street under Gordon Brown's chief spinner became a prototype political mud-making factory.

Lying, cheating and dirty tricks are not tools of campaigning and should not be used. The fabrication of sleaze to attack your opponents is not only beyond the pale, it is criminal. Most reputable politicians and campaigners draw a distinction between targeting an opponent on the basis of their policies, performance and values and 'personal/character' attacks.

But even if you don't lower yourself to the depths of Mr McBride and friends, engaging in negative campaigning can easily backfire. Think of the 'Demon Eyes' and 'New Labour, New Danger' in 1997. The attack backfired on the Tories with Labour capitalising, allowing capture of the moral high ground and reinforcing negative perceptions of the Tories. This was a rare own goal for the Conservatives, as for the previous twenty years, they had been very successful at remorselessly attacking Labour.

Whatever you want to call it, it is campaigning. And whether you are running for the local parish council, the upcoming general election or President of the United States, you need to be aware of how to deploy negative tactics, whether you should engage negatively and, more importantly, how to rebut your opponents.

But don't ever admit you're campaigning negatively
Admit that you are engaging a negative campaign and you're more burnt than toast in a Blackpool hotel. Essentially, if you admit you do it, you're a fool. If you don't, you're a lying fool.

And, whatever the tone of any negative material produced by your campaign, you will find the biggest detractors won't be the media or your opponents but your core supporters. Party members hate negative advertising and whinge until the cows come home when their party engages negatively. Ignore them. Politely.

Ironically, sometimes negative campaigning allows you to accuse your opponent of using negative campaigning while you are engaged in the same. President Obama is the most recent embodiment of perfecting this technique, especially when it came to the issue of race. To this end, President Obama is seen to have run by the chattering classes a clean campaign. Where he was very good was using his race to imply that others were racist. The classic example involved Obama claiming that the Republicans would try to scare voters as he looked different to 'all those other Presidents on the dollar bills'. A clear reference to race.

McCain's team exploded with indignation, attacking Obama for playing the race card. Obama calmly responded that no one thought he was making accusations of racism until the McCain operation 'started pushing it', thus reversing the 'attack' and at a stroke becoming the victor of the Republicans.

Why do people use negative campaigning?

So if it has such a bad reputation, your own supporters hate it and no-one admits to doing it, then why are we even having a discussion? We could be doing something far more useful like learning Etruscan or joining the jury team. Campaigners and politicians engage in negative campaigning because, when used properly, it works in a number of ways:

› It can be effective in suppressing the vote of your opponent.
› It encourages people to vote against something. By this I mean it is easier for people to vote against something that threatens their values and way of life than to vote for something.
› It enables you to define your opponent before they have an opportunity to define themselves and their values.
› It helps you raise money. As we've seen with Jesse Helms, negative campaigning allows supporters to donate to causes or protect their values, even if they're not within the electorate.
› Most importantly, it helps you set and control the agenda and the message. If your opponent is being forced on the defensive and is responding to negative attacks then they're no longer talking about their issues.

When should you use negative campaigning?

Negative campaigning has to have a purpose and be designed to move voters in a strategic direction. It should never stand alone but if you are minded to campaign negatively it must be part of your overall communication and election strategy.

Labour and Ken Livingstone in the 2008 London mayoral

election were incredibly negative. Clearly they wanted to motivate their base and suppress the second-preference flows to Boris Johnson. Labour used 2008 to trial their class war campaign, with Boris accused of any combination of 'toff, posh, Eton educated, Oxford educated, right-wing, racist, homophobic', as Ken Livingstone tried desperately to hang onto power.

In addition, Labour trawled through Boris's every written word to find negative attack points. As an aside, the most surprising 'attack' was using Boris's admission that he had pocketed a Tariq Aziz cigar case from the ruins of the former Iraqi Foreign Minister's Palace to lodge a complaint with the Met that Boris was guilty of war crimes by plundering Iraq.

But Labour's attack failed. While research showed voters did have certain views about the personality of Boris, these views subsided because Boris was talking about his plans for London. His plans on crime, transport, the environment and so on were used by his campaign team to 'define' a 'serious' Boris. If Labour had connected concerns over Boris's ability to run London (as opposed to their cheap character attacks) to critiques of his manifesto then the result might have been different. Don't forget that negative campaigning needs to be believable.

Linking your opponent to an unpopular politician or policy is a common technique. Prior to the 1997 general election, Conservative PPCs and council candidates downplayed their party connections as a method of defusing Labour attacks linking them to the Conservative government. Likewise, at the coming general election expect to see the Conservatives target Labour MPs and their links to Gordon Brown while Labour MPs reinvent themselves as 'community campaigners', minimising their government links.

It is not just about linking to an unpopular politician. Prior to the 2005 British general election the Labour Party released a graphic ('internally' to Labour Party members as part of a poster competition) in relation to the Conservative Party's economic proposals showing flying pigs with the faces of Michael Howard and Oliver Letwin. Both men are Jewish. The Labour Party denied allegations of anti-Semitism, but reminding Britain's Muslim minority of the Jewish links in the Conservative Party is just another example of negative campaigning.

That said, be wary of using negative campaigning in areas of small or settled population. And this is particularly relevant in many parts of Britain. Importing American-style attacks would probably be self-defeating. In such areas, any negative campaigning would need to be more subtle with a tone of disappointment rather than shrill attacks.

Get your bad news out there before others do

As mentioned above, an important aspect of dealing with negative campaigning is controlling the agenda. If there is some aspect of your past that could be construed as negative then there is a reasonable chance your opponents know. So you have a decision to make. Option A involves you ignoring the problem, thus allowing your opponents to 'release' the issue at a time most damaging to you. Option B would see you release the issue at a time and through a mechanism convenient to your campaign.

During the 2007 Ealing South by-election the Labour Party released details of the Conservative candidate's previous financial support for Labour only days before polling. The timing was crucial – minimising any chances of a decent response from the Tories. But that's not the story. The Conservatives knew about the donation, and instead of releasing it at their timing – 'Labour donor now supports the Conservatives' – thus allowing a positive story, they sat on the issue and hoped it would not come out.

Oh no, my opponent is campaigning negatively against me

You can either ignore or respond – depending on the issue, your tracking in the polls, the time left until polling day and whether the issue is getting traction. My gut reaction, though, is always to fight any allegation and any inference of negative campaigning.

Conclusion

Attempting to define your opponents (or name calling) will always be with us. And not just in Western democracies. In the

Maldives, previously if you wanted to raise doubts about someone's commitment to or fitness for public life you called them a 'Christian' or a 'Christian supporter'. While I was working for the opposition in 2008 in the Maldives, the then Maldivian government in three press conferences over a period of thirty-six hours labelled me a 'Christian Terrorist' – in one stroke agreeing with Mrs Johnstone, my former fifth-grade Religious Studies teacher and showing their desperation.

Whether you are running for office or are running someone's campaign for office, you need to maximise your chances of winning, and sometimes that will involve negative campaigning. The question you need to decide is how far you will push the line to win.

James McGrath is the deputy director of the Liberal Party in Australia

14

Effective photo opportunities

Shane Greer

A picture paints a thousand words. Tempting though it is to avoid the use of that obvious cliché when writing a chapter about photo opportunities, to do so would be a disservice to the inherent value of the statement. It might be one of the oldest clichés in the book, but it's also undoubtedly true.

Think about it. We've all experienced the power of evocative photography. Perhaps you've picked up a photo from your childhood when you were on a school trip or playing with friends. Suddenly the memories, the emotions and the joy of that occasion come flooding back, like a tidal wave washing over you. Or perhaps you turned on the TV last night to see the image of a starving child thousands of miles away in a country where food is in desperately short supply. Unless you're inhuman, odds are you felt pity, sadness, perhaps even a sense of moral outrage. Who knows, maybe you even felt compelled to make a donation to support that child. Or maybe you've seen an advertisement for a new product and for some indescribable reason felt compelled to purchase it. As powerful as words are – powerful enough to change the course of history – the power of effective imagery is undoubtedly greater. And for those standing for public office, this knowledge should act as a call to arms, a constant reminder that if you're failing to incorporate photo opportunities into your activities you're punching far below your weight and handing an advantage to your opponent that they neither earned nor deserve.

The case for using photo opportunities in campaigns couldn't be more compelling. Former Conservative party strategist David Canzini has explained: 'These days people have less and less time, so messages need to be communicated quickly, people won't always read the article about your campaign in the newspaper or your piece of campaign literature.' He adds: 'A strong photo op allows you to tell the story without people having to read anything.' What's more, as Jo Tanner, director of iNHouse PR says, a strong image will make an enormous difference to the page: 'A photo op immediately increases your presence on the page of a newspaper, rather than being restricted to the text alone.' I've lost count of the times I've received a leaflet in the post only to throw it in the bin seconds later without so much as a second thought. But someone, somewhere, spent time designing that leaflet, writing the text, choosing the pictures (if there are any), deciding on a colour scheme, determining the dimensions of the leaflet, and all in the hope that I and thousands of others would take the time to consider what they've said. Why did their leaflet fail? Simple. Nine times out of ten, it simply didn't grab the recipient's attention. It didn't pop out and scream PAY ATTENTION TO ME, I'M IMPORTANT. How could it have achieved this? Simple. By including a strong photo which literally commands the recipient's attention. Of course, leaflets aren't the only place for strong photos. Websites, newsletters and, as Tanner indicates, news stories benefit from them too.

But knowing why photo opportunities are useful isn't the same thing as knowing how to stage one that will actually be useful. Political history is lined with the corpses of photo opportunities that undermined, and in some cases destroyed, candidates, campaigns and politicians. Some of my personal favourites are, in no particular order, the now iconic image of William Hague riding a log flume wearing a baseball cap, Michael Dukakis destroying his US presidential campaign with a poorly executed photo of him driving a tank, and Gordon Brown with a swastika behind his head.

OK, so those are some textbook examples of how not to do it; but how do you get it right? For a photo op to be successful you must first determine, precisely, what story it is you want to tell. Is it the problem of litter in the local park, a protest outside the local council buildings, or perhaps a petition you're collecting to draw attention to a particular issue? Whatever it is, your photo should tell the story. If it's about a protest, for example, perhaps you could stage a shot of you and some fellow campaigners picketing outside the town hall (ideally on a miserable day to demonstrate your commitment!). And don't be afraid of using props; they can be tremendously effective. I know one local councillor who has, what he describes as, a 'box of tricks'. Inside the box you'll find everything from a hard hat and hi-visibility vest to a cycling helmet and Wellington boots! Needless to say, no matter what photo op he wants to create he'll have something in the box to help craft the perfect image. A problem with construction, the hard hat goes on; a problem with cycle paths, the cycling helmet goes on. Your picture needs to tell your story, and props can help make that happen.

On most occasions it's a good idea to include other people in the photo op. As David Canzini has explained, you need to 'humanise the story'. What's more, the involvement of other people serves to demonstrate that your campaign has popular support. But don't include just anyone in the photo op; think about who you're communicating with. Is the image targeted at young people, old people, women, an ethnic minority group, teachers or nurses? When choosing people to stand with you in the photo, make sure they properly reflect the photo's ultimate audience. One word of caution about including other people though, make sure you know who they are. As Canzini puts it, you should 'always research the people who appear in the photo op in case there are any negative connotations that come with them. You don't want to get caught by something unexpected.' After all, the last thing you want is to find out in the papers that the GP who stood with you in a recent photo op is under investigation for fraud! Stranger things have happened.

The thing that most often undermines an otherwise brilliant

photo op is the backdrop, or rather the unintended consequences flowing from the backdrop chosen (witness the example given above of Gordon Brown sitting in a school classroom with a swastika appearing to the left of his head). As Jo Tanner has counselled, 'always check what's in the background, and check from every angle . . . photographers will find the worst shot possible given the opportunity.' Candy Piercy, a Lib Dem media trainer, says: 'You should always look for things like exit signs, or adverts that can be cropped, things that could send an unintended negative message. For example, don't stage a photo op with a political candidate in a "hot air" balloon.'

Often, a new candidate will spend a day going around the constituency to take photographs in various locations with a range of local people. This can be a great use of time and provides a useful stock-file of photos which can be utilised throughout the campaign. But a bit of advice. If you are going to spend a day doing this, make sure to bring several changes of clothes. If you're a male candidate this could be as simple as bringing a range of ties, but if you're a woman you may need several outfits. By changing clothes you give the impression that your activity in the area is more than a day long charade.

A recent example of a photo op which was well executed is from a campaign by Guide Dogs for the Blind. Its purpose was to get the Mayor of London to stop funding a 'shared surface street' design in the capital. Shared surface streets have no definition between road and pavement, and for safety rely instead on people making eye contact to determine who should move first. The issue, from Guide Dogs for the Blind's point of view, is obvious. While hundreds of blind and partially sighted people marched on City Hall in London to register their opposition to the scheme, the photo op (overleaf) involves only three protesters, each with a guide dog, with their backs to the camera, looking at City Hall in front of them. The photo communicates a David and Goliath battle between a minority group uniquely and negatively affected by a policy being driven forward by a colossal and powerful institution. Standing outside the seat of power their physical exclusion reflects the exclusion visited

Reproduced by kind permission of The Guide Dogs for the Blind Association

upon them by the policy they oppose. This one simple photograph tells the tale of an underdog's struggle.

The challenge for you, of course, is to create images of similar power and impact!

Shane Greer is the executive editor of Total Politics

15

Writing winning literature

Hopi Sen

A lot of people in politics hate writing to voters. Are you one of them? Perhaps it makes you nervous of making mistakes – or just scared of writing something tedious.

The purpose of this chapter is to try and help you through some of the pitfalls and stresses of developing campaign literature. It will focus on how to make the process easier and more effective, through eleven simple, practical tips.

What you say in your campaign is a subject to your politics, your personality and the issues you think matter. The purpose of this chapter is to help you find the right style and voice for your campaign literature.

Know your audience

You are not the most important person in a campaign. The voter is. So when you're writing, you need to keep your audience at the front of your mind.

Whatever you're thinking of writing, first ask yourself who you are writing for. Think carefully – you probably have a more detailed answer than you suspect.

Perhaps you know that a third of people won't vote whatever you say, while many others already know how they'll vote. So is your audience everyone, or just those who are undecided?

If you're talking to undecided voters, do most of them *usually* support your opponent or are they people who generally support your party but are unhappy? Do they want reassurance or inspiration?

If you're writing about a particular subject, are your readers interested and well informed about it, or do you need to capture their attention from the very first line?

The more you know about your audience the easier it is to know what to say to them.

Know your purpose

Writing to your voters isn't like writing to a friend. When writing a political message, you have a *purpose*. You want your readers to vote for you, and every piece of literature you put out should help persuade them to do just that.

If you can't sum up the purpose of what you're about to write in one sentence, the chances are you'll write something flabby and boring.

Before you begin writing, sum up what you want people to think at the end of reading your leaflet. Do you want readers to know that you are a seasoned local campaigner who is in touch with local issues? Do you want voters to be shocked at your opponent's extreme views? Or perhaps you want residents to know what the consequences will be for their family if they don't vote.

Try it: What's the purpose of the next leaflet you need to write? Is it 'I want people who read this to know that I am passionate about bringing green jobs to the area'? 'I want people to know that I oppose the building of the new estate nearby, while my opponent supports it'? 'I want people to know that I was born and brought up here, and know the area inside out'?

If you know your purpose, you'll write sharper, clearer copy.

Ask questions, and listen to the answers

Research used to be hard. Now it's ludicrously easy, so there's no excuse to be ignorant.

Almost every local newspaper is online, while Google records newspapers, media, blogs and research papers. If you have access to them, Lexis-Nexis and Factiva store every newspaper story. If you're a candidate for a major party, your party will provide policy guides, briefing notes, campaign notes and key quotes.

If you know your audience and your purpose, it won't be hard to find evidence to support your case. Make sure you do.

Want to talk about crime? There will have been dozens of local newspaper stories to highlight the issue. Think your opponent has opposed money for a new school? Check Hansard, or the local council voting records.

There's one other vital way of doing research – listening to people. Whether it's surveys, canvassing or community meetings, simply listening to people and noting down what they say is a mine of quotes, information and insight. If you want to convince people you're part of the community, proving that you've listened isn't a bad way to start.

You should also keep the dialogue going. Always give people a way to get in touch with you, whatever you're writing. It might be a feedback form, a survey or a tear-off slip to send back, but make sure people know you want to listen as well as talk. Often, what they have to say will write your next letter or leaflet for you.

Decide your format

There's another decision to make before you start typing. It's an important one. What format are you going to choose?

Maybe you know it's a leaflet – but *what kind* of leaflet? If you're standing for a major party, they might provide leaflet and letter templates, so you know how many words, picture and headlines are needed. If you can, use these formats. They're designed by professionals, and having someone do the hard work for you will save you valuable time in an election campaign.

If you're standing for a minor party or on your own then make sure your leaflets have impact. Nothing is more offputting than a wall of text. Big snappy headlines, lots of space for pictures and a limited amount of text is the order of the day. It doesn't have to look designer, but it should grab people's attention.

The format you use changes the tone and language you write in. A Risographed handwritten note should sound different to a carefully considered letter on policy. Use your audience and purpose to choose the right format for your copy.

Deciding your format might even mean changing who the letter writer is. People often write 'introductory letters' to show they're part of the community – but those letters are more powerful when they come from someone who people know already.

If I boast that I know your area, you'd be sceptical – but you might believe a neighbour who says 'Hopi's really active round here'.

What about in a leaflet? If you want to grab attention on one big story, you don't want something long and complex. You need to keep your message simple, direct and punchy. One story. Short sentences. Lots of emphasis.

Think in pictures

Whatever campaign literature you put together, make sure you know what images you want to go with it. Your story needs to be complemented by the images you use.

Make sure that you have lots of stock pictures on the campaign trail, especially of you talking to people, at local landmarks, with residents, with police, nurses or teachers, or at local schools, hospitals or libraries. These can be used to illustrate a wide range of stories.

Vitally, wear different clothes for different pictures. If you're wearing the same thing in every picture of you, everyone will think you had your pictures taken on the same day. Also, try and have someone with you in most pictures.

If you've got a particular story in mind, make the effort to get a photo specifically for it. You might be doing a photo opportunity for a newspaper story, or just one for your own leaflets, but treat the photo as a key part of your literature – worthy of as much effort as the design and writing.

If you can't get a photo – design a stock image. Is your opponent rarely seen in the area? Then a simple Clip Art silhouette with a question mark on it will get the message across.

Message, message, message

You know your audience, you know why you're writing, you've got a couple of key facts to back up your argument, and you know your format.

Now you're ready to go. Start your engines *an-n-n-n-d* write. But make sure you stick to what you meant to say. It's easy to wander off at a tangent. You can start indulging your pet theory or get diverted into trivia. That might be great if you're writing a comment piece for the *Telegraph*, where your purpose is to show off your eclectic knowledge, wit and range, but it's terrible if you need people to know why you want a new cottage hospital.

It's your message that matters to voters. Make sure every sentence does something to deliver it.

Use drama

What makes a message come to life? Drama. Drama is about conflict – whether it's conflicting desires, needs or ideas.

Think about an exciting news story – perhaps there's a villain who needs to be stopped, whether a swindler doing old ladies out of cash, a heartless businessman defrauding the vulnerable or an officious jobsworth denying kids a place to play.

Or the focus might be on people trying to do something worthwhile or noble – the parent trying for a better school or the child standing up to bullies.

In each case there's something at stake, something important to the reader – and it's in danger.

So what is the drama in your message? Is it that a school is under threat, or that we need to stop the menace of fly tipping, or the risk of repossession or regulation throttling business?

Whatever it is, you should use drama to bring it to life. Who might suffer? Why does their fate matter to the voter?

Consider the difference between these two paragraphs, both forty-five words long:

An increase in business regulation will lead to lower growth and a reduced number of small business start-ups, according to leading researchers. I believe we should reduce the burden of red tape on entrepreneurs to increase the chances of economic recovery here in Ourtown.

Tony Jacks runs Ourtown's butcher shop. He's afraid he'll have to close. Tony told me: 'I spend more time filling out forms than I do on my job. My life's almost impossible.' We need shops like Jack's Butchers in Ourtown – not even more red tape.

I know which is more likely to go on the *Economist* letters page, and which in a campaign leaflet.

Watch your language

There are some easy ways to check if your language is going to keep people interested. One way is focus on your sentence length

Short sentences make writing easier to understand. The *Sun* is the most popular British newspaper. A sentence in a *Sun* editorial is usually ten to twelve words long. Short sentences keep things punchy. They don't confuse or complicate.

Ironically enough, for most of us, writing short sentences is harder than writing long, complex, unwieldy sentences. Brevity requires much more attention than waffle. For some purposes, complexity and shade is important. In most election campaigns, you'll want to keep things as clear and direct as you can.

Another way is to focus on your choice of words. You can tell if your text is interesting by writing and then checking the words you've used.

If you find you've written words like Outrage, Anger, Shock, Horror, Afraid, Delight, Amazed, Hero, Disgusted, Disaster, Miracle, Confusion, Deceit, U-Turn or Victory, then there's probably some drama in your piece. If you've written words like Statistics, Percentages, Caveats, Reminders, Discussions, Reviews, Meetings, Processes or Feedback, then your reader's eyes will be glazing over. Of course, if you're trying to bore your reader into submission, that's a good thing.

Use repetition
Repetition is one of the oldest rhetorical tricks in world literature. Go to Homer and you'll find that the Iliad includes dozens of repetitions – like 'Rosy-fingered Dawn', 'Swift-footed Achilles' or 'Wily Odysseus'.

If repetition is good enough for the greatest work in world literature, don't go turning your nose up at it.

Why is it useful? Because repeated use attaches the meaning of the words and issues back onto you.

The Liberal Democrats are perhaps the best British exponents of this technique. You rarely see the name of a Liberal candidate without the epithet 'local campaigner' prefixed to it. And the 'local campaigner' is usually 'working all year round' because they're 'on your side'.

If you use these phrases often enough, they become yours. If someone else tried to introduce themselves as a 'local campaigner' who 'works all year round', voters would just be reminded of you. These perceptions can be established quickly, if repeated frequently enough, as anyone who's campaigned against the Liberal Democrats in a by-election can tell you.

Repetition can work for an issue too. An issue can be raised, a survey done on it, the results of the survey reported, the refusal to listen denounced and victory declared, all in the same tone. Even if you're not paying attention to the issue you'll know that the 'local campaigner' is passionate about it. When you're sick of saying it, a lot of people are just starting to get the message.

Don't be afraid to reuse your leaflet and direct mails again and again. Repetition is nothing to be scared of.

Edit
The political world is full of disaster stories caused by a failure to edit properly. One 1997 Labour candidate famously printed 40,000 leaflets with the unusual pledge to 'deliver fast track punishment to the young unemployed'.

Politics is high pressure, especially during an election campaign. You're being asked to do a thousand things at once. It's unlikely you get to compose your article or letter in peace. It's usually the last minute, and you should be at a community forum.

If you write something yourself, you will find it harder to see its flaws. So get someone else to find them for you. Don't just restrict them to finding typos. Tell them what you're trying to do with the copy, and who the audience is, and let them loose on it.

Don't stand on ceremony. The annoying American intern might be the only person you can get to look at it. But you need another pair of eyes, so use him.

You don't have to agree with every change that's suggested – but more often than not, people will spot mistakes, strange gaps, misspellings and non-sequiturs that you missed. Often, you'll get really good suggestions.

Perhaps you're like me and find people telling you what's wrong with your writing annoying. Strangely, even though my editors are always idiots, every time they edit my writing it gets better.

Edit it again
I did say not to be afraid of repetition, didn't I?

One you've written and edited your copy, put it away, even if just for a couple of minutes, and go over it again, to check for sense and errors.

If you can get three or four pairs of eyes to check for mistakes, then all the better.

However, a word of warning: make sure only one person in your campaign finally decides what goes in and what's kept out. Someone has to be able to make a decision, because an election campaign is a pressured situation and you're operating to deadlines.

The only thing worse than a poorly edited leaflet is one that doesn't reach people in time to influence their votes.

So there you go. Eleven simple tips to help you write more effective leaflets and Direct mail letters. Now get started.

Hopi Sen is the former head of campaigns for the Parliamentary Labour Party

16

Politics 2.0

Mark Pack

In the early twentieth century, large public meetings and lengthy public speeches were expected of – and needed by – parliamentary candidates fighting vigorous campaigns. A century on, candidates fighting vigorous campaigns frequently get by without organising any public meetings or giving any public speeches longer than a few minutes of opening remarks at a local organisation's hustings.

Yet although these forms of personal, direct contact between candidate and voter have declined sharply over the last century, the opportunities for such contact via the internet have increased sharply in the last few years.

We are already at the stage where voters find it surprising if a candidate is not online. Candidates who do not make good use of the internet face losing out on votes, helpers and money.

The two key insights for an effective online presence
First, people increasingly look online for information – so the information a candidate wants to put out needs to be in those places where people look.

There is a saying that anglers use – you need to fish where the fish are. The same applies to politics. You need to put information where voters are or can be attracted. There isn't much point putting huge effort into nurturing a presence on Orkut (Google's social networking site) if Orkut is shunned by just about everyone in the area.

But second, you cannot simply put information online and then sit back and wait. Some people will come, but far more will come if you also effectively promote it.

Who is the audience?

Turning both of those insights into practical steps starts with understanding who the audience is, or might be, for a candidate's online presence.

It usually has three key parts. Arguably most important of the trio is *media* – because if journalists pick up information online and then use that in their own stories, that information almost always gets before a much bigger audience than the original online audience. Just look at the number of views which local candidate films on YouTube receive; it's a rare clip that gets more than 1,000 views, but it is a rare local paper which has fewer than 1,000 readers.

Another part of the audience is the *internal audience*. Whether it is councillors, activists, members, helpers or donors, they all need to be kept happy and motivated. The online world offers many opportunities to do just that, and to turn that extra enthusiasm into extra offline campaigning. This was the big success of the Barack Obama internet campaign. It mobilised people online to give money (largely spent on TV adverts in the offline world) and to go and knock on doors, make phone calls and deliver leaflets (all also aimed at the offline world).

The final part of the audience are the *floating voters*. The media and the internal audience are ways to get at floating voters too, but there is also a direct online audience.

In previous general elections it has been fairly small for most candidates most of the time, but the audience is growing – and even a small audience is vital in a close-run election. Lynne Featherstone, who gained her seat in 2005, found her online audience then was already larger than the number of postal voters, and audiences of that size are becoming increasingly common.

What information does the audience want?

It is easy to get lost in the blizzard of different online services: websites, blogs, Twitter, instant messaging, email, Facebook, YouTube, Digg and more. Not even Barack Obama's massive team effectively made use of them all. (Look at his Twitter account during the election campaign for an example of boring, uninteractive minimalism).

Labour candidate Luke Pollard puts it well: 'Some candidates get obsessed with Facebook or Twitter. Answer is to ignore the channel and concentrate on the content.'

The best starting place is with a blank sheet of paper and three rows: 'media', 'internal audience' and 'floating voters'. Write in each row the key pieces of information which they want or which you want them to have.

This list should then guide choices about what is put online and where. It is particularly important to have such a list if one or more technologically savvy people help out with the online campaign. Often such people are relatively new to political campaigning and not that plugged in to the rest of the campaign – so without this list it is easy for the online work to go off at a tangent, drawn along by the clever things the technology can do rather than the key things it must do.

Sample lists

Media

They want to know: name of candidate, photo, brief biography, contact details.

I also want them to know: why we can win, five local campaign pledges.

Internal audience

They want to know: how the campaign is going, how to help.

I also want them to know: success of efforts they've made, why they need to help more.

Floating voters
They want to know: name of candidate, biography, contact details, views on local hospital, attitude to local school closure.
I also want them to know: why we can win, five local campaign pledges, where to vote, how to get a postal vote.

There will usually be a large overlap between what a candidate wants people to know and what people actually want to know, but a candidate should aim to do more than just simply provide people with the information they already think they want.

As a final piece of preparation, take a look around the existing online presence from all political parties, the council, the local media and other local news sources (such as bloggers and local organisations). This may highlight gaps in the provision of local information which a candidate can usefully fill.

Many local councillors, for example, have very popular blogs fuelled by the provision of very local information about their area which fills in a gap in the local media coverage. A good example is http://stevebeasant.mycouncillor.org.uk, who provides local information which in previous decades would probably have been found by people via local newspapers. However, if there is already extensive similar information provided online then a candidate supplying such information too is going to get much less benefit from it.

Website, blog or something else?
Armed with your basic sketch of the audience, the information to supply and the gaps in the information already out there (which professionals in this field may recognise as a hugely simplified version of the persona and information architecture processes they commonly use), good decisions can be made about what online presence to build.

At the heart of it needs to be a web page of some sort. It could be a website, a blog or a combination of the two.

Blogs often suit the personal tone of voice, which is handy for getting over conviction, beliefs and sincerity.

In addition, blogs are to websites as newspapers are to books. They are best suited for regular updates, often briefer stories and building an audience which expects a new edition most days.

This all means blogs require a regular, personal contribution from someone who can write well, and so they are not the best answer for everyone. More traditional websites are more suited to those with less of a writing style or with less time or news to impart. It is a matter of juggling skills, priorities and resources.

Some candidates end up with both a website and a blog, but this rarely works effectively (two different sites to look after, too fragmented an online presence) unless they are closely integrated. Liberal Democrat MP Lynne Featherstone even has the same system – WordPress – driving a closely integrated website and a blog (www. LynneFeatherstone.org).

Whichever option is chosen, populate it with content based on the list of information to supply to the target audiences.

Extra online content: a checklist
That list will give you most of what you should put online, but here is a checklist of other items to include:

> Email sign up box
> Online donations (see Chapter 23, Online Fundraising)
> Ability to volunteer to help (see Chapter 10, Building an Army)
> Links to other local sites from your party, councillors and the national/regional party sites
> Election imprint and data protection disclaimer
> RSS (or news feeds) – these provide an easy way for people to sign up to automatically receive new content in future. Any decent website or blog system will provide RSS options.

Don't forget the photographs. . .
A picture is still worth a thousand words. People skim-read online just as they do with printed matter. Photographs catch the eye even when the carefully nuanced sub-clause is not read.

Good action photographs are a must online. The photographs

should illustrate the main messages overall and also present the candidate in a positive light.

That sounds obvious, but if you take a quick browse around some candidate websites or blogs you will see that far too often the photo of the candidate looks more like something out of a regional news crime report than an image conveying a positive message. A candidate claiming widespread popular support does themselves no favours being photographed on their own all the time. (And don't think you can get away with using a member of staff to be the public in a photograph, as Conservative candidate Jacob Rees-Mogg found to his cost with a lengthy exposé in the *Daily Mail*.)

I have seen plenty of photographs where the candidate is a tiny, unrecognisable smudge. But I have yet to see one that makes me recoil, saying: 'I really don't want to see that far up your left nostril, thank you very much.' The photographer can always take at least one step closer.

. . .nor the importance of good headlines

Again, as with print, people will skim-read so powerful headlines that attract attention are important. It is also the headlines which people may see when viewing links to your site from other sites or from an RSS reader. Without a good headline they may never come to the site to read the full story.

Finding good advice

In putting together a good website or blog, there are a large number of technical issues to get right. For a candidate the key is not to attempt to learn all of these themselves but to hunt out at least one person who can assist. Beware, though, the self-anointed expert who isn't! A genuine expert will understand and be able to help with the items in this short checklist.

Technical checklist

› Does the site perform well in search engine results?
› Does the site meet basic accessibility standards? (It's not only

those with limited or no sight who benefit from this; good accessibility standards often overlap with general good practice.)

› Is this site backed up regularly?
› Are traffic statistics available for the site, including how many people visit the site, which are the most popular pages and where the traffic comes from?

Promoting your site

Although the single most important step is providing good quality content, that is not enough on its own. People base whole careers and businesses on promoting websites and blogs, but there are many simple steps a candidate can take.

› **Printed literature:** leaflets are an excellent place to start. Don't just stick the address on a leaflet; include stories which give people a positive reason to visit a site online. For example a story about school admission rules might include a link to further details. A good tip when giving web or blog addresses (URLs) is to capitalise words as this makes them easier to read, remember and type – www.MarkPack.org.uk rather than www.markpack.org.uk.
› **Verbal promotion:** whether it is canvassing, meeting voters in the high street, visiting groups or making speeches, most candidates will find plenty of opportunities to mention their URL. This is a good reason to have a URL which is easy to say and easy to work out the spelling of. If you have a name that is neither, then also get the URLs which are common mistakes and point them at the right site too.
› **Use the media:** the days when simply launching a website made for a local news story are mostly gone, but with a little imagination stories can often be found. For example, launching an online survey can be a great way of getting a URL in the local newspaper. Remember also your internal audience and look for publicity on other sites that they read. Sites such as Conservative Home, Labour List and Lib Dem Voice often mention new sites from candidates or MPs and in amongst comments on such pieces you can also often pick up good tips.

> **Email:** I have often said – and still believe – that I would rather run an election campaign in which the website and blog failed than one in which the email setup failed. Nearly nine in ten UK internet users are on email. That is far more than visit blogs or political websites. Gather up email addresses (with consent to use them) from members, local journalists and voters. Then use them to let people know when significant new content has been added.

> **Make content shareable:** increasingly people read content online because someone else has recommended it to them. At a technical level you can assist this by having 'share this'-type buttons on content, such as to send a post to Twitter, Digg or Facebook. It is also about content: think about what content your audiences might want to share with others. Only the very best political rants (or the very worst!) get shared. Useful local information is usually a much stronger bet.

> **Make use of social networking:** this chapter focuses on websites and blogs, but the logic about fishing where the fish are applies very strongly to using Facebook and possibly also other social networks such as Twitter and YouTube (depending on your audiences). You can use those to drive traffic back to the main site.

> **Comment on other sites:** many websites and blogs take comments and this can be a good way of taking part in the conversation where the audience already is. It is also likely to expose you to conflicting views from others, which can be a useful check against falling into the myopic mindset about how your party is fantastic and everyone in other parties are the spawn of the devil. As Terence Eden (@edent on Twitter) puts it: 'Leave sensible comments on other blogs using (a) your real name and (b) a link back to your website. Get known and stay visible'. Wise advice.

Promotion works best when someone is consistent across different online services. You may be called both Sam and Samuel, but pick one to use consistently, whether in the name of a blog or in a Facebook profile. As it is the name of the candidate on the ballot paper, first and last names should usually be used rather than Eloise4MP, though with common names you may have to be inventive if your name has already been taken on various services.

Consistency also applies to messaging. The online audiences will also be reached by offline campaigning, so the messages in each should compliment – and certainly not contradict – each other.

Privacy

Flick through the coverage of election candidates getting it wrong online and one theme repeatedly dominates media coverage: supposed exposes of what someone has got up to in their private life based on what has been found online. Some exposés are justified (an election candidate who dresses up in a Nazi uniform should, at the very least, have a very good explanation), while others which are more hypocritical are not.

As long as there are producers and consumers of such content, it is wise to be aware of how online information may be fuel to their fires.

Candidates are politicians, private individuals and also often employees. What is said or done with one of these hats on can easily affect the others. Working for a trade-union-busting employer may well result in questions being asked of a candidate, but also over-the-top political vitriol about how all members of another party are deceitful can come back to bite a politician at work if they are after new business from. . . a supporter of that 100 per cent deceitful party.

The two basic steps any candidate should carry out are to search for their own name in Google to check what is out there about them and to check the privacy settings on their own social network profiles, such as Bebo or Facebook, to be sure that only that which they'd be happy to appear on the front page of a newspaper is being shared with anyone other than very close friends and family. To be extra safe, if in doubt do not put something online at all.

Three candidates/MPs to take a look at

1. Charlie Elphicke (Conservative candidate for Dover & Deal) – a site that is demanding in terms of technology and content, but

a good example of what to aspire to, even for candidates who should settle for something less ambitious.

2. Lynne Featherstone (Lib Dem MP for Hornsey & Wood Green) – an unsurprising choice perhaps given that I've helped her out over the years, but also an excellent example of how to integrate a blog and a website.

3. Derek Wyatt (Labour MP for Sittingbourne & Sheppey) – a pioneer in online campaigning and particularly effective with his use of online video branded 'Derek Wyatt TV'.

Internet usage is now so high right across the UK that in fact more people use the internet than vote in elections. So wherever you are, if you want to get on in politics, get online.

Mark Pack is the co-editor of Liberal Democrat Voice

17

Getting out the vote

Luke Akehurst

GOTV (Getting Out the Vote) is what seals the deal on any campaign.

I learned this the hard way in the first general election campaign I worked on, in Bristol North West in 1992. As a Labour student activist I declined an offer to run a GOTV operation in safe Tory Westbury-on-Trym ward. I didn't realise this meant there would be no GOTV in one of the constituency's wards. On polling day itself, working in low-turnout Labour Southmead ward, we shut up shop at 9 p.m. because it was dark and voters were getting grumpy about us knocking on their doors. We lost that parliamentary seat by forty-five votes after several recounts. An operation in Westbury-on-Trym or carrying on 'knocking up' in Southmead or anywhere else for the final hour until close of poll would have pulled out the extra forty-six Labour voters needed. And nationwide, Labour winning Bristol North West, and just ten other seats where almost as narrow margins had occurred, would have created a hung parliament rather than a Tory fourth term. We didn't know it, but stopping knocking on doors one hour early in Southmead had altered the result of the general election and given John Major five more years in Number 10.

You can have the best leaflets ever, the most canvassing, the greatest candidate, the finest policies and messages, and the most expensive advertising, and none of this will matter if you can't get your supporters to vote.

Of course there are some countries, notably Australia, where voting is compulsory so turnout is not affected by what the political parties and candidates do, and there are those who advocate such a system here, but until or unless that comes about, GOTV is an essential part of any campaign.

Of course all the other elements of a campaign feed into GOTV: canvassing provides the database of known supporters; candidates, policies, messages, literature and advertising convert voters to your cause. But you still need to turn expressions of support into ballot papers cast.

GOTV is the element of the campaign which is most a science and least an art. It is the most mechanistic part of an election, where the candidate becomes just another activist knocking on doors and the agent or organiser and their allocation of resources rules supreme.

It is also the element least changed over the years – fundamentally the same process as Joseph Chamberlain invented in Birmingham in the 1860s.

GOTV has become more, not less, important in recent years as turnout has dropped from a norm of 70–80 per cent to 59–61 per cent in 2001 and 2005. With overall turnout lower, any party that can use GOTV techniques to increase their own supporters' relative turnout gets a huge differential advantage.

Unfortunately declining turnout has been accompanied as a sociological phenomenon by declining levels of party membership and volunteer activism. This presents a big problem for campaign organisers at all levels – voters need more and more contact and effort to persuade them to vote, yet the number of people available to do this most labour-intensive of political tasks is declining.

This is driving changes in the way in which GOTV is organised and points to the science at the heart of any GOTV operation – putting the limited human resources you have into the places where they will have the most impact on turnout of your own supporters and where this will have the most impact on the number of seats won.

In an ideal world with limitless party activists there is a model way of doing GOTV. The mythology is that this is how it was done nationwide in the 1950s in an era of mass-membership Labour and Tory parties, but I suspect even then it was only properly done in key marginal seats. In 1997 Labour was able to run the full system in all seventy key target marginals. In Edmonton for instance the Labour agent had so many helpers from twinned safe seats that he had over 900 volunteers on polling day – a ratio of one party worker per thirty Labour voters – not quite man-on-man marking but not far off it! This kind of intensity of operation is still possible in marginal seats if they get external help and in one-off parliamentary and council by-elections (I had 110 helpers on the day in a 2009 ward by-election in Hackney) but becomes more difficult when you face all-out parliamentary or council elections.

The traditional model of GOTV operation consists of the following polling day elements:

› A rota of 'number takers', i.e. a person with a party rosette and a pen and writing pad who sits or stands outside every polling station asking voters their polling number (the number than identifies them on the electoral register) and recording these. Council returning officers often insist that voters are only asked this question as they leave the polling station, and that blank rosettes without slogans are worn. The number takers from different parties usually co-operate to ensure no one misses a number. Some voters refuse to disclose their number. In some regions there is a tradition of voters handing in a card distributed by the party they support and marked with their polling number. In a typical constituency with ten wards each having four polling stations this part of the system requires forty volunteers at any one time – and given most people won't want to do this job for more than a few hours during the fifteen hours of polling, many more are required in practice.

› Runners, usually one per ward – on foot, bike or car – take the lists of numbers collected back to the relevant campaign HQ every hour or so.

› At the HQ – usually there is one per ward, known historically as the 'committee room' – an organiser cross-references the lists of people who have voted against a list of known party supporters obtained earlier in the campaign through canvassing. Nowadays this can be done on a computer using the party's database systems but until recently a paper-based system was used. This consists of lists of supporters printed out (hand written until the advent of home PCs!) onto multi-part sheets of carbonated paper laid out on a large table or board in polling number order, with a sheet or more per street. The organiser crosses out any numbers on these sheets that have been recorded as already having gone through the polling station. Thus the uncrossed-out names and numbers are the people who still need to be visited and reminded to vote.

› The organiser identifies which streets or estates are not turning out fast and still have known supporters in them who need to be reminded to vote. He tears off sheets for those streets if using the manual system, or prints them off if using a computer. He then sends teams of activists out to visit the party supporters who have not voted yet and encourage them to vote.

› Thus as the polling day wears on party volunteers are visiting with increasing frequency a smaller and smaller group of their supporters who have not voted, and time is not wasted on those who have already turned out.

This system is known in the UK as the 'Reading system', named after the campaign in which it was invented by Labour left-winger Ian Mikardo – the parliamentary election for Reading in 1945. It only works with a large number of volunteers and with good canvass data.

In the USA an equally labour-intensive but rather lonelier variant of the system is used. Instead of working as a team from a central HQ, each activist is given one block or street where they repeatedly visit party supporters throughout the day.

Given the difficulties some local parties will face in staffing such an operation, the political parties have come up with a number of organisational shortcuts.

First, it is possible to dispense with number taking and committee rooms and just focus on sending all your volunteers to visit supporters. Basically you knock on doors blind without knowing if the person has already voted, and if they say they have you just take their word for it as you have no evidence from the polling stations. This is obviously a good way of handling polling day if you are short of activists, but you do waste time talking to people who have already voted – and you risk aggravating them.

Second, you can address a lack of canvass data, i.e. a failure to identify who your supporters are, by using commercially available demographic datasets overlaid onto the electoral register to identify neighbourhoods with socio-economic characteristics making them more likely to vote for your party. You then go and visit voters in those households. In some places this is so obvious that you don't need expensive software e.g. it is a bit of a no-brainer that low-turnout Labour areas and council estates are usually the same thing. Still, there is a risk of GOTVing your opponents' supporters.

Third, you can use phones instead of visiting voters in person. Possibly less effective, and it's increasingly difficult to obtain numbers due to the decline in landline use and the spread of the Telephone Preference System opt-out from cold calls, but it's a lot, lot faster than pounding the streets, and a lot warmer.

Fourth, you can start GOTV earlier than polling day, leaving you under less pressure on the day itself. The 1997 Labour campaign in key seats was based on finishing canvassing before the month-long 'short campaign' started. This was so that the entire month of the campaign was one long GOTV process: visiting and delivering materials to known Labour supporters to increase their likelihood of voting, and contacting undecided voters to try to persuade them to plump for Labour.

Where there are large numbers of registered postal voters an early start to GOTV is of course a necessity, not a tactic. This is because postal voters will have either voted or binned their ballot paper as much as a fortnight before the final polling day. Now that there is postal voting on demand, and where councils or political parties have run drives to increase registration for postal votes, this could affect up to one third of the electorate. So you need to organise

GOTV visits to them, timed for immediately after the returning officer tells you they will receive their ballots, to encourage them to post them back. Quite correctly, given recent scandals involving postal vote fraud involving all political parties, postal vote GOTV is an area under great scrutiny from the police and returning officers and is coming under increasingly strict legal control. Anyone visiting postal voters needs to be familiar with the law, the protocols agreed between the parties and the Electoral Commission nationally, and the local guidance from the returning officer. The basic rules are that you should never handle a postal vote (call the council electoral services department to arrange collection if a voter really can't take their completed ballot pack to a post box), should not watch how the voter votes (this is a breach of the secret ballot) and should not enter their home (if passers-by can't see that nothing untoward is happening you could lay yourself open to charges of 'attempted undue influence'). All you should do is remind the postal voter to vote and advise them on the technicalities of how to vote and when they need to return the ballot.

A side-effect of the availability of postal voting on demand is that it almost completely negates the need for anyone to have a proxy vote. A proxy vote is a system where a voter nominates a friend, relative or activist of the party they support to vote on their behalf. In almost all circumstances now it is better for a person who can't vote in person because of illness or absence from the constituency to have a postal vote.

Similarly, postal voting on demand means there is far less need to organise car calls than in the past, when parties had to organise a fleet of volunteer drivers to transport the elderly and infirm to the polls. Usually one car per ward is enough nowadays other than in very rural areas where polling stations are sparsely distributed.

Another dying art is the loudhailer. Back in the days when whole communities used to back one or another party consistently there was some sense in literally talking to the whole area by shouting out or broadcasting a recording of an appeal to vote through a handheld bullhorn or a car-mounted loudspeaker. Now that communities and even households vote in fragmented and diverse patterns this is just as likely to GOTV your opponents as your supporters. Similarly risky, unless you are in a rare area of monolithic support for one party, are outdoor polling day activities such as walkabouts, street stalls and leafleting bus stops and train stations – they can all remind the opposition to vote when GOTV should be focussed on your supporters.

A script is necessary for contact with supporters on polling day. This needs to go beyond 'please go and vote for my party' and give details of where the polling station is and when it closes, and more important reasons why busy people should bother. These reasons can be organisational ('it's really neck and neck here', 'it could be your vote that makes the difference', 'your vote could stop the other lot / put our wonderful candidate in') and political ('vote today to save the local hospital / get more police on the beat / send the government a message / cut the deficit').

The same combination of facts about how to vote (e.g. names of your candidate(s) and their position on the ballot paper, and a map of where the polling station is, as by definition low turnout voters won't often have been there!) and organisational and political reasons to bother voting are needed on any literature handed out as part of GOTV. Leaflets are needed on the day to be handed to supporters you talk to or stuck through doors when no one is in. You need several designs as you could visit some slow-to-vote households multiple times. The Lib Dems swear by dawn-of-poll leaflets delivered before voters have breakfast but I'm not convinced the effort of getting up that early is justified. Far more effective are reminders to vote – as personalised as possible – delivered in the forty-eight hours before polling day.

The key thing about effective GOTV, though, is strategy and having a strategist who people will trust and whose judgement about where they should go they will accept. That's why at this stage in any election the agent or organiser becomes temporarily more important than the candidate (disparagingly known as the 'legal necessity' by agents!). Campaigns don't have limitless human resources, and the trick under our first-past-the-post voting system is to place the people you do have in the places to do GOTV where they will most affect the overall result. That means the areas where supporters of your own party with a low propensity to turn out are concentrated, within marginal parliamentary seats or council wards. The organiser then concentrates his activists more and more in the constituencies or wards where the pattern of voting suggests the outcome is tightest as the polling day progresses, so that by the end of the day all effort is focussed on those areas where the result remains in doubt.

Luke Akehurst is a Labour councillor and blogger

18

How to win or lose with grace

Stephen Twigg

This year, in Liverpool West Derby, I will contest my fourth consecutive general election – and I'll be hoping for a third win rather than a second defeat! I fought Enfield Southgate three times so I have learned from experience some lessons about how to deal with both winning and losing. Ideally, this should mean magnanimity in victory and dignity in defeat. In either situation, I would advise candidates to be gracious and respectful both to their opponents and to the local electorate.

The general election result in Southgate in the early hours of 2 May 1997 was voted the third greatest television moment ever – after the first man on the moon and the day that Nelson Mandela was released from prison. Michael Portillo was extremely dignified and gracious in defeat, even managing a wry sense of humour at the election count. As is customary, once counting was complete, the returning officer gathered the candidates together, gave us the result and then enquired 'Is everybody happy?', to which Michael replied 'Ecstatic!' Eight years later, when I lost the seat, I did my best to match his good grace and humour. In 2005, he sent me a text with his advice: 'May I recommend a by-election?'

Partisan triumphalism is rarely attractive to the wider population. In 1997, Labour people did feel a sense of triumph after eighteen long years out of office. I hope, though, that we managed to combine our celebration with good grace. I recall, in Southgate, paying tribute to Michael Portillo and the other candidates who had fought the seat and pledging that I would be there as the MP for all the constituents – not only those who had voted Labour. During the 1997 campaign, I would lie in the bath and draft my fantasy acceptance speech. I never thought I'd get to deliver that speech but I am glad I had bothered to at least give it some thought. The speeches at the declaration are the first public opportunity to demonstrate good grace. Many general election declarations are televised so this adds another element of significance to the speeches. It is definitely worth spending time on preparation for what is a very important speech.

In victory, it is essential to be constructive about the other candidates, grateful to the local electorate for their support and to demonstrate a clear understanding that as the Member of Parliament you will be there for everyone – not only your own supporters. The newly elected MP's acceptance speech sets the tone for their work over the subsequent four or five years. If the sitting MP has been defeated, this speech is an opportunity to put the divisions of the campaign to one side and thank your predecessor for their work. This can be expanded upon once the new MP makes their maiden speech in the House of Commons.

In defeat, the challenge is arguably much greater – to pay tribute to the person who has won (i.e. defeated you!), to show respect for the outcome but also to thank and rally your own supporters. In 2005 I was expecting to hold the seat – albeit narrowly. Defeat that year came as much more of a shock than it would have done in 1997 or 2001. I used my speech at the count to congratulate David Burrowes, the new Conservative MP, and to thank the people of Enfield Southgate for the opportunity to serve them in the House of Commons for eight years. I wanted also to rally local Labour members and supporters so I said that while I had been the first ever Labour MP for Southgate I was confident that I wouldn't be the last. I hope this turns out to be a wise prediction rather than empty rhetoric – either way it served to cheer up Labour supporters at the time.

Immediately after the declaration, it is likely that the media will approach winning and losing candidates alike – either at the count itself or in the days immediately following the result. For a winning candidate this is a great opportunity to flesh out the points made in your acceptance speech and to identify some key priorities for your new job as the local Member of Parliament. In defeat you are probably less likely to feel enthusiastic about talking to journalists. Michael Portillo's interview with Jeremy Paxman in 1997 has become the stuff of legend. In 2005 I did not speak to the media on the night but had interviews with local papers and *The Times* in the days after the election. When I spoke to the press about my defeat I had had time to reflect on it and also started to think about what I might do next in my life. I was fortunate that the Holocaust Centre/Aegis Trust, the Foreign Policy Centre and Progress gave me opportunities to move on in the months after defeat.

Volunteers are of crucial importance in election campaigns. Whether a candidate has won or lost, it is vital to thank and show gratitude to those who have given up their own time to help. On the night itself, some activists will be at the count but others might gather at the campaign HQ or in someone's home, watching the results come in on television. In 2005 my speech to my campaigners was in some ways a tougher task than my earlier concession speech at the count. When a sitting MP has been defeated their supporters' emotions will often run high. At our HQ in 2005, we were joined by a very emotional Green Party candidate who was anxious to express his regret that he might have taken votes from me (though, to be fair, the total Green vote was less than the Conservative majority). Even in defeat the candidate has a responsibility to show political leadership and to give people a sense of hope for the future.

Election results are influenced by a broad range of factors: the national swing, local organisation, personalities, demographic trends, particular issues in the constituency. When I was elected in 1997 I knew that very few people (if any) had cast a personal vote for me. True, my Dad and sister did live in the constituency but both of them would have voted Labour anyway! The result was primarily based on the huge national swing. Similarly, in 2005 most of those who switched from Labour were at great pains to tell me that it was no reflection on my work as the local MP but was because of national issues. Despite this, at a personal level defeat can be difficult. I loved the job and missed it from Day One. I had been heavily involved in a lot of local issues and local organisations and I had to decide what level of involvement to maintain. I did not want to let people down but I realised that I wanted to take on some new challenges in my life.

Now, five years on from 2005, I keep in touch with some Southgate groups like the truly inspirational Chicken Shed Theatre Company. I continue to chair the annual Livia Award, which was established by Giulietta and George Galli-Atkinson in memory of their daughter Livia, who was killed by a car. I was delighted that they wanted me to continue with the Livia Award and equally pleased that my successor David Burrowes joined me on the award panel. Local political campaigning can be very partisan, reflecting real differences in policy, priorities and values – but on many issues it is possible for politicians to work together on a cross-party basis. The Livia Award is a fine example of this.

In 2007, local Labour Party members in the West Derby constituency in Liverpool voted to select me as their candidate for the forthcoming general election. It is an enormous privilege for me to have this opportunity and I hope that I have been able to learn from my experience of being in Parliament before in ways that will be positive for the local community in West Derby. If I do win I will do my best to be magnanimous and dignified.

There is a desperate need to rebuild a relationship of trust and faith between the British people and their politicians. This will take years to achieve and there is no single panacea. How politicians behave has an important influence on people's perceptions of the political system. At the 2010 general election, 650 candidates will win and thousands of others will lose. Win or lose, all of those candidates have the opportunity to make a positive contribution to the renewal of our politics. Between now and the election we can do so by engaging seriously with the people on the big policy challenges facing our country. On election night itself we have the opportunity to react with good grace to the result and when the new House of Commons convenes, politicians from all parties can work together to restore the reputation of Parliament itself.

Stephen Twigg was the MP for Enfield Southgate from 1997 to 2005 and is now the Labour prospective parliamentary candidate for Liverpool West Derby

19

Surviving life in the fast lane

Melanie Batley

So you're one of those curious creatures that decided to embark on the gruelling occupation of political candidacy, subjecting yourself to months, sometimes years, of intense stress, exhaustion, and personal sacrifice. As a member of this species, you have actually chosen to leave the comfort of your home and family to spend hundreds of hours shaking hands, making speeches to unpredictable audiences, and walking the streets for hours on end repeating a mantra to unappreciative strangers.

Far from the common perception, life on the campaign trail is not at all glamorous. It's physically exhausting, mentally and emotionally taxing, and at times, stressful enough to push you to the edge of sanity. Nonetheless, there's no shortage of competition for this dubious privilege, and if you are serious about succeeding, you must take steps to ensure that your campaign's most valuable asset (i.e. you) has the stamina to perform well and the energy to finish the race.

Taking active steps to maintain physical, mental and emotional health must be a priority, in spite of the immense pressures and frenetic pace, and there are specific ways that candidates can do this.

Back to basics: prioritise diet, sleep and exercise

At the most basic level, a healthy diet, adequate sleep and regular exercise are the fundamentals to maintaining good health, and for a political candidate subjected to the intense pressures of life in the spotlight and the punishing schedule to go with it, failing to prioritise these basic needs could fatally compromise an otherwise promising political campaign. These are the guidelines:

> **Get plenty of sleep.** It's difficult to follow this advice, especially as election day approaches, but it's a must if you are to maintain focus and energy and avoid potentially costly mistakes. Know how much sleep you need each night and make sure you get to bed at a time that will ensure you get the required number of hours. Of course there will be days when it just isn't possible, but keep those to a minimum. In addition, learn to sleep anywhere, really anywhere, and grab opportunities to nap when you feel exhausted, even if it's on an air mattress in the back of the campaign office.

> **Eat healthy meals and snacks and don't skip meals.** As with most things, preparation is the key to success. Make your meals in advance or ask someone to do this for you so you aren't grabbing unhealthy treats on the go when you get worn down. Alternatively, see whether a member of staff or volunteer will take responsibility for buying your food and reminding you to eat it. For very long days when you'll be out for hours, bring along a cool bag with healthy snacks to get you through the day. Though sampling local fare is one of the first obligations of the keen candidate, make it just that – a sampling. It's important to avoid consuming too much throughout the day or eating empty calories that could contribute to weight gain and ill health.

> **Exercise regularly.** Yes, you do have the time. If the President of the United States can fit in a daily workout, so can you. Aside from maintaining your fitness and building your endurance, it's a great stress reliever.

Protecting your physical health is crucial, so make it a top priority. However, even for the most health-conscious candidates, life on the campaign trail is stressful and wearing, so family time and downtime are the other two critical areas to prioritise.

Staying grounded and sane

Campaigning is emotionally and mentally gruelling and involves long hours away from the people you love. It can knock your confidence and wear you down. Meanwhile, just when you need the support and comfort of your family most, your schedule will dictate that you see much less of them, which in turn can put strain on even the best relationships.

Make it a priority to spend time every week with family and loyal friends. It will help maintain your confidence, reduce your stress levels, and offer you a safe haven when times get tough. Though time with family and friends will be severely curtailed, if you set aside the time every week, it will help maintain the strength of these critical relationships. With luck, family and friends will be understanding of your schedule and supportive during the time they see less of you.

All work and no play makes Jack a dull boy

Set aside time to do things you enjoy other than campaigning, or you risk burning out. Make it part of your weekly schedule to practice a hobby, go out for dinner, or just enjoy a good book. Your mind and your spirit need a break from the pressure and relentless pace of the campaign.

There have been numerous recent examples of serious political candidates that managed to maintain a Sabbath even during very high profile campaigns, so don't dismiss this as a possibility. After all, even God rested on the seventh day!

Scheduling and time management are the keys to success

Effective time management and proper campaign scheduling are at the heart of your ability to thrive as a candidate and manage the pressures on the campaign trail. Major political campaigns have a team of staff dedicated solely to scheduling. Aside from putting together a programme of strategic events and campaigning priorities, the staff and candidate block out time for everything from family gatherings and mini-breaks, to meals, work-outs, naps and even bedtimes.

You may not have the resources for a scheduling staff, but set aside at least one hour at the beginning of each week to sit down for a scheduling session with your campaign manager (or by yourself if you're running the whole show). The schedule must start with the basics of making time for the needs discussed, so start by blocking out work-out times, meals and slots for family and friends. Try to make these regular and sacred, refusing to allow other events and day-to-day urgent campaign issues to crowd these out.

There are times when you might have to be flexible to accommodate very critical or last minute events, or to deal with a (real) crisis, but otherwise resist the temptation to let other things encroach. Remind yourself that time for eating, sleeping, exercising, socialising and relaxation is crucial, and in many cases may be more important than that extra hour of glad-handing or additional events that could drive you to exhaustion.

Next, go through invitations and schedule important events. Before accepting any invitation, ask yourself whether it will further your campaign goals or serve a strategic purpose. Some events have fixed dates and times, while other campaign obligations, like meeting voters or important officials, have flexible timings. Consider putting similar activities in blocks together. For example, schedule an afternoon of meetings with voters, rather than scattering them throughout the week, so you don't have to switch gears or locations and waste precious time. Protect your time and be in control of it: just because the phone rings doesn't mean you need to take the call now; do things at times that are convenient for you and your schedule.

As you schedule your week, consider the length and pace of each day before committing to activities. Is it wise to spend eight hours campaigning on a day when you have to make a major keynote speech in the evening? Also, if you have more energy at certain times of the day, consider those times as good slots for taking on the tougher parts of the job, for example, media interviews that require you to be on top form.

While days will be inevitably busy, you will be anxious and exhausted if you pack too much into one day without time to reflect or prepare for events. Schedule 'appointments' for thinking, reading, briefing, and meetings with staff or volunteers so you can maintain effective management of your campaign. Meanwhile, fiercely protect your diary and strictly limit the number of people with the authority to schedule events for you.

Finally, delegate. You may be a person that likes to do everything yourself, but ultimately, to relieve stress and make your campaign efficient, delegate what you can to staff and volunteers. You will get more done and maximise your effectiveness if you build a competent organisation to support you.

Thriving in the fast lane

As a candidate, your first responsibility is to take care of yourself. Successful candidates take pro-active steps to minimise the impact of the inevitable pressures of campaigning, and the potential for burn-out, illness or breakdown.

Keep your priorities straight through careful planning and proper campaign management, and you will have the energy to run an impressive campaign and maximise your effectiveness on the trail.

PS. Don't forget to pack your hand sanitiser.

Melanie Batley is a journalist and former US campaign advisor

Part IV

Raising money

20

Personal solicitation

Shelley Tidmore

One of the hottest topics surrounding the McCain campaign was the large gap between its fundraising efforts versus Obama's results.

Economic strain heavily mounted during one of the most historic presidential campaigns America has seen, both nationally and abroad. Many donors of political campaigns large and small contracted gifts and hesitated to wage their bets. As a John McCain 2008 staff member I caught a glimpse of this crisis, and at some point we all experienced the shift. Everyone recalls the moment that McCain's campaign, due to lagging fundraising ability, all but sank and was miraculously rehabilitated. Campaigns are not immune to our economic global crisis. The smaller the campaign, the more you are affected. Your success depends on your ability to adapt to the economic crisis and nurture your donor's needs.

There is a direct correlation between your campaign plan and your fundraising agenda. Your budget, fundraising plan and donor pool should fit the size and shape of your individual campaign. Without a well-oiled fundraising plan and without a sustainable pool of financial contributors, your vision may go unrealised and at a costly rate of time, energy and debt from expensive campaign programmes.

You're about to learn the practical fundraising methods of political experts in today's turbulent times to increase the impact of your campaign, cultivate new donors and grow more cohesive donor relationships.

First let's cover some of the main fundraising strategies and where they lie on the scale of effectiveness. Various ways to fund raise include fundraising events, direct mail, video direct mail, social media, e-fundraising, telemarketing, better known as 'dialling for dollars', and personal solicitation. Let's quickly discuss why some work only part of the time, while personal solicitation works *all* of the time when approached with the finesse you'll learn in the rest of this chapter.

Fundraising events are acceptable when held with two purposes, first when done at cost or through in-kind donations of time, food, beverage and space to alleviate overheads. That is to say when you're able to organise an event without using the funds of the campaign to front the cost, you're able to net funds rather than spend your overhead. These events work only if you're not competing with other event activities and only if you've planned well enough in advance with enough publicity to gain the attention of free press, voters and donors alike. Secondly, your purpose in holding an event should be to gain momentum in the eye of the community for your candidate or cause. An event-heavy campaign is typically a failing campaign so you should ensure you only have one or two larger events held by the campaign, but if firms and associations would like to sponsor events entirely to help gain endorsement and support, by all means let them do so. This can only mean more campaign funds for you.

Direct mail and telemarketing are typically the most expensive forms of fundraising, as these strategies typically cost upwards of 70 pence for every pound that comes in as a result just to conduct. Telemarketing is fast being outgrown by other forms of technologically advanced fundraising methods, such as video direct mail and e-fundraising.

Video direct mail, also a costly venture, provides a snappy documentation of the vision of your candidate or cause. Since you want to evoke emotion within your target audience, video direct mail has been a major hit in the United States. It is both tangible and visible and gives a voice to typical mail. Your limitations include production cost and time spent developing the mailing programme for the video that the would-be donor will watch. You may even use video direct mail in your e-fundraising campaign, where donors can watch online by linking the video to your website, and even forward to other prospective donors.

Direct mail is an effective form of fundraising for targeted one-issue voters and our elder generation (65+), who use the internet, or email for that matter, much less frequently and are less likely to watch a video direct mail. This generation tends to vote more than any other but lags behind younger generations in the technology curve, thus postal mailed letters are far more appealing. These types of letters should first be mailed to a small universe of readers who have been targeted for specific issues pertinent to the candidate or cause. One such issue may be a couple who have lived in a particular neighbourhood their entire lives, or to a single mother of three in a neighbourhood which has seen an increase in crime. Stopping crime in the readers' district would be an obvious issue to highlight in this direct mail piece, followed by a request for a gift to help in the battle against crime in her neighbourhood. Likely because this issue speaks personally to these neighbours and evokes the emotion of hope for a neighbourhood safe once again, they may send a contribution. The more financially effective direct mail in a test 'universe' of recipients becomes, the more I recommend expanding your universe for further growth of your direct mail programme.

E-fundraising is much the same in that rather than utilising postal mail, you're targeting issues voters and sending similar mail to them via the internet about their issues of choice and guiding them to your website where they can then make an instant donation. This type of fundraising programme has the ability to become viral in that readers can forward direct mail to others, which may expand your prospecting. The downside is that e-fundraising is much less personal than other methods. Fundraising is much more effective when adding a personal touch, as in personal solicitation, which is what we're focusing on in this chapter.

Each of the fundraising tactics mentioned above are needed, although they are costly and much less individual than personal solicitation. Fortunately, personal solicitation costs nearly nothing, and because campaigns are emotional and personal, personal solicitation should be the flagship of your donor relations. Your candidate should devote up 65 per cent of his or her time to this, spending the rest of the time only focusing on connecting with voters.

Many candidates mistakenly use other fundraising methods in the place of personal solicitation out of fear of rejection, and cost the campaign greatly. In this chapter you will learn all you need to know to overcome these reservations and open the floodgates of confidence in fund raising through personally asking for financial gifts to your campaign.

You first need to understand your financial environment and how best to convey your message. Next, conduct precise donor research, collect as much information as possible on prospective givers using lists ranging from a candidate's personal holiday party to lists you've gathered from your church, business relationships and other parties within your coalition of support. Finally, carefully determine the most important role besides the candidate – the finance chair. And build a finance committee of sales proficient members from diverse successful industries across differing areas of the community in order to cast the widest net of fundraising possible.

As you solicit your donor for a potential gift, you'll note their most consistent concern focuses on whether the goals of the candidate once in office will match up with their goals – that usually being our economy. Others may rely on your efforts to press for change in social issues while others give for party loyalty. The greatest reason for giving is informational access and to feel a sense of ownership of the campaign. Personal solicitation focuses on your largest donors, most of whom you have already built strong relationships with. They tend already to be the power players, which will translate in your campaign through the intellectual equity they will take. They often have strong personalities with an appetite for access to information. Simply put, power players are an integral part of the funding of your campaign's plan. You will successfully grow your relationship with these individuals simply by staying in touch with them every couple of weeks by phone or personal visit. Provide them with information like polling, how their funds have been used so far and how they'll be used moving forward. Think of your contributors as venture capitalists investing in your success. Even better, affluent people know affluent people, and thus may refer you to others— if you ask. Once introduced, you begin the process all over again and cultivate new relationships through other fundraising means. Candidates and surrogates should focus primarily on large donors while fundraisers focus on building relationships with prospective donors who give small to medium donations. I remind fundraisers who have a tendency to ignore smaller donors that simply because a donor sends £50 after receiving mail on the issue that touches her most doesn't mean she is unable to send £5,000. These are undeveloped relationships and larger gifts may be obtained simply by nurturing this initial financial gesture and letting the donor learn more about the campaign.

Let's now determine who within a campaign conducts research, nurtures donors, and examine how we close the deal.

Realistically, most campaigns cannot hire Obama's finance chair, the Hyatt Regency heiress Penny Pritzker. You need a finance chair who can aggressively sell your campaign's plan to other affluent people, but also knows the candidate well and truly believes in him/ her. Ideally they're also a model top donor.

The candidate, finance chair and committee should scour collective lists of prospective donors and known donors from sources ranging from your personal Christmas list to borrowed lists from allies in coalition organisations (making sure to stay within the bounds of data protection laws). Donor list notes include the donor name and multiple telephone numbers, frequency of gifts, the most recent contribution, to whom it was made, the reason they gave, and simple details like profession, number of children and other interests. More sophisticated software such as Razors Edge provides the researcher an even more intimate view of prospects such as net worth and home equity to determine potential giving. In the States we have a website called OpenSecrets.org used to analyse gift-giving trends. Use of OpenSecrets.org is the gold standard in American politics.

The candidate is the best choice to solicit the donor, but in case the candidate isn't already acquainted, the finance committee person who knows the donor may make the first call introduce the candidate. It is always ideal to close the deal over the phone, but if a visit is required it's better to oblige than to end up empty handed.

Candidates typically dislike soliciting funds for various reasons such as fear of rejection, the (otherwise) social taboo of asking, the sense of begging, or because they feel asking could damage the relationship. Contrary to belief, the primary reason to ask is that you're offering a chance to invest in the future and without meeting your budgetary needs, you simply can't win. Regular donors already understand this and already anticipate the opportunity to invest in the future of politics. Once you begin to understand this, you'll experience greater returns on your fundraising efforts. Ultimately you must close the deal. It is helpful practice to prioritise a call list from easiest solicitations to hardest to gain practice prior to the more challenging calls.

There are three steps in closing the deal. First, talk about the donor's interests first, whether their passion is sports, their profession or their children. This builds a rapport and lets them know you care about their lives. They're likely crunched for time so take care that you aren't spending excess time discussing personal details. Once it feels natural to transition, mention your campaign and your purpose for calling. Their donor notes should cue their interest in your campaign so you'll know how best to appeal to that interest. Finally, request a specific amount and ask high. You should never ask less than their highest gift. You won't insult the donor by asking more than they can give – they'll feel complimented you assumed they could give more. You could, however, insult them if you ask for less than they could give. You may not get the amount you request, but you'll have started with room to negotiate and have less chance of ending up empty handed. Throughout your conversation, remember positive energy feeds positive energy and the opposite is true. If the conversation turns negative, always spin the conversation to positivity and never broach negative topics. Always place the donor's interests first. If they're unwilling to write a cheque, keep the door open by asking to call again and ask to send further information that may relieve any reservations about giving. Offer a payment schedule. Just don't leave empty handed.

The global impact of our economy is likely the main reason people fail to give more. In Britain individuals give between £1,000 and £5,000. To increase your impact in fundraising, first and foremost tell your donors that you need them to shepherd your flock. Explain that other donors are giving more even though their resources have been cut nearly in half due to recession, and how others have given despite not having many resources. Explain that you need those who can to shepherd a weaker flock to be able to see victory on election day. This approach today has proven successful above other approaches and above all else, I recommend conveying this particular reason to give when speaking to your donors.

Now that you've learned the psychology of giving in today's times and how to overcome reservations, I want to share my method of practising what you preach before going 'live'. I've taught these same methods to over a thousand students and worked with countless clients. Where time allowed, I provided an opportunity for my students and clientele to role play the methods they learned. In my experience with clients, I would ask them to call a friend the night before beginning their donor calls and have the friend pretend to be a hard-nosed nay-saying donor, with reservations, who only gives to the best candidate. I'd ask them to go over several phone calls and practise their conversation a few times before trying out a real one. This was the 'ice breaker' for most of them, which helped personal solicitation become an empowering experience rather than a nervous experience. To begin with I provide a list of calls that started with easiest 'yes' to the most difficult. Once the more difficult calls began, the candidate had already fallen into a comfortable gate, rather than stumbling around trying to turn a 'No' into a 'Yes'. The old adage 'Practice makes perfect' is true in most cases so practise as much as possible with a friend or colleague first.

Finally, it is best to make a list of ten most likely asked questions and have them pre-answered to avoid not sounding well informed. These questions include 'What are your plans after you win?', 'How many calls are you making?', 'Who has endorsed you?', 'What is your strategy to win?', 'How much money have you raised so far?' and 'How many votes do you need to win?'. Donors like to ask questions about your strategy, and you don't want to be caught sounding ill informed. My most important piece of advice is to prepare. Have your spreadsheet open for note taking and your campaign website open for navigation during calls. Once you feel comfortable, nothing can stop you from achieving the results you need for success!

Shelley Tidmore is the founder of the Tidmore Group

21

Direct mail fundraising

Shane Greer

If you're a political candidate, when it comes to raising money you'll find yourself punching far below your weight if you don't take advantage of direct mail (literally sending letters to people in which you ask for a donation). Yes it's old school, and yes it has a much higher cost attached to it that the other fundraising methods discussed in this book; but the simple truth is this, if you miss out direct mail you'll be missing out on a powerful income stream. What's more, you'll be missing out on a tremendous opportunity to identify some donors who are capable of giving, and who will give, significant sums to your campaign. OK, so direct mail fundraising is important, but how does it work?

Unsurprisingly, the first challenge in any such fundraising effort is determining who you will send your fundraising letters to. My response to this question has always been 'What kind of people do you think might give you money?' Do you have a pre-existing list of supporters (whether financial or otherwise)? Do you have a list of people who subscribe to a monthly/quarterly newsletter? Are you a member of a club whose members are likely to support you in a personal capacity regardless of politics? I could go on, but suffice to say when you begin your search for potential direct mail donors you should start by identifying lists already in your possession. To do this you should sit down with some of your closest supporters and brainstorm options (don't forget, some of the people who are already throwing their weight behind you might have some lists of their own which you might be able to use). Outside that, consideration should be given to lists available from list rental companies. Again, you need to identify groups of people who you think will be sympathetic to your cause. Perhaps you're standing in a rural area and country sports are a significant issue. If so, can you rent a list of subscribers to a country pursuits magazine? Or maybe a local hospital faces closure and you're leading the campaign to stop that from happening. In that case, can you acquire a list of medical practitioners in the area? Get creative: really spend some time identifying the kind of individuals who are likely to want to support you and then find somebody who can rent a list to you. Whatever lists you decide to use, though, make sure you comply with data protection laws.

At its heart your direct mail operation will have two elements: prospecting and house file. Prospecting involves sending letters to individuals who have never given to you before in an attempt to find new donors. Every person contacted during a prospecting effort who gives money is then moved onto your house file (the list of people who have given to you on one or more occasions). The members of your house file are then contacted regularly (about once a month) and asked for further donations. Your prospect mailings will almost always lose money. You make money by growing your house file and maximising the number and level of donations from these individuals. One thing to bear in mind, though: just because somebody doesn't give you a donation when you first prospect them doesn't mean they won't give you a donation if you prospect them a second, third or perhaps even fourth time. On occasion I've even managed to secure a donation from somebody I've previously prospected by sending them exactly the same letter as before! And you should never put all your eggs in one basket. If you're prospecting a list of, let's say, 15,000 individuals you shouldn't mail them all in one go. You need to test the list, perhaps taking three samples of 1,000 individuals and sending them each a different letter. For all you know the list might be a complete dud. Just because you think it's a solid list and are convinced they'll start throwing money at you doesn't mean it is and that they will. Proceed with caution. If one of your test letters outperforms the others then clearly you should roll that letter out to all 15,000, but if none of your letters work it's probably the case that the list just isn't going to work for you (or that you write really bad copy!).

Having identified the individuals you're going to send your fundraising letter to, it's time to start writing. Above all else, a direct mail fundraising letter should be crafted to read like a personal communication from the person signing the letter to the person receiving it. If it comes across as a piece of 'one to many' correspondence it won't work. Needless to say, when you're writing to thousands of people this isn't an easy thing to do. The starting point with this is to ensure, where possible, that letters start with the donor's first name. Dear James comes across a lot better than Dear Friend or even, in many cases, Dear Mr Smith. A word of caution, though: if you're writing to individuals who expect their title to be used, a retired army officer for example, your letter should start with their title. And if you're writing to older individuals it's usually best to defer to their age by starting the letter with title and surname rather than just forename. How will you know what to do? As the paragraph above outlines, you need to run tests. In any event, the salutation alone does not a personal letter make. Think about the words you use. When I was first introduced to direct mail in the States (at an organisation that raised over $80 million through its direct mail programme) I was instructed on pain of death never to use 'we' in a letter, as it's far too general. Instead, the magic phrase was 'you and I', much more specific; you the reader, and me, the person writing to you. It sounds silly, but it really does make a difference. Using the individual's name within the letter also helps to personalise it (but be careful not to overuse this technique as it can come across as very slimy). Then there's the signature. Where possible, the letters should be signed in blue ink. It's astonishing the difference this makes. And when they can't be hand signed (or machine signed – yes, you can get machines that sign letters using your signature), the signature should be laser printed with blue ink.

The number and ways of personalising a letter is vast, and the value of employing them, is incredible.

One additional thing to consider with the signature on the letter is whose signature it should be. You might think that because you're the candidate that it should always be your signature. But not so. Sometimes it helps to have the letter signed by an individual who resonates with the those being mailed. Using the country sports example above, perhaps there's a well-respected member of the country pursuits world who carries more weight with the individuals you're writing to than you could ever hope to achieve. If so, and provided they're willing, then that person should sign the letter. It shouldn't be a letter from you at all, it should be a letter from them asking for their peers (or perhaps even fans) to support you. Similarly, let's say the current MP is standing down, you're now their party's prospective parliamentary candidate, and you want to send out a direct mail letter to some of the current MP's past supporters. You could sign the letter yourself, but wouldn't it be better if the current MP signed it?

Your letter can't just say 'I'd like you to give me money for um. . . something'. You need to be specific. Mailings often fail because the 'ask' is too general. People are much more likely to give if they can see how their donation of £10, £50 or £100 will make a tangible difference. For candidates, for example, this could mean asking for donations to cover the cost of new office equipment or a leaflet to local residents rather than for their campaign in general. And don't forget to actually ask for a donation. Perhaps it's the British thing about being embarrassed to talk about money, but it's astonishing how often mailings ask for some vague form of support rather than a very specific monetary donation. As the saying goes, if you don't ask you don't get.

The most important part of your fundraising letter is the opening sentence, followed by the PS (all letters should have a PS). They both need to tell the donor why you are writing to them and what specifically you want them to do. They are essentially hard-hitting summaries compressing the totality of your full letter into a few words. I've literally spent hours in the past writing and rewriting the opening sentence of a direct mail letter and then yet more hours writing and rewriting the PS. But time spent doing this is time well invested. When you get it right your mailing can soar; when you get it wrong it can tank.

Your letter should, structurally, be easy on the eye. This means short sentences and short paragraphs. I remember when I was first introduced to direct mail in the States, and the person who made the introduction told me that sentence and paragraph length should be like skirts (imagine the confused look on my face at the time): 'long enough to cover the essentials and short enough to keep it interesting'. You should also have a few paragraphs which comprise only a single very short and powerful sentence.

The isolation of these paragraphs really adds to their power.

Crucially, you should also have a single line of space between each paragraph. And never finish a page with a full stop, as it really jars the reader. To make sure this doesn't happen you should force sentences to break into two pieces so that the first piece is on the end of one page and the second piece is at the start of the second page.

Then there's the font. Don't just go with Office's default setting. For example, in the States when we wrote to older donors we used the Courier font (reminiscent of the typewriters from their youth) and when I tested it over here it worked fantastically. Should you use Courier for younger recipients? Probably not, it would just look weird. For them Calibri or Arial might work best. Again, you won't know until you test. Another great trick is underlining important phrases in the letter, placing emphasis on the most emotive portions of the text. You shouldn't overuse underlining, but used well it can transform a letter into an incredibly effective call to arms.

You shouldn't just send out a letter. You also need to send a donation form. This is where the donor writes their personal details and indicates how much they are giving you. It also instructs them on how to make out their cheque and allows them to pay by credit card (or if you have the facility, direct debit). But whatever you do, don't for a second think that the donation form is nothing more than a technical necessity. It's much more than that. It's another opportunity to reiterate why you *need* their donation. And you should grab this opportunity with both hands, tell the reader why you need their money, why you are deserving of their support, and what a difference their donation will make! Crucially, on the portion of the form that lists donation options (i.e. £100, £50, £10 etc.) you should start with the highest figure first. Donors are much more likely to give a higher sum than they might otherwise be inclined to do if you arrange the figures in this way. Along with the donation form you should also send a Freepost reply-paid envelope. The easier you make it for people to donate the more donations you will receive. Simple.

The envelope. Yes, that's important too. People get bombarded with mailings these days. Whether it's bank statements or junk mail, our doormats are awash with letters vying for our attention. And unsurprisingly, they aren't all successful. When sending out a direct mail letter you need to give it the best chance of being seen. In other words, you need to do everything you can to make sure the recipient opens the envelope. Cost is always an issue, but to the best extent possible you should try to make your letter look like a personal communication. So, like the signature, you should, where possible, handwrite the address (or rather some campaign interns should do the writing!). If you can't handwrite the addresses, use a machine. If neither of those options are possible then you'll simply have to print the address on the envelope (and that means not using a windowed envelope!). Also, if you can, use real stamps. Once again, though, make sure you keep testing different things. Perhaps you'll find a completely new technique that works brilliantly every time!

You should take the time to build up as much information about each donor as possible. Once someone is on your house file, you should work hard to find out the issues that matter most to them. That way you can segment your house file by issues when you next mail them. Those interested in the environment would receive one version of the letter while those motivated by fox hunting would receive another. This allows you to include issue-specific paragraphs and sentences into your letters without alienating anyone. And as suggested above, the more personal you can make a letter the better your returns will be. Think of it this way: you're much more likely to get the money you need if you ask a friend for a fiver than you are if you ask a complete stranger on the street. The difference? A strong personal relationship.

With your house file you should also constantly strive to increase the amount being given by each donor. One way to do this is to create different versions of the same donation form discussed above. If a donor has previously given £500 then that donor should never receive a form that has £500 as the highest donation option. Equally, someone who has given £5 is probably not in a position to drop £500, so the highest option on their form should be much more modest (perhaps £20). By tailoring the donation forms in this way you'll find that many donors will give a little bit more than they might have otherwise. And don't forget to leave a space on the form where the reader can fill in a different amount that they would like to give. You'll be surprised what this can bring in. I once got a donation of £5,000 from one guy as part of a prospect mailing (needless to say that was a very good day!).

Finally, it should go without saying, but donors should be thanked and they should be kept up to date. If someone gives you £20 it costs very little to send back a very short thank you note. Aside from anything else they deserve to be thanked. But also, by thanking them you help to cultivate your relationship. Equally, you shouldn't forget that donors are essentially investors, and to keep them happy and to retain their support you need to demonstrate that their money is being used wisely. A regular newsletter is a great way to do this.

Shane Greer is the executive editor of Total Politics

22

Fundraising events

Chris Younce

Many times when one thinks of a political fundraising event, two images come to mind. The first is the large, expensive gala featuring the President or other national political figure with guests who have paid tens of thousands of dollars to attend. The second is a poorly attended fundraiser for a local politician with a few people standing around a cheap buffet. Neither of these events is necessary. A campaign can have a successful fundraising event that raises plenty of pounds without being cost prohibitive or unbearably cheap and boring.

Before we begin discussing the types of events and how to put them on, some time needs to be spent talking about why events are necessary and also, what they will not accomplish.

First, the bad news. Events can cost a lot. From room rentals to food, decorations etc., events can be an expensive way to raise money. Besides the monetary investment, events can take a lot of staff or volunteer time, which can and should be dedicated to other campaign duties.

Next, events are used, usually by losing candidates, as an excuse not to personally solicit donations. Candidates who are not willing to personally ask for donations should not run. Truth be told, if a campaign does an event the correct way, the candidate will still have to solicit personal donations (for more on this, see Chapter 20, Personal Solicitation).

It may sound like events are never worth doing; that assumption is incorrect. Every donor to a campaign is different and some will only give if they can attend an event. They like the access to the candidate or they like being seen by others.

Some events, especially small events, are good ways to bring new donors into your campaign organisation. These new donors can then be asked for additional assistance later on in the campaign.

Finally, fundraising events can demonstrate to the press that the campaign has momentum. The media loves to report on these 'horse race' stories and less on the issues of the campaign. Events with big names can prove to the media that your campaign is for real. These 'big names' do not need to be as big as the Prime Minister. A local celebrity can serve very well as a draw to your event.

Now that we have touched on what events are good for and what they are not for, let us talk about the types of event. The first type is the small, more personal events.

These events are generally hosted at someone's home or property. The host also is usually responsible for most of the planning of the event. This makes them much easier on the campaign staff.

The host will use their personal Rolodex as the start of the invitation list. They should be people whose beliefs are politically similar to the candidate and the host. The host should also feel comfortable asking them for money. The campaign will also supplement the host's Rolodex with people in the area that should be invited.

There are many different themes you can use for a small event. A favourite has always been a barbecue (if the weather's good!) or a coffee morning. These can also keep food costs down. Hamburgers and hot dogs or coffee and biscuits are the norm. These events are usually very casual and allow the candidate to spend a little time with everyone in attendance.

I have always enjoyed having a birthday party for my candidate if their birthday is during the campaign cycle. During one campaign, the candidate was turning forty-seven years old. We asked for a donation of $47 to attend his party. It was a great success.

If you live in an area that has a large following for a particular sports team, a watch party can be a good event for a small fundraiser. During a break in play, the candidate can take a few minutes to thank everyone for their help.

Other types of activities for small fundraising events include a luau, a wine tasting, a Scotch tasting, or even a morning with the candidate hunting waterfowl (although the latter is best restricted to rural constituencies!). Be creative. There is no limit to what you can do.

The second type of event is the large event. These are the events that are more likely to get noticed by the press. They are big and expensive and will involve more people in the planning.

Large events require more preparation. In many cases, one person on the campaign will spend most of their time organising these large events. However, almost everyone on the campaign staff will be involved with the event in some way.

As with small events, you have to decide what type of event you would like to have. The most popular is the large dinner. This involves renting a banquet hall and serving a multi-course dinner to the attendees. During the dinner, the candidate and any special guests will speak.

You are not limited to holding dinners, though. In fact, many of these events are quite boring. A casino night could be fun (using fake money, of course). I have been to some golf tournaments that were incredibly successful. If your candidate has a good sense of humour, have a roast. As with small events, be creative.

One thing you should remember when planning a large event: you are going to raise a lot of your money from the base donation amount. Most of your money is going to come from the host committee and those that donate more to get something extra from the event. We will talk about each of these.

The host committee is a vital component of large fundraising events. These people will be your largest supporters. The candidate will have to personally ask each person to join the host committee and donate to the campaign. To learn how to do that, refer again to Chapter 20.

After someone agrees to become a member of the host committee, get a list of potential donors from that person. Supplement these lists with the list of your current donors plus any prospects you have from other lists.

In addition to your host committee, you can encourage your invitees to give a larger amount for something extra at the event. A popular extra is a photograph with the candidate and the special guest. Or have a VIP reception where only those that gave at the higher level are invited.

A huge mistake people make is to reserve a room that is too big. Which headline would you rather have in the paper: 'Weak crowd attends candidate fundraiser' or 'Candidate rakes in thousands in front of standing-room-only crowd'? A crowd of 150 always looks better in a room that holds 100 than it does in a room that holds 200. Ideally, reserve a room that has dividing walls so they can be opened or closed based on your attendance.

If your event is outside, the same effect can be achieved by enclosing off your space with ribbons, banners or a tent. This helps to create the same effect as being inside, making your event look full.

Now that you have an idea of the different types of event you can hold, let's talk about some things you need to remember for any type of event you hold.

Costs can easily get out of hand with any event you hold. Since most events will not raise large amounts of money, you can blow any profits by overspending. Create a realistic budget and stick to it.

Invitations may seem like a small thing, but for most people, it is the first time they heard about your fundraising event. Make them colourful and exciting. If your event has a specific theme, make the invitation correspond to the event's theme.

Use different-coloured paper and an envelope other than a standard white or brown C5 (spice it up!). If possible, handwrite the addresses on the envelopes. Always use proper stamps on the envelopes. All of these small details increase the probability your invitation will be opened, which increases the chances your targets will attend the event.

People are busier now than ever before. Many plan their schedule weeks, if not months, in advance. This means you must send out your invitations with enough time for people to plan. A good rule of thumb is to send out invitations about four weeks before the event.

In each of the invitations, make sure to include a reply device. The reply device should have the option to donate for each tier you have and a place to donate without attending.

Name tags are essential for any event. People love to hear their name spoken. Studies have shown that a person's heartbeat changes slightly when they hear their name.

Every name tag should have the attendee's first and last name easily readable. When they meet someone, that person will be able to greet them by name. It also allows the candidate and any special guests to greet and thank the donors by name. People will think the candidate remembers their name when in fact, they just forgot they were wearing a name tag.

Another thing you should place on name tags is something to designate what donor tier the person gave in. It could be as simple as different-coloured borders or stars on the name tag (examples include a gold star for host committee members, a silver star for middle tier donors, and blank for general attendees). This allows the candidate and campaign staff to easily tell what that person gave and thank the donor for their generous gift. Also, because people are competitive, they will ask why some have different name tags and how they can get one too.

People in general will not do anything unless pushed. Sending an invitation to an event is a great first step. It must, however, be followed up with phone calls. Phone calls should begin about two weeks before the event.

Event hosts and host committee members should make follow up calls for the people that came from their lists. Campaign workers can make follow up calls for current donors or other prospects.

Follow-up calls should continue until you get a definite answer from every person on your invitation list. Some people may need several calls because you need to leave messages, they do not have their diary with them, or they just do not want to commit yet.

Because many of the people will have RSVP'd by telephone,

you will need to collect cheques at the door. This is easily done by getting a couple of campaign workers to staff a check-in table. As every donor walks into the event, they should be greeted and, if they have not paid, politely asked if they can write a cheque.

Sometimes they will not be able to pay at the time they check-in. Whether by accident or deception (yes, some people will try and get into events without ever paying), they do not have a cheque or cash to pay at the event. Don't make a scene about it. Give them their name tag and allow them in. Make a note that they did not pay and let them know you will follow up with them after the event.

The day after the event, send a short reminder to those that did not pay. Say that you hope they enjoyed the event and remind them of their pledge. Include an envelope and a reply device. After a week, if they have not sent in a cheque, follow up with a phone call. Continue to call until the person sends in a cheque.

Do not make the mistake that just because the event is over, your work is done. It is not. One of the most important things after the event is the thank you note. You have many people to thank.

The first people to thank are your donors. Thank them for attending your event and for supporting your campaign. For those that were not part of the host committee, a simple form letter thanking them is sufficient. Thank you notes should also be sent to those people that paid and did not attend and those that just sent in a contribution. For the host and host committee, a personal letter from the candidate is needed. Finally, if your event had a special guest, do not forget to thank them.

Fundraising events can be stressful. You are trying to juggle many things at the same time. You are worrying about all of the other campaign activities you need to get done. But if you plan appropriately, your fundraising events can be successful, less stressful, and put more pounds in your campaign war chest.

Chris Younce is the founder and president of Grassroots Strategies LLC

23

Online fundraising

Jag Singh

Candidates in elections know the problem all too well: you need money to grease the campaign machine, but you also need the building blocks in place before you can dream of approaching complete strangers – usually masquerading around the web behind silly usernames – for money. The phrase 'online fundraising' often conjures up images from US presidential elections, with Barack Obama's campaign riding on millions of donations totalling nearly half a billion dollars. In reality, the online fundraiser's role revolves as much around pinching money from well-off contributors as it does with invigorating the grassroots – the bottom line is a direct function of people's emotional attraction to a specific cause, or a candidate who champions that specific cause. While it is true that online fundraising cannot exist in a vacuum by itself, the rewards can be extraordinary, bearing in mind the relatively low overhead cost of soliciting online donations and the immediate availability of funds when compared to the offline options.

Throughout this chapter on harnessing Web-based technology to assemble and sustain productive donor relationships, you'll notice four recurring themes that are often heard as maxims to live by on the campaign trail:

1. Follow the money.
2. You have to spend money to make money.

3. The KISS principle: keep it short and simple for the donor.
4. The FUD factors: fear, uncertainty and doubt are great motivators.

The fundamentals

Prior to embarking on this magical journey, campaigners must recognise that it is absolutely imperative to have a compelling story and narrative that attracts people to your cause. Online fundraising isn't just about placing a little 'Click here to donate now' button on the side of a campaign website that links to a static PayPal form (PayPal is an online payment gateway that enables anyone to accept credit card payments via their website). Like offline fundraising, where a campaign must commit to offering a range of messages and donation choices, the online flavour also requires making the Web a focal point of engagement with potential voters: in other words, you have to lay the groundwork before trying to convince voters to donate to your campaign. At the very least, you'll need a website, an email marketing solution, and a method to accept donations online, but most importantly you'll want to give people a reason to actually donate to your cause.

It is vital for all communication with donors and potential donors to take place across both online *and* offline channels – you want to reach out to them on their terms – while simultaneously maintaining an integrated approach for fundraising, which means you need to continuously synchronise media and co-ordinate consistent messaging across all platforms. To extend your brand and reach constituents where they reside, you'll need a campaign presence, and the first online step involves having an intuitively navigable and useable website.

You then need to consider broadcasting and pushing your message out, and email is the medium considered to be the cheapest and most suitable (and as case studies indicate, it is the most successful) for fostering a personal relationship for soliciting online donations. This means you'll also want an email marketing solution that affords you the ability to segment and target emails to your list on behavioural and contextual levels, i.e, you'll want to send people living in one part of the constituency a different email to the one sent to users in another area, and you'll also want to send a different email to people who haven't previously donated to your campaign. The campaign website should also be optimised to coerce visitors into subscribing to your email list. You'll want to constantly monitor exactly who opened the email, what they clicked, and who didn't open your messages – and this is all possible with most email marketing solutions. Donation forms must always be one click away, and always reassure donors about the security of the form.

This leads us to the last point – the need for people (and by extension, a voice) in the campaign. You'll need to develop a real strategy, preferably with a professional fundraiser, but asking people to pull out their wallets will require authentic voices making the case for your campaign or cause.

Fundraisers in the UK all agree that people don't particularly enjoy giving money to lost causes. You need to credibly prove that others can visualise the candidate or cause as a 'champion' or winner, but don't forget, you'll want to share your success stories with the world. Achieving a target shows people your campaign has legs, and that you're capable of attracting other people to donate to your cause. And nothing does that better than a statement in a broadsheet along the lines of 'fuelled by the power of the grassroots'.

How you actually do it

Fundraising is essentially about building relationships, and it's important to note that all relationships, be they online or offline, are built on trust. Your goal here is to reach out to as many people as possible on an emotional level – making them feel special, and subsequently 'investing' in your candidacy or cause. Too many candidates focus on just being relevant, and instead don't consider adding value to the conversation or proposition. It all boils down to this: campaign donations are a form of political consumption and involvement. As a part of the Web-enabled generation of candidates, trying to convince a generation of Web-enabled voters to vote for you, you will need to tweak your strategies to enhance your relationships with constituents, and provide value while offering transparency as to how and where campaign funds are being directed. What charities have found when operating in this space is that people are more inclined to give to very specific causes – say, buying a goat named Billy for a child named Joe in a particular sub-Saharan country. The political equivalent involves sharing with a potential donor the number of volunteers a donation of £10 or £50 would feed during a canvassing run.

Political fundraisers often reflect on the 'four Cs' when soliciting online donations – customisation, content, cultivation and conversion. Here's how it works: you'll want to customise and tailor different content (or 'asks') to specific users by cultivating your relationship over an extended period of time, and improving the effectiveness of the process by tracking your conversion rates. Conversions are defined in percentage terms as the rate of people who perform an action you've specifically defined, out of all the people who have been exposed to the messaging. If you send an email or buy an advert that is seen by 100 people, and if one person out of that pool eventually donates, you'll have had a 1 per cent conversion rate. Industry conversion averages range from 0.05 per cent to 0.1 per cent, but finely tweaked and optimised campaigns can often yield rates of up to 10 per cent. You'll need a database to keep track of all this, and thankfully a Google search will easily allow you to explore the available options and suppliers. The ability to continuously test and tweak your campaign means all the difference between a 0.1 per cent conversion rate and a 10 per cent conversion rate.

This leads us to what I term the 'relationship pyramid' principle of breaking groups of people into smaller segments. The Obama campaign called it the 'relationship ladder' while the McCain campaign referred to it as the 'relationship pathway'. To compel people who haven't donated to your cause, you'll want to gradually increase the involvement of the potential donor up to the actual point of donation, and then augment that relationship further by offering something back that involves them even more with your campaign. It's worth considering that online fundraising appeals can and often do bring in additional volunteers into the campaign's fold, and that the act of volunteering should be considered a donation.

It is unrealistic to expect a message to go 'viral' on its own, and when it comes to broadcasting and pushing your messages out, campaigns need to spend money on their marketing efforts. Given a campaign's budgetary considerations the trick to success involves knowing exactly how much you're spending and also understanding the rate of return, while constantly tweaking your messaging to ensure the strongest return. If you spend £1 and make £2, as with any other strategic investment, you'll want to keep on spending and reinvesting as much as possible. It is advisable that someone monitor this closely, as the return rates can turn negative very rapidly and you'll want to use your targeting and segmentation tricks to channel resources into any medium that yields the highest rate of return – be it via email blasts or advertising media buys in local newspapers and high-traffic blogs. Monitor your success rates, and tailor your activities to follow the money. If you've bought an online ad, be sure to track where donors are coming from, and shift your resources to sites and platforms that convert well. If you notice a sudden surge in traffic from your Facebook profile to a landing page about a specific issue you'll want to try experimenting with more content relating to that issue. If emails you've sent relating to specific causes are converting well, it should be obvious by now that your speech at an offline fundraising event should focus a little more on that topic. Timing is everything, and you'll want to always be quick to roll out your campaign to other platforms.

The KISS principle relates to something we do in life every day – keeping it short and simple. When soliciting donations online, you'll want to bend over backwards to make it as easy as possible for donors to donate, primarily by employing a visual call to action that's always prominent – be it on a website or within an ad or even within an email – but simple to understand. A call to action is essentially a link that entices a user to perform a specific task.

In this atomic age your potential supporters are busy consuming information from – and you're busy competing with – a thousand other sources, which means you'll want to regularly bring up the call to action early in the conversation. Composing an email that reads like it has been written only for the eyes of the recipient takes some practice. It usually requires keeping the message short and engaging, with a call to action (a link, or maybe even a picture) that compels the recipient to donate or get involved with the campaign, and it's important to vary the options. When soliciting donations, the call to action should redirect immediately to a page that provides a tiny bit of information and asks for credit card details, and you must not burden the user with filling a form that takes hours to complete. It's important to note that contextual targeting tends to increase conversion rates. If the email approached the topic of your opponent's failure to rectify a problem within the constituency then the landing page should also only mention that specific issue, and the donation form should also be visually relevant. The concept of continuity is an important one, as you'll want to track the donor as having an interest in the issue, and continue the conversation around this (particularly relevant) issue. The relationship pyramid comes into play here, as the donor is likely to know other people with an interest in that issue that first compelled them to donate, which suddenly gives you an opportunity to increase your yield from that one initial conversion.

If users aren't donating, you'll want to broaden your base and make fundraising appeals more tangible and compelling. The best thing about working with the Web is that you're able to track exactly how many people are coming to your site, how often they are coming, where they're coming from (both in terms of geographical location and the website that referred them to your site), and how long they stay on specific pages of your site. Use that information and experiment with different types of appeal – make your campaign stand out and compel an immediate response.

Fear, uncertainty and doubt are among the most successful motivating factors for fundraising in politics, and they all rely on one element – emotion. For example, the capacity to craft a sense of exigency lends itself to the nature of the online environment, where information flows at the speed of light, and artificial deadlines can play a major role in establishing a reason to give. Over the next few years, we will see a shift toward peer-to-peer fundraising, where individual voters are empowered to solicit donations from those who trust them and direct funds to the specific candidates and causes they champion, instead of broad-based political parties and organisations. This will require candidates to reach out beyond their existing constituencies, perhaps even creating an arbitrary pool of people to draw funding from. The act of giving to a political candidate or cause requires an amount of emotional attachment or investment, and your focus as a candidate should be to do everything you can to augment that emotional attraction, regardless of where those people are located. We often hear that money isn't everything. But when it comes to campaigning, it is all about the money. Think about this: what if you had five times as much money as you had now to run the campaign? What could you accomplish?

Jag Singh is the founder of MessageSpace and a former advisor to the Democratic presidential campaigns in 2004 and 2008

Part V

Life in the spotlight:
dealing with the media

24

Navigating the media

Paul Richards

The interrelationship between politics and the media comprises a complicated series of symbiotic connections between individual politicians and journalists, and between political parties and news organisations, based on mutual distrust.

In a speech at Reuters in June 2007, just days before leaving office, Tony Blair said: 'Not to have a proper press operation nowadays is like asking a batsman to face bodyline bowling without pads or headgear,' before describing aspects of the media as behaving like a 'feral beast'.

To succeed in modern politics, you have to understand the structure and culture of the media, and what floats journalists' boats. That includes the pressures they're under from editors, the constant demand for news, the need for exclusives, splashes and scoops, the tyranny of deadlines, and the rivalry between hacks. In the current climate, some sympathy for the precariousness of their employment status might also be appreciated.

The journalist you're most likely to encounter is the reporter (either a local reporter, or one of the lobby correspondents based at Westminster). They will be questioning, sceptical and focused on getting the story. They seem brusque, or even rude. They are always on a deadline; they need information and quotes fast. A journalist is less likely to take care with your side of the story if they have no relationship with you, and if they think they will have no relationship with you in the future. That's why politicians invest time in their relationships with journalists, helping them out when they can, sharing secrets and gossip, and answering their calls.

You might be contacted by a researcher or producer from radio or TV. In a TV studio, you'll meet an 'anchor' or perhaps a famous interviewer like Andrew Neil, Jeremy Paxman or Kirsty Wark (as well as floor producers, assistant producers, technicians and the make-up artist). You might also come across the big name commentators (who comprise 'the commentariat'): people such as Polly Toynbee, Steve Richards, Simon Jenkins, David Aaronovitch, Peter Riddell, Rachel Sylvester or Kevin Maguire. These journalists write a regular column for a newspaper with trenchant opinions on the story of the moment.

Politicians have to deal with the media for a very simple reason: the media is powerful and influential and can make or break a politician's reputation. The way we interpret politics and politicians is significantly influenced by what we read, see and hear in the media. Voters are guided by their own value systems, personal experiences and conversations with others, but the media remains a colossal influence on voting behaviour.

As John Lloyd writes in *What the Media Are Doing to Our Politics*:

> Nothing – not religious belief, not political debate and argument, not even conversation with friends and family – possesses the command over mass attention that the media have taken as their own. Their themes dominate public and private lives. Their definitions of what is right and wrong, true or false, impose themselves on politics and on the public domain. Their narratives construct the world we don't immediately experience – which, for most of us, is most of the world.

Broadly, you can predict what kind of media different social groups are consuming, which means you can reach certain types of voter via specific types of media. Just as companies buying advertising space to sell products and services know in scientific detail what their target consumers are watching, listening, reading and logging on to, so political parties are always trying to reach key sections of the electorate. A newspaper, commercial TV or radio will have an in-depth understanding of their consumers: their incomes, social values, spending habits and personal likes and dislikes. It's not for nothing that Iceland (the shop, not the country) advertises during peak viewing times on ITV1, whereas the aristocratic restaurant Wilton's in the upmarket St James's area of London places a single advert every week in the *Spectator* magazine. Each knows its audience.

This explains politicians' enthusiasm for appearing on GMTV, *Loose Women* or Mumsnet as a way of reaching important segments of the electorate, mostly women, who don't listen to *Today* and have never heard of Polly Toynbee.

The main thing that you need to know about the British media is that it is becoming more diffuse and specialised, with the audiences fragmenting and disaggregating. In the mid-1990s ten million people watched the evening news bulletins on BBC or ITV; now it is half that. Fifteen years ago more than 200 television programmes had audiences over fifteen million. At the close of 2009 even *Strictly Come Dancing* could only manage 9.7 million (although *The X Factor* was watched by over fourteen million).

Newspaper circulations have declined from their 1950s heyday, when over sixteen million people read the *News of the World*, the *Sunday People* or the *Sunday Mirror*, and over seven million read Sunday papers that don't even exist any more: the *Sunday Dispatch*, the *Sunday Graphic* or the *Empire News*.

The big news is of course the rise of the internet as the place for politics to be conducted: news, debates, gossip, fundraising and 'citizen journalism'. It is almost impossible to believe that as recently as the mid-1990s the internet was irrelevant to politicians and political parties. Today Twitter, Facebook, YouTube and the myriad of political blogs are as important to politicians as, if not more than, the mainstream media.

Here is the basic shape and structure of the British media.

National newspapers

We can divide national newspapers into broadsheets, middle-markets and tabloids. They are listed below, with their circulations in 2009 according to the Audit Bureau of Circulations (ABC) in brackets. It is worth noting that more people read the *Star* than the *Guardian* and *Independent* combined, and more people read the *Sun* every day than all of the broadsheets put together. On a Sunday morning, over five million people are reading the *Mail on Sunday* or the *News of the World*, but fewer than 200,000 are reading the *Independent on Sunday*. In Scotland the national newspapers produce Scottish editions, and there are established Scottish titles such as the *Scotsman*. Wales and Northern Ireland have their own respected and well-established newspaper titles.

Broadsheets (sometimes snobbishly referred to as the 'qualities')
> *Daily Telegraph* (783,210)
> *Times* (617,483)
> *Financial Times* (426,676)
> *Guardian* (358,844)
> *Independent* (215,504)

Middle market
> *Daily Mail* (2,200,398)
> *Daily Express* (736,340)

Tabloids (or 'red-tops')
> *Sun* (3,146,006)
> *Daily Mirror* (1,366,891)
> *Star* (768,534)

Sunday newspapers
> *News of the World* (3,031,025)
> *Mail on Sunday* (2,134,809)
> *Sunday Mirror* (1,244,007)
> *Sunday Times* (1,198,984)
> *Sunday Express* (646,971)

Sunday Telegraph (602,306)
The People (594,552)
Observer (427,867)
Independent on Sunday (178,798)

Metro is given out free in sixteen city centres for commuters every morning, including Bath, Cardiff, Glasgow, London, Nottingham and Sheffield. *Metro* has the fourth highest newspaper circulation in the UK.

Regional newspapers

Regional and local newspapers have suffered in the recession. Falling advertising revenue and declining readership sales have hit them hard, which has meant fewer journalists doing more of the work. Every city and most counties and towns have their own title, for example: the *Argus* (Brighton), the *Birmingham Mail*, the *Cambridge News*, the *Derby Telegraph*, the *Hull Daily Mail*, the *Hampshire Chronicle*, the *Lancashire Evening Post*, the *Liverpool Echo*, the *Evening Standard* (London), the *Manchester Evening News*, the *Oxford Mail*, the *Sentinel* (Stoke) and the *Yorkshire Post*. There is also a plethora of local newspapers, covering stories everywhere from the Hebrides to Cornwall. These are important outlets for politicians to reach their voters with local campaigns, news stories and photo ops.

Television and radio

Despite the explosion in TV channels, political coverage is still the preserve of the major organisations: BBC, ITV and Channel 4. No one has yet started a specialist political channel with significant audience. The main news channels all cover politics from their base at 4 Millbank, yards from the Houses of Parliament. Politicians can spend an hour in Millbank, and do interviews for several stations under the same roof (and afterwards go to the popular juice bar on the ground floor).

There are also important political programmes which break big stories, and conduct interviews with politicians. These include the

Today programme on BBC Radio 4, *Newsnight* on BBC2 and *The World at One* (known as 'Wato') and *PM* on Radio 4. GMTV starts at 6.00 a.m. every weekday, and attracts heavyweight politicians to sit on the famous sofa in its South Bank studios.

On a Sunday, you can take your pick from *The Andrew Marr Show* on BBC1 at 9.00 a.m., *The Politics Show* on BBC1, *Boulton on Sunday* on Sky News at 10.00 a.m., and the *Westminster Hour* on Radio 4 at 10.00 pm. Every Saturday night, government ministers, special advisors and No. 10 spin doctors take part in a conference call which goes through the Sunday papers' first editions and agrees 'lines to take' for those ministers appearing on 'Marr', *The Politics Show* and 'Boulton'.

Braver politicians, or those who feel they have the popular touch, can subject themselves to late-night phone-ins on TalkSPORT, or BBC Radio 5 Live (for example the Tony Livesey show from 10.00 p.m. Monday to Thursday).

For the true political aficionado there is *The Daily Politics*, presented by Andrew Neil and Anita Anand on weekday lunchtimes when Parliament is sitting, and for insomniacs there is *This Week* at 11.35 p.m. on a Thursday with Andrew Neil, Michael Portillo and Diane Abbott.

And for ritual humiliation you can watch or listen to politicians squirm on BBC1's *Question Time* on Thursdays or BBC Radio 4's *Any Questions* on Fridays, or see them try (and usually fail) to hold their own on BBC1's *Have I Got News for You* (HIGNFY).

Magazines

Political magazines preach to the converted, rather than reach the electorate, but politicians like to appear in them because they know their peers are reading. The *Spectator* for the right, and the *New Statesman* for the left, are the main weekly titles. But you can add to those a host of small circulation titles, including *Progress*, *Tribune*, *Standpoint*, *Fabian Review* and *Red Pepper*, representing different political standpoints and factions within parties. The exception is *Total Politics*, produced by politicos across the spectrum, aimed at anyone interested in politics.

The Press Association

PA is the predominant 'wire service' in the UK, supplying online news to news organisations such as local newspapers. If you can get a story on PA, it will appear on the desktops in every newsroom in the UK, and you may find it getting coverage all over the place. Politicians also use PA to get quotes into the public domain.

Online

The rise of online media, social media and political blogging has been the most significant recent development, even since the last general election. Millions now get their political news, views and gossip online. As well as the traditional news outlets now all appearing online, we have a growing market in political blogs and websites. There are seventy million blogs online (not all about politics), with 120,000 being created every day. They vary greatly in quality of fact-checking, standards of journalism, numbers of readers and frequency of posts. Some are produced by MPs (Nadine Dorries, Tom Harris or Tom Watson), others by candidates, councillors, journalists or those observing and commenting on politics.

Everyone has their favourites on their 'blog roll', but these are a few of the most influential and readable:

> Iain Dale (www.iaindale.blogspot.com): Tory blog run by political publisher, broadcaster and sometime candidate.
> Guido Fawkes (www.order-order.com): Vicious satire and genuine scoops from a libertarian point of view, much copied by lazy newspaper diary writers.
> PoliticsHome (www.politicshome.com): A political news aggregator, bringing together all the latest political stories and commentary in one place, updated all the time. Can save hours of scouring newspapers and websites.
> PoliticalBetting (www.politicalbetting.com): A site dedicated to gambling on political developments; interesting insights, polling analysis and the latest odds on all kinds of political contests.
> ConservativeHome (www.conservativehome.blogs.com): Grass-roots voice of the Conservative Party.
> LabourList (www.labourlist): After a difficult start, now the

Labour Party equivalent of ConservativeHome, where Labour's supporters can get their news and views.

If you were to predict one thing about the notoriously difficult-to-predict realm of politics, it is that political blogging and sites such as Twitter and YouTube will not only reflect and report on future elections, they will shape their conduct and outcome. You can expect the carefully crafted campaigns to be derailed by politicians' embarrassing off-the-cuff remarks broadcast on YouTube, citizens haranguing candidates in public spaces, and then broadcast across the internet, and political leaders tripping and falling over things to be watched by millions.

The online media makes election campaigns almost impossible to media-manage: this will be the most anarchic election since the days of rent-a-mobs, professional hecklers and rotten tomato-throwing. The age of spin is over.

Paul Richards is the author of Be Your Own Spin Doctor

25

Dealing with journalists

Paul Richards

Successful politicians need to cultivate and nurture their relationships with journalists, because journalists can make or break the reputation of a politician.

Individual journalists have their own personalities and foibles. They are at different stages of their careers and lives – from eager 'cub' reporter keen to make a name, to veteran newshound with a thousand scoops under their belt. Successful journalists have a combination of skills: they can write fast and accurately; they can get people to say things they don't want to say; they have a 'nose' for a good story; they can turn base metal into journalistic gold; and they can do it day after day.

A look around the 'Lobby' of the Houses of Parliament (the journalists accredited to work in parliament covering politics) reveals a group of talented and motivated men and women. Many are in their thirties and forties, with young families. Most have university degrees, and post-graduate journalist qualifications (usually an NCTJ qualification). All have worked as journalists on local or national newspapers, radio or TV before joining the Lobby. Most have worked for other news organisations within the Lobby, and moved around jobs in a journalistic game of musical chairs. They are predominately middle-class, white, and pay their mortgages on homes within the M25. The Lobby is sometimes described as a cosy club, or worse, by the new breed of insurgent bloggers. Actually it is a fiercely dog-eat-dog place to work – more like cage fighting than a comfy armchair in the Reform.

What political journalists want most of all is to be good at their job. They want to be able to write sharp, readable news stories or create punchy, clever broadcasts. They want to 'scoop' their rivals (getting a story no one else has got). They want to create regular 'splashes' (the main story on the front page of a paper). They want to interpret and shape events. They want their names to be in lights, and a way of gaining promotion, or keeping their jobs.

Politicians can help journalists be good at their jobs, and thus earn their gratitude, by being ready with news, views, leads, quotes, secrets and gossip. Most of all, politicians need to understand that all journalists divide the world up into useful people and time-wasters. Useful people can help them do their jobs faster or better. Time-wasters clog up the email or telephone, and make meeting the deadline harder.

Here are some tips on dealing with journalists.

Do your homework

A little time Googling the name of the journalist you want to talk to is a good investment. You can discover some useful facts. Let's take a political journalist at random: Kevin Maguire of the *Mirror*. Within a few minutes you can ascertain that Kevin Maguire works for the *Mirror*, was born in 1961 in South Shields, is married to Cambridge-educated author Emma Burstell, has three children, has been on HIGNFY, and has worked for the *Telegraph* and the *Guardian*, and written for the *New Statesman*. You can read all of his columns and see the kinds of stories he covers. You can get his email address (kevin.maguire@mirror.co.uk). You can even see the average word length of his articles (195 words). In other words, you can build the kind of pen-portrait within minutes that would have taken days in the library just a few years ago.

This means if you are dealing with a particular journalist, you can have up your sleeve all kinds of titbits of knowledge that might come in handy. You might discover a connection, or a mutual friend or interest. At the very least, it will allow you an opportunity for sycophancy. All journalists are flattered when someone says they read their recent article or column and enjoyed it.

There are some things the internet won't tell you. For example, some journalists read their emails and react to them; others ignore them, so a news story idea sent by email will simply not get read.

Speed kills

In 1992, the Clinton campaign slogan was 'speed kills'. It was printed on the backs of the T-shirts of the rapid rebuttal teams who issued their devastating rebuttal to George Bush's convention speech *before he had even said a word*. They fed the media beast with enough rapidity to stop it getting hungry.

Journalists' lives revolve around deadlines. The mainstream media has a ruthless system of deadlines. Towards the end of the afternoon, most lobby journalists are tense, frenetic and desperately trying to file their stories. On the Sunday papers, Friday afternoons and Saturday mornings are the most anxious times (and Monday is a day off).

On the BBC News Channel (what used to be called News 24) or Sky News, or news-based websites, the news is updated all the time, twenty-four hours a day. Deadlines are a constant. This creates a voracious appetite for news and comment. It also means that false stories can be reported in good faith before corrections can appear (hence the slogan given to 24-hour news stations by their rivals: 'never wrong for long').

This is a recent development. As Tony Blair has commented: 'When I fought the 1997 election . . . we took an issue a day. In 2005, we had to have one for the morning, another for the afternoon and by the evening the agenda had already moved on.' In coming elections 'news' will not be an event or a programme, but a process, relentlessly moving forward. Any modern politician needs to know the deadlines of the journalists they deal with, and be sympathetic to them.

News

Journalists need news like a plant needs water or Tiger Woods needs women. There are various definitions of what makes a good news story. One is that news is 'man bites dog' – if a dog bites a man, then so what, that's what dogs do all the time. But if a man bites a dog, we are intrigued and want to know why. The phrase is variously attributed to British newspaper owner Lord Northcliffe, to *New York Sun* editor John B. Bogart, and others. Allied to this definition is the idea that you never read about planes that don't crash or laws that cabinet ministers don't break. It is the unusualness of the incident that makes it newsworthy.

Arthur Christiansen, editor of the *Daily Express* from the 1930s to the 1950s, told his reporters: 'Always, always, always tell the story through people.' People doing things, saying things or being affected by events. Much of modern political journalism is influenced by the famous investigation by Woodward and Bernstein of the *Washington Post* into the break-in at the Watergate offices of the Democrat National Committee. The unravelling of a plot which brought down a president, thanks to persistent, old-fashioned investigative journalism, makes many political journalists believe plots are endemic in politics, and their job is to unearth them. News, as the old saying goes, is what someone, somewhere doesn't want you to know.

Most news stories can be boiled down into one or more component parts (or 'news values'):

› Novelty – anything new
› Unusualness – man bites dog
› Conflict – wars, rows, sports, divorces, business takeovers
› Celebrities
› Scandal – financial, sexual
› Triumph over Tragedy (TOT) – earthquake and plane crash survivors
› Danger – everything from the recession, climate change and swine flu to killer bees
› Superlatives – the biggest, shortest, fattest or thinnest
› Milestones and anniversaries – the millionth customer, ten years since. . .

Take a look at today's papers and you will see what I mean.

The secret to getting stories into the news is to mould the story to fit one or more of these news values. Most of all, your news story must contain people. This could be quotes from residents, the offer of interviewees, case studies and personal testimony. Local papers in particular need photographs, so take them yourself with a decent digital camera, and if they contain people in interesting settings, you will see them appear.

News isn't annual reports, sets of financial figures, minutes of meetings, or the text of speeches. This may be the meat and drink of politics, but it adds up to a big pile of 'so what' to a journalist.

The tricks journalists play
Journalists say there are no tricks, just good journalism. However you label them, these are some of the journalistic techniques to watch out for.

'Would you say that. . .?'
It is a convention of journalism that any statement put to you by a journalist, if you agree, or even fail to disagree loudly enough, can be reported as your own words, as though you had spoken them yourself. If you hear the words 'Would you say that. . .' it should set alarm bells ringing. The way to handle this is to use a phrase such as 'I wouldn't say that' or 'Those are not words I would use' and then say what you want to say.

Pinter pause
In normal conversation, a lengthy pause is a social embarrassment. People will come out with almost any banality to keep conversation flowing. Journalists use this social nicety to get people to talk. They pause, and allow you to keep on speaking, in the hope that you say something interesting. Just 'pause' back, and see who cracks first.

Wood for the trees
If you find yourself being interviewed by a print or broadcast journalist, beware a series of easy questions at the start. They are almost certainly designed to put you at your ease. The hard, or

'killer', question is coming down the track. This device also worked for the mac-wearing 1970s LAPD tec Columbo.

I know your boss

Journalists sometimes pretend to know your own peer group, or boss, well and suggest that they've told them the story already. This might make you think it's alright to speak freely. The police in films use this technique to force confessions from suspects, by making them think their associates have already confessed (or 'squealed', 'sung like a canary' etc.)

The 'old pals' act

Appeals to old friendships are seldom intended to achieve anything other than to loosen your tongue. You can be as friendly as you like with journalists. Have a drink or a meal. Tell them gossip. Share secrets. But never forget they are not your friends.

Time for a drink

It is a well-practised ploy for a journalist to conduct an interview with a politician, and then theatrically turn off the recording device as though the interview has finished. At that point, a politician might think they can relax, speak freely, or perhaps share a bottle of wine with their interviewer. It is of course a trick, especially the wine part. Everything you say is on the record, and there may well be a second recording device whirring away. If you share your views about the marriages, financial affairs or mental stability of your colleagues with a journalist, you can confidently expect to have shared them with the public.

Some final pieces of advice

Take notes

It is impossible to complain about a misquotation or inaccuracy if the journalist has a short-hand note of the conversation and you are relying on your memory. If you are talking to a journalist on the phone, take a note of the conversation, and let the journalist know you are doing it. Towards the end of the conversation you can ask for a 'read-back' of the journalist's notes. This is the time to make any clarifications or corrections, not once mistakes have appeared in print.

Never wrestle with a chimney sweep

That's one of the Benn dynasty's axioms, and it should be your guide to dealing with the media. Be honest, play it straight, refuse to engage in dirty tricks and underhand briefings, and you might just survive in politics as long as the Benns. If you are tempted into dirty tricks, be prepared to see your political career end in ignominy, and without sympathy. Who lives by the briefing dies by the briefing.

Paul Richards is the author of Be Your Own Spin Doctor

26

Dealing with bloggers

Phil Hendren

JOSH *(on phone to blogger)*: This is Josh Lyman, and this is off the record.

TOBY (White House Press Secretary): She's not a. . .

JOSH *(on phone)*: There may be more disreputable ways to make a living than trafficking in gossip and clandestine photos, but none spring to mind. My and this administration's environmental bona fides are well established. To use this incident to imply otherwise is scurrilous and irresponsible – cheap and easy irony from what I can only surmise is a cheap and shallow person. . . I said this was off the record.

TOBY: She's not a journalist.

JOSH: *(on phone)*: You're gonna post this?

DONNA (Josh's assistant) *(refreshes screen)*: She's posting it now.

Taken from *The West Wing*

There's something to be said for getting your media handling advice, or more accurately 'blogger handling advice', from a hit American TV series, but the truth is you could do no worse than heed the lesson within that little conversation.

We are bloggers, we don't follow rules other than our own. In fact, we are for the most part, just ordinary people. Yes, some of us have links through our blogs to the political world. Some of us may have been activists at one time or another, but really we're just individuals who've jumped on the crest of a new media wave.

If you want to deal with us then the following eight rules will hopefully help you along the way. The rules are by no means exhaustive, there are probably other rules that other bloggers could offer, but they provide a good starting point.

Rule No. 1: Bloggers are not journalists

Sounds obvious, doesn't it? Forget it at your peril, though. When you tell a journalist that something is 'off the record' then it's pretty much a given that it will remain the case. If you say it to a blogger you can never be quite so sure; it all depends on what type of blogger they are (see Rule No. 4 below).

Bloggers do not operate within the usual rules of engagement that journalists do. They have ethics of course, but they're not bound or constrained by things like the Press Complaints Commission. If they get a story, regardless of whether they can stand it up in the traditional way or not, they may still post it in one way or another.

Unlike your friendly neighbourhood hack, the blogger most likely has a job already doing something else. They may have zero connection with the party political world apart from the subject of their blog. The blogger may have no desire to become a journalist or gain access to the world in which you operate.

This rule shouldn't just be read by those who want to be politicians but also those who want to be political press officers. The Conservative Party only started including bloggers on press releases after a blogger was told he was not important by a press officer and other bloggers started screaming about it.

Rule No. 2: Find supportive bloggers

While bloggers are not journalists and you should assume that everything you say to them might one day appear digitally, this shouldn't stop you seeking out friendly and supportive bloggers.

True, you may have restrictions from upon high about your dealings with the media, but there is nothing to stop you adding bloggers aligned to your political way of thinking to your press release distribution lists. They'll appreciate the fact you are telling them something; just remember that they may contact you to query a press release, and that means Rule No. 1 comes into play.

One important thing to remember when seeking out blogs that might give you support is to assess whether they're really relevant to what you're campaigning on at a local level. Telling nationally focused bloggers that you've been delivering leaflets and talking to people about dog fouling in the local park will get you one of two responses. You'll be ignored, or you'll be ridiculed (possibly both if you send them lots of press releases).

Rule No. 3: Offer to write articles for supportive group blogs

If you want to be a politician then you want to get yourself noticed. One way would be to write some sort of insightful commentary for the national newspapers. Let's face reality, though: you're the prospective candidate for the constituency of 'Little Place No One Has Ever Heard of Unless You Live There' so what chance do you have unless your Dad writes commentaries for a national paper he used to be the editor of?

This is where group blogs come into their own. Group blogs are often a useful platform for the unknown and wannabe politician to make a name for themselves. They exist across the political spectrum, with editors running them but inviting anyone and everyone to contribute.

Find the group blog that is in keeping with your inherent Thatcherism/socialism or sit-on-fenceism and ask them if you can write an article for them on some news issues of the day. You might even want to offer up some policy idea too – just remember that if it's out of step with the High Command of your political party (assuming you're in one) it could get you into trouble – unless of course you want to be labelled a 'loose cannon' or 'maverick' before you even get started.

Remember this, though: whatever you write will most likely be ridiculed by political opponents in the Comments section, so you'll need to be referring to Rules No. 5, 6 and 7.

Rule No. 4: Know Thine Enemy

OK, so you've found some supportive blogs locally. You've sent them some stuff, and you've built a bit of a relationship with some of them. What about the ones who vehemently disagree with everything you stand for? Ignore them, right? Wrong!

Fair enough, you don't have to go out of your way to engage with them proactively, but you need to be aware of what they're saying about you. Remember, they'll probably be part of Rule No. 2 for your political opponents. Find out what blogs are out there and start reading them and getting to know them, because one day they might contact you about something you've said that can be turned into a story that will embarrass you. You might also find something on them that you give to your newly found group of supportive bloggers.

Rule No. 5: Beware of mentally unhinged bloggers

Not all bloggers are normal people, some of them really are the clichéd bedroom-sitting sad gits screaming to be noticed. You may not realise that the blogger contacting you is a corner flag short of a football pitch at first but it will become apparent eventually through constant emailing and lengthy posts about you where you will always be wrong no matter what you say.

They may even start to call you or your office, constantly asking ever more insane questions where they quibble over the definition of 'is' in an answer you have given to them. Eventually they'll set up a website dedicated solely to you, and they'll probably make videos about you on YouTube.

They'll also attempt to take the moral high ground against you while simultaneously publishing personal emails from you and perhaps clandestinely recorded telephone conversations they have had with you (see Rule No. 1). They'll also make sure as many other blogs that might disagree with you write about their mad ramblings (see Rule No. 4). So what can you do?

It's simple, and it may seem counter-intuitive, but ignore them. They want you to react, and when you don't it annoys them more. When you do react you will never say the right thing anyway and that will just annoy them some more. You're caught between a rock and a hard place. You are in the wrong, they are in the right, and that is how it will be until the end of time or until they take their next dose of anti-psychotics.

The light at the end of the tunnel is that they will go away eventually as it dawns on them than you're not paying them any attention. Unfortunately their activity might mean that people read their rantings and ravings if they search for you on Google. There's nothing you can really do about that in the short term. Just remember to save their mad emails, along with perhaps time records of their phone calls, so that if anyone ever asks you about them you can show why they're mentally unhinged.

Hey, you want to be a politician, don't you? You're going to have to take the rough with the smooth in this new media world. Sorry.

Rule No. 6: Remember the Blog Pyramid

Never heard of the Blog Pyramid? It's a very simple concept derived from the nationally known blogger Iain Dale. It notes that while a small independent and local blog may not have a readership as high as the national ones, all it takes is a for a good story to appear at the base of the pyramid and it could filter up in a big way.

The pyramid works in the same way as the national newspapers often feeding off stories in the local press. There have been many examples of local candidates who have become national blog stories after appearing on local blogs. Likewise there have been locally sourced blog stories that have managed to smash their way onto the front pages of the nationals because of the pyramid.

The pyramid is something you can use to your advantage just as much as it can work against you.

Rule No. 7: Know when to quit when responding to a blogger on their blog

So you've just discovered that someone has written about you on a blog that opposes you (see Rule No. 4) and they've jolly well been nasty about you, calling you foolish and many other cruel names, so you decide to leave a comment. Before you know where you are you're involved in a full-blown argument, commonly called a 'Flame War' online.

It's very easy to get carried away defending yourself. Don't. However right you might think you are, you'll only make it worse. Remember what Rule No. 4 says, and don't forget your mentally unhinged blogger in Rule No. 5 is probably storing everything you're saying for his or her next tirade against you.

If you feel you must respond then do so once and only once, and make it clear that you have no intention of continuing to do so – tell them that you're choosing to ignore the insults too. Do not swear, cast aspersions or insult anyone, and under no circumstances revisit the post after you have returned from an evening in a local drinking establishment. That way lies pain and hassle you really don't need.

Say your piece (sober) and get the 'Hell out of Dodge'. Capiche?

Rule No. 8: Don't become a twat on Twitter
Everyone who is anyone has a Twitter account these days. It's like blogging, only in micro-form because you're only allowed to use 140 characters. All previous rules applicable to blogs apply to microblogging.

Twitter is not a replacement for proper conversation, and getting lost in Twitter-Land thinking that it is will probably gain you only a handful of votes if any. But it will ensure that those linked to Rule No. 4 have yet another means to bombard you and distribute nonsense that you may feel compelled to respond to (see Rule No. 7 for dealing with this).

When David Cameron infamously said 'too many twits make a twat' there was a hidden truth in there. The pyramid in Rule No. 6 is even more applicable to microblogging on Twitter than on blogs themselves. It's fast and furious, and what you say could be popping up on a national journalist's screen within minutes of you saying it.

Move away from the keyboard, put the BlackBerry down, take a breath and think.

Phil Hendren blogs at DizzyThinks.net

27

Getting in the news

Sarah MacKinlay

Getting ready to make the news

Today every politician must be the master of their own media. You need to know what makes a good story and how to sell this into the press.

To enter office you need to have confidence that your story is one that people will want to listen to. Without this, your interactions with the media will appear insincere. And in a crowded market your press release or pitch will make it no further than the journalist's spike.

Misguided confidence can be very damaging. So a media-savvy politician will equip themselves with a critically constructive, highly literate and articulate aide who will guide them through the media maze and develop a sincere message. This will ensure that media appearances are frequent. And that a clear and simple message is articulated in a controlled and carefully managed way.

Relationships with individual members of the press are key to the successful dissemination of your message – a personal briefing and chat over a coffee is worth twenty press releases and is far better at ensuring your story gets the exposure and accuracy it deserves. This method of getting into the news is so important that it has a whole section devoted to it below.

Targeting the right journalists in order to build a relationship is straightforward: choose the ones most likely to print your story. This is likely to be the political or community correspondents from your local papers and broadcasters, the trade journalists from the trade magazines of your specialist area, and the writers on political magazines such as *Total Politics*, the *Spectator*, *The Economist* or *Tribune*. Building up a specialism in one area will establish you as the reliable expert voice to turn to for authoritative comment.

What is a good news story?
A good news story must be 'new' to readers. It should:

› surprise
› entertain
› change the reader's perceptions.

Every story should be pitched to appeal to the audience you want to attract. It should be of direct interest to them and contain essential ingredients such as people, money, drama and extremes – for instance latest, first, biggest, fastest – which are most likely to attract the attention of journalists.

Journalists also like figures, so a good way to ensure coverage is to do a survey and present the results within the press release. They are simple and inexpensive to do these days and you can use programmes such as Survey Monkey to do this. But above all – it should inform.

You can decide whether your story really is worth telling by exploring some of the following questions:

› Is your story of interest to the audience you want to attract?
› Has something new happened to the story which may already be in the public domain?
› Is there a strong human interest element to it?
› Is it just your comment? This is rarely of interest unless it is particularly controversial. And journalists will spot self-promotion a mile away.

An interesting story will be full to bursting with new facts. Be careful not to introduce scandal, it's not your job to do this. Just present the information in a clear and unbiased way. If the journalist is good enough, he or she will do further research, find the scandal and make the decision how to use it from there on.

Get ahead or get overtaken

If getting to know your media is not top of your agenda at first, then you will make life far more difficult for yourself in the long term. You will give opponents the opportunity to jump ahead of you and build a successful relationship with the very journalists you want to sell your story to.

Of course if you have a good story a journalist will look at it. But you will have missed out on the prior opportunity to build reputation and favour with the journalist, which rightly or wrongly may influence the way they cover it.

Getting yourself on the media radar

Journalists are bombarded with badly pitched, inappropriate and useless emails, press releases and calls. To stand out from this clutter you need to clearly differentiate between what's of interest to you and what's of interest to your target audience. You need to grab their attention in less than ten words and put this in your email subject. The first words you say on the phone and the heading of your blog should also be brief.

The best way to begin your press activity is to set up a blog, and advice on how to do this is covered in Chapter 16. It will give you the chance to act as an editor, help you to begin to think like a journalist (what makes them tick) and increase your profile.

You'll learn what kind of stories you should cover from the level of activity on your site. This understanding can be used when trying to get stories into other areas of the press, such as your local newspaper.

A blog will go some way to increasing your profile but it is somewhat one sided, a tool for promoting yourself and the good work you undoubtedly do. Far more balance will come from straightforward news reports, so preparing and distributing press releases for your local paper, for example, will help you to gain coverage.

Think local

The importance of regional newspapers should not be underestimated. They are widely read and respected within local communities, and some even outsell the closest national newspaper in their regions.

As you begin your political career you would be well advised to familiarise yourself with all your local and regional newspapers. Even though local papers have been hit hard in the recent recession, many still have local government and political correspondents. You need to know who these people are. Read a selection of their stories online and find out what kind of things they cover and the stories they run and how they tell them.

Writing the news

Once you know what makes a good story you will need to develop a theme and create a structure so that you can write your own press release. There is no hard and fast rule for writing the perfect press release but there are some things you would be well advised to observe.

Think of a press release like peeling an onion. You tell the story in layers: first introduce it, revealing a little more in a longer second paragraph, providing details you had to omit from the first paragraph for brevity. Then introduce the second, punchiest point of your story, in the third paragraph. Finally summarise and add any other essential details before adding a quote.

Just one quote in the release will suffice. A press release shouldn't be seen as an opportunity to write a long set of quotes just to satisfy the ego of the people featured in the story.

A press release rarely needs to be more than four paragraphs long, five at most. And you should start questioning your understanding of 'essential' if it spreads beyond one page of A4.

The first sentence should contain the essence of the story in

25–30 words, if possible. I received a press release recently where the first sentence was a staggering fifty-one words long. I thought I might stop breathing before I'd reached the end of it! The person writing it had obviously tried to tell the whole story straight out, but the most interesting, newsworthy part of the story did not appear until the final paragraph.

Use strong active language when writing your release. Journalists have very short attention spans and they'll look at a press release for an average of three seconds before deciding what they'll do with it. 'Local politician saves life of young woman following knife attack' is far punchier than saying 'A local woman who was attacked with a kitchen knife has been saved by a local politician'.

Avoid flamboyant words, keep it informal and use everyday language. It is tempting to write in a way that will show you have great knowledge of the subject area, but it's far better to write simply and clearly. This does not mean patronising people, but if you want to show you understand what you're talking about and get people to listen to your message then you will inspire far more confidence if you are able to tell the story succinctly.

As a rule of thumb, if your story is aimed at a local paper or tabloid, the press release should be easily understandable to an eight-year-old. For a trade magazine, broadsheet or financial title a twelve-year-old should be able to pick up the story and get a good understanding of what's going on.

When you reach the end of a release it should be marked clearly with 'ENDS/'. After this point you should write 'Notes to editors'. The most important things to put under this heading are the contact details for further information. Make sure you put out-of-hours contact details here. Journalists don't work nine to five, and if they can't reach you to verify or give more details to the story it may end up not making the news cut for the next day.

'Notes to editors' is where you should also give concise, relevant background information, such as biographical details of the person or organisation the release relates to and supporting facts and figures relating to the story.

Images are also a good tool to sell a story; strong unposed

shots help to create a narrative and can strengthen a press release. However, be careful not to clog up journalists' inboxes with large images. Always send over a reduced size image and add a note to the editor that high-resolution images are available on request.

Once the email is complete, factor in time before sending it to ensure there are no spelling, grammatical or style errors. It is incredibly embarrassing to be caught out on these and in the world of social media and blogging you can pretty well ensure that if you disseminate your press release thoroughly any mistakes will get picked up. I always double-check my use of 'tenants' and 'tenets' after an embarrassing slip-up.

Releasing your news

A scattergun approach when emailing out your press release will not win you any favours and could potentially damage your political reputation. Email is the only real option for sending press releases to journalists and should be backed up by web and social media.

Target your release by drawing up a list of journalists who are likely to be interested in your story ahead of when the release needs to be sent out.

Make sure whoever is on this list is interested in this particular story either for immediate publication or knowledge building. Don't send a release on the local scouts prizegiving at which you were asked to give awards to a journalist at *Practical Caravan* magazine. But in addition to your local paper, *Scouting* magazine or another special interest title might also find an interesting angle relevant to its readers.

Use medialist.co.uk to pull together a list of emails and phone numbers of journalists to send your press release out to.

You should also include any relevant stakeholders, such as party activists, party press officers and bloggers, on your press release list as many of them will spread your news for you. You should also publish it on your website so it is easily referenced in future and put a link to it on Facebook, Twitter and LinkedIn if possible.

Writing the perfect release and identifying the right people to send it to can be scuppered at the last minute by sending it to a journalist who is off on holiday or sick leave. Or one who is just so busy they don't notice it in the deluge of emails they receive every day.

Following up your release with a phone call can make the difference between your story ending up in the bottom of an inbox or the front page. You may get a few journalists on deadline being rather short with you on the phone but ignore their abrupt tone and press on.

Most often picking up the phone will help you to build your relationship with the reporter. A really helpful member of the press will even give you some pointers on why your story works or why it doesn't, to help inform your next attempt at making the news. You can always use this point of introduction to put a date in the diary to catch up for a coffee or drink in the future.

Why it's worth it

Increasing your media profile might seem like a chore but if planned and carried out well it should be a worthwhile and rewarding task. Regular news stories about your campaigns and activities are essential to the democratic process and they let constituents know what you're up to. After all, the ultimate aim is to reach out and speak to your current or future constituents and you have a duty and are in a privileged position to do this.

Sarah MacKinlay is founding editor of Total Politics *and director of the political communications firm Journalista*

28

Developing a media strategy

Ed Staite

A good media strategy will enable you to set not only the tone of your campaign, but the entire election battle. A well-disciplined strategy can establish the rhythm of a campaign, maintaining a sense of urgency and driving momentum while at the same time helping to marginalise your opponents. It can define who you are and what you stand for and carry the all-important call to action for voters to put their cross next to a name.

Being honest about your objectives and your chances in achieving these are crucial to being successful. Are you looking just to win or to win big? Is this achievable or should you be developing a longer term strategy to whittle down an opponent's majority over time? Is the campaign part of a wider party strategy, aimed at making other parties divert valuable resources to your ward or constituency?

Your media strategy is not an end in itself but should support your campaign objectives. The term 'strategy' is often misunderstood and also frequently misused. A strategy is the overall approach taken. A strategy comes after the objectives have been set but before tactics.

All good campaigns are based on honesty. A candid situation analysis is the ground on which any media strategy will be built. Once this has been undertaken a message can be developed to frame the choice in voters' minds.

The most important element in a campaign is the message. This isn't to suggest that a communications strategy is a substitute for a well-thought-out set of policies, but modern elections are not won by chance; they owe a great deal to the effectiveness of the communications strategy. Without this strategy in place the voters are unlikely ever to know what your policies are. Framing the choice voters face drives the message and who you are as a candidate. This shapes your media strategy and subsequently your tactics.

Every day we are exposed to many thousands of messages through a constant stream of information via television, radio, social media, advertising, direct interaction, newspapers and magazines. This puts political parties increasingly at a disadvantage. The success of the communications industry to sell the modern world to consumers has marginalised politics. Recognise this and adapt. Take every opportunity that comes your way to get your message across.

Very little of today's massive flow of information makes its way into our consciousness, and anything which makes a message hard to understand makes it less likely to be noticed. Simplicity will help you to communicate effectively.

To the same extent do not be afraid of repetition. Through a relentless determination to hammer home their message the Labour Party succeeded in making 'sleaze' inherently linked to the Conservative Party during John Major's government.

A campaign message must be written down and understood by all working on the campaign, especially the candidate. Test your message for use in a variety of situations so that it is memorable and punchy without sounding fake or contrived. Your message must sound right in a quote given to a newspaper but also as part of what you say on the doorstep to the voters.

Ask yourself whether what you are saying is interesting. Does what you are saying really matter? What will people think of you when they hear you use your proposed campaign messages?

A useful point an experienced TV news journalist once told me is that every time you appear on television you should see it as like being a guest in someone's home. So act accordingly. Use this tip in devising your campaign messages. Make them relevant, easy to understand, but also the kind of thing you wouldn't mind saying to someone's face over a cup of tea.

To maximise impact you should summarise your messages in three key points which can be constantly repeated. The Labour Party went as far as publishing their pledges on wallet-sized cards pre-1997. Alongside this repetition remember that successful communications are all about storytelling: use interesting narrative or human interest stories to make your point. Use language people can connect with, not language that shuts them out of the argument.

A key pillar of any campaign strategy is the need to define a candidate. Voters don't like uncertainty or ambiguity – they fear the unknown – so a candidate's character should be the clearly defined embodiment of their principles, what drives them and what they are selling the voters. Perhaps I'm old fashioned but I believe political ambition is a noble calling which deserves candidates who are driven by principles. If these are in place then you have the foundations of a very good message and subsequently an excellent tactical campaign.

In recent years some candidates have led social action projects as a way to not only define who they are, but also demonstrate action and create another rich source for potential media stories. Tactics like this should ensure a campaign is not reliant on press releases to grab media attention, while an issue of real relevance to voters can define a campaign in a positive way rather than restricting it in the minds of the electorate.

George Osborne famously talked about following Labour's 'playbook' as part of the Conservatives' moves to modernise. He believed the Conservatives could learn a lot by how Labour operated in the build-up to the 1997 general election. Finding a chink in your opponent's armour can be crucial for landing a telling blow that may define an election campaign. Spotting an opportunity such as a poor radio or newspaper interview can be your way of moving your opponent off their home territory to allow you to seize control of the campaign.

The key question to ask is: 'If you were in their shoes, what would cause them the biggest nightmare?' If you can answer this then you have your approach for a well-targeted tactical attack. Put your opponent on the defensive and they are not going to be communicating their key messages effectively.

Disciplined man marking is a useful exercise whatever level of political campaign you are involved in. Know your opponent and what they are doing; know their policies as well as you know your own. This way you can stay one step ahead and don't have to use valuable resources reacting to media stories. Your aim is to shape the media narrative, not have your campaign shaped by the media.

Effective monitoring of your opposition should be a key pillar of your media strategy. Whether this means reading the weekly paper as it hits the doormat, listening in to local BBC or commercial radio, keeping an eye on influential blogs and other new media or having in place a large team working twenty-four hours a day to monitor every national broadcaster, blog, newspaper and news wire, intelligence used effectively in any campaign means you remain in control of your own destiny.

Even if you are part of a small team on a local campaign, technology can help you. Google alerts or RSS feeds (instant updates from blogs and websites of your choice) can do the trawling through cyberspace for you – now all you need to do is react quickly to this intelligence, in the right way.

Speed kills. This isn't just a tag line from a road safety campaign but also a key factor in the success of any campaign. Speed should drive how you observe events and the campaign in general, arrive at the right decision when reacting to developments and then, most importantly, act.

In the recent presidential election in the United States one of the most common themes for media commentators was who had the momentum – the 'Big Mo'. If your campaign develops a system where you are doing things faster than your opponents then you hold the momentum. You can then set the agenda, be on the front foot and so be more likely to land damaging punches on your opponent(s).

Technology can hinder as well as help a campaign; understanding the impact new technologies can have on a media strategy is essential in today's fully integrated media world. Citizen journalism has existed as long as journalism itself, but the rules of the game have been redefined by technology. In the age of 24-hour rolling news, where the appetite of the press and media can never really be fully satisfied, there is a real danger that during a general election an individual candidate or the entire campaign of a political party could be derailed by one opponent, a misplaced word and a mobile phone.

In a matter of minutes footage can be posted on a blog or social networking site before finding its way into the mainstream media. The Labour Party used these tactics to target Boris Johnson during the 2008 London mayoral campaign. I have experienced first hand how control can be lost of the media narrative, momentum stalls and you are thrown onto the back foot. Remember message discipline is important no matter what your audience. Also remember why you are making huge efforts to man-mark your opponents. Expect them to do the same.

Understanding what the media narrative is and how you fit into it is essential in implementing a media strategy successfully. This means you need to get close, though not too close, to journalists. In my first few weeks of working in the Conservative press office a very senior Lobby journalist wished me luck in my new role and, with a smile and a twinkle in his eye, added a bit of helpful advice: 'Remember, no journalist is ever your friend.'

At the same time journalists are not your enemy; they are an additional resource for you to use to ensure you are getting your message across. A street-wise media team are your eyes, ears and sixth sense. If they are doing their job properly they will have a network of contacts in the media who will be able to warn them of impending trouble as well as identify areas of weakness in your opponents.

If you don't have the luxury of having your own press officer, make time to add this important task to your to-do list. Ideally, as soon as you are selected for your seat you will be building relationships with key journalists. Investing time in a coffee every now or then with your local newspaper editor is certainly not a media strategy in itself but it is an essential pillar to building one.

Once you have got your message right it needs to be correctly targeted. I am not advocating that you say one thing to one group of people or one part of your constituency and not to another, just that you realise it is possible to dial up or down parts of your message.

Strategic targeting is essential to a successful and impactful campaign. This in turn drives your tactics to ensure efficient allocation of resources. If you understand your audiences and what motivates them, you can prioritise your message appropriately to emphasise the different elements of your message for the different audiences.

When this has been completed you can look at which media you will use and to what extent. This should be linked to your 'Get Out the Vote' strategy to ensure you have the focus right. Don't be afraid to evaluate your successes and failures constantly. Recognising when tactics are not working and revising them is the sign of a good campaign. Revising your strategy, however, is a much more drastic step and should be avoided. If your message has been properly defined then your strategy should be robust enough to work as long as the tactical implementation is reaping rewards.

It is clearly advantageous to have a web strategy in place even on a very local campaign. This should be linked to, and developed in parallel with, your media strategy as a tactical part of your overall campaign.

Arguably the first campaign to recognise the shift in focus necessary for a successful modern campaign was the Clinton presidential election campaign of 1992. Their belief, shifting perceptions as well as using resources to inform the electorate about policy, has become an essential weapon in a politician's armoury.

Voters, and the media, get their information on campaigns from surprising sources nowadays, all of which shape their perception of a campaign, party or individual candidate. Voters, more than ever before, make their choices not based on fact but on perceptions. Adapt accordingly. Tony Blair was much maligned for appearing on chat shows or daytime television but his media team were just putting their man in front of their target audiences. You should do the same. Recognise that how you are perceived by your target voters is shaped as much by where they see you as what they hear you say.

Perception management is an essential strand of any media campaign, as journalists are influenced by multiple external influences and increasingly by bloggers. Whatever your industry, there is always a media narrative that will shape the context of any story. It is essential that you are aware of this narrative but also how it is developing. Then you can start to influence it.

Engagement with bloggers is tricky. The old rules of engagement with journalists rarely apply, meaning background briefing is difficult and fact-checking a story cannot be relied upon. This does not mean you ignore them and, as with key journalists, bloggers can be a helpful resource as well as a useful opinion former to have on side. Identify those that may influence your election early and then try to find out what makes them tick. Who knows, they may even become your greatest cheerleader. (For more on this, see Chapter 26, Dealing with Bloggers.)

Another element of perception management is communicating through the image a campaign or candidate conveys to the electorate. A picture is worth a thousand words. Today, when we are all bombarded with comment, news, blogs and gossip, perhaps this is truer than ever; a good picture can cut through all this.

Modern politicians are frequently attacked for an obsession with photo opportunities but the reality is they work and should be a consistent tactical strand running through your media strategy. This doesn't mean that you embark on a mad rush around your potential constituency to kiss as many babies as possible. Make the pictures meaningful so all images of you during the campaign are consistent with your campaign messages. This discipline ensures that, even if you have been campaigning for weeks or even months, when a voter finally registers who you are their first perceptions of you are the right ones. The first thing they hear from you is a key message. Remember, this one interaction may be your one and only opportunity to influence this voter before Election Day – don't waste that opportunity.

For every policy announcement you should have a long list of tactical actions in place to communicate the news. This will ensure you communicate the substance of your policy and your overarching message and will help to shape the perception of who you are in an integrated and complementary way every time.

The implications of a poorly devised media strategy cannot be overestimated. Any campaign should be as obsessive about getting its media relations right as they are passionate about why they embarked on the campaign in the first place.

Discipline is essential, as is a well-developed but simple message targeted in an effective manner. At the same time evaluate constantly and be fleet of foot in your tactical implementation. Campaigns are intense and sometimes physically and mentally bruising. The knocks you take will be far less severe and the blows you dish out will be far more damaging if your media strategy is right from the day one.

Ed Staite is senior media advisor at Fleishman Hillard

Part VI

Life in the spotlight:
the perfect presentation

29

Public speaking

John Shosky

Control the setting

A few years ago, Mother Teresa spoke at the National Prayer Breakfast in Washington. She was introduced by President Clinton. The event was broadcast live to the nation over C-Span. There were several hundred people in the audience. This was a big speech by any definition.

But the speech failed; it flopped. The delivery was good. The message was clear. But the podium height was set for the tall Clinton, not for the significantly shorter main speaker. When she walked to the podium, Mother Theresa disappeared. You could hear her give the speech, but you couldn't see her, just the tip of her hat and an occasional disembodied hand that would rise in gesture to the top of the podium, wave, then evaporate.

Stories about the failures of the physical setting are legion. For example, recently a cabinet member in the United States spoke from a podium that looked like it was designed for little children, only rising to his belt. The microphones were scotch-taped onto the podium. He had to bend down to give the speech!

Another well-known speech, a bit more vintage, featured a speaker placed in the middle of an enormous stage, which itself was many feet from the first row of chairs in the audience. The speaker looked like a miniature figure seen through the wrong end of a telescope. The physical division between the speaker and the audience was too vast to overcome.

These are mistakes that undercut the speech itself. After all of the time preparing and practising, the speech is ruined because other people made poor decisions about the physical setting, decisions on behalf of the speaker but without regard to the actual needs of the speaker. The speaker was passive, not involved or present beforehand, allowing others to make important decisions about the speech, then just accepting the physical setting at the time of delivery.

Most speakers just show up and give the speech. This is a typical. You put the speech on your schedule and then maybe show up a few minutes early to look over the room and the audience. This forces you to immediately adjust to the room, podium, microphone, cameras and other aspects of the setting of the speech. And sometimes those adjustments are wrong, because you are giving the speech and can't see your image or hear your words from the perspective of the audience. For example, if you have to ask 'Can you hear me?', then the magic of the speech is already gone.

Very few speakers ever preview the physical setting. Few actually look over a room and try to understand it before giving the speech. Few speakers walk around the room looking for possible problems. Few speakers have an advance person to look over all of the elements of the physical setting of the speech and the means of transmitting the words and images that make up the speech. And, frankly, many advance people don't know what to look for when they preview the setting. And many candidates don't have 'people' to help out, often don't have the time to check out the location beforehand, nor do many have the desire to do so. In fact, I recently spoke of this need to an audience of communication and public affairs personnel for a government agency in the United States. Many argued that advance work was not part of their job profile. Some were indignant: no time for such detailed efforts. Fairly common responses. And the absence of control inevitably leads to preventable problems.

So what can a candidate do? Political candidates must become more paranoid about controlling the setting, worried about

Murphy's Law, because if something can go wrong it probably will. Candidates must eliminate the passive approach and seize the setting. . . make it your own. I literally mean that – candidates must make the physical setting most advantageous for the speech through direct and strategic decisions and adjustments about every significant aspect of it. Rather than simply accept decisions made by others, speakers must become more aggressive in altering the setting to suit the needs of the speech!

Here are some things to think about.

First, one or more of the campaign staff must perform advance work. Controlling the setting becomes part of their job.

Second, make the backdrop more favourable. Find out about the backdrop. Get a photograph if possible. This will allow the candidate to know the message displayed behind the speech. Make sure that message is consistent with the speech itself. There have been many speeches where the backdrop actually contradicted the message of the speech. The campaign should consider changing any backdrop to better emphasise its own message. That backdrop can be creative. It doesn't have to be a waving flag or a dot.com address. It can be a photograph, an emblem, a slogan. It can be anything. It can also be nothing. . . a neutral, solid black or blue. The point is to make sure it is what the candidate wants, not what someone else outside the campaign thinks the candidate wants. And the candidate should dress to stand out from the backdrop, to look good, to offer a sharp and compelling visual. One famous comedienne for whom I wrote came to a ballroom to be filmed. Her dress was exactly the same pattern and colour as the backdrop. When she stood in front of it her body was gone, with only a head and hands remaining. She looked out at me and said: 'Always tell someone about the backdrop.' Good advice, that.

Third, get the right podium. Perhaps buy a proper podium and lug it to events. The podium anoints you as the speaker. It is a functional tool to hold a manuscript and a symbol of your task to be the speaker, to be the expert or advocate for a position or party. The podium may also display a logo or emblem of office or a message on the front. So there must be some thought about the podium.

Just as a church has a pulpit or a teacher a desk, this is where the candidate will work from, the place that makes us different from the audience. It is a tool of the trade. Get the right tool for the job. There are podiums of every shape and size. Some are wooden poles and planks from another era. Some are so technologically advanced you need an instruction manual. There are thousands of possibilities in between. My advice is to get a podium that will adjust to height, will look good in a photograph, allows the candidate enough room for work, and gives the candidate control of technology, such as the microphone or the Powerpoint remote.

Fourth, use a microphone that makes the voice sound good. Speaking of microphones, they are not all equal. There is vast variation. Some make a candidate's voice sound deep and rich, like Darth Vader. Some raise the voice, making the candidate sound like a heavy metal rocker hitting those falsetto notes. Some microphones make the sound muddy, others clear. The campaign needs to know which brand, style and make of microphone works best for the candidate. That comes with trial and error. Ask around. Get some professional advice. With each microphone the speaker will have to discover how to use it and what it can do. The speaker needs to know whether to speak across it or right into it, or whatever. This search should extend well beyond the fixed microphones for the podiums. Look into clip-ons and headset models, too. When you find the one that works, insist on it for all the candidate's speeches. Obviously, the sound system in each room will vary. Know the capabilities and performance quality of the sound system in use. The candidate will want to have the right microphone that provides the best overall sound quality, with 'quality' defined as the best presentation, in your view, of the candidate's voice.

Fifth, fix the lighting. Recently, one of my clients was scheduled to speak before a large audience. The day before I went to the room and tried out the podium. When the lights came on I could not see anything. I couldn't see more than two feet in front of the podium. The lights were blinding and created a wall of glare. I spoke to the events people, who replied: 'Well, we have to illuminate the speaker so everyone can see him.' Yes, the lighting people do have that task. But the solution to their problem is not to create a visibility problem for the speaker. So the lights had to be configured in a new way. Many speakers complain about lighting that blurs the manuscript. That needs to be fixed beforehand. Some lighting is too 'hard', making the speaker look too old, weary or wrinkled. Some celebrities bring their own lighting people to interviews and speeches, replacing the usual bulbs to produce 'softer' lighting that makes their skin glow and look younger. That is good control of the physical setting.

Sixth, mind the gap. There is space between a speaker and the listening audience. Make sure it is the right amount of space, close enough for connection without violating any territorial imperative. Think of the back row as well as the front row. How close is too close? At this moment, the trendy answer is to place the speaker among the audience, the 360 look, creating an image of intimacy and contact. When the audience is all the way around, it gives a backdrop of people. But such a backdrop makes eye contact tough, and can be claustrophobic for everyone, speaker and audience. Make sure the trade-off is worth the cost.

Seventh, understand the room. Where should the speaker stand so the audience can see the best? Move the podium there. If there is no microphone, find the acoustic 'sweet spots' where the voice sounds best. The candidate must speak from there. Where will the cameras be placed? Do they have a good visual angle to get their pictures? Alter the setting to give the photographers what they want. Where will the media be seated? The candidate must look often in that direction during the speech. Show concern about them. And, of course, know how to get in and out of the room. Nothing is more pathetic than a speaker who cannot find their way out of the room.

This list is abbreviated. There are many more worries about the physical setting. See it beforehand. Study the setting. Make decisions that empower the speaker. Don't let others make key decisions without consulting the campaign. Change the setting to best suit the needs of the speech. Control the setting; don't let it control the candidate.

Preparing the manuscript

Some speakers are naturally gifted. But most of us need to work at it. A great speech requires more than composition, audience analysis and memorable prose. Often successful public speaking is a matter of the preparation of the manuscript. Murphy's Law is at play too: if something can go wrong, it will. So in an effort to improve delivery and to avoid mistakes, here are some ideas about the delivery manuscript, the actual text in front of the speaker during the speech.

First, increase the font size of the text. Typically a draft speech in preparation is constructed and circulated in 10–12 point size. Yet, for delivery, the font size in the manuscript should be much larger, between 22 and 36 points. This allows for easy viewing of the manuscript, which in turn allows for more eye contact and fewer verbal gaffes. If the speaker is squinting to see the manuscript or has to break away from eye contact to read the text more closely, then the font size must be increased in the manuscript. Personally, I like the size of the text to be around 22 point. It allows me to see the text very well, even if I walk a couple of steps away from the podium.

Now, think of what this means to the speaker standing at a podium, the speech 2–3 feet away, speaking to a room full of people. The speaker wants to persuade the audience to adopt an action or belief, or to vote in a particular way. The speaker should be reacting to the feedback, fine-tuning the language to the atmosphere of the room, gesturing meaningfully, sometimes walking away from the podium, leaning forward, moving back, searching every face, sensitive to each person in the audience, and making adjustments in eye contact and emphasis. The speaker doesn't need to complicate matters by reading small print or losing the thought in the manuscript. The speaker needs the words to pop out in a user-friendly fashion. When a speaker cannot see the words then the problem is self-inflicted, rhetorical stupidity. It is easily avoidable. But some speakers are so lazy or stubborn that they fatally doom the speech because they cannot read the text for persuasive delivery.

Yes, larger print size does mean more paper. But the trade-off is worth it because the speech is delivered more fluently, which should mean more effectively. If the speaker thinks that 22 point is too large (or too small) then experiment until you find the right text size. And that means the right size at the podium, not while formatting the speech in the office or using a portable printer on the road. Each speaker needs to find the text size that works best in the action of delivery itself, not what looks good before the action starts. I have found a hesitancy to use more paper until disaster strikes. Then speakers get religion about font size. Why not preclude problems with a preventative approach that includes font size?

Second, increase the spacing between lines. Create space between lines of larger text. Some speakers like double spacing, which is what I recommend, although I know some speakers who triple space. Again, the reason for this is to create more ease of viewing the text during the speech.

Obviously, increasing the size of text and spacing between lines invites use of shorter words and shorter sentences. One of the great advances in public speaking in the twentieth century was the use of more concise sentences. Compare speeches from the eighteenth and nineteenth centuries with those given today. Look at speeches by William Pitt the Younger or William Gladstone, both great speakers, and both speakers who typically liked to use punctuation to string together epic sentences that never seemed to end, although often it looked like they might, but such expectations were merely an illusion, a mystery of missed opportunities, savaged by the need to speak more profusely and stretch out the allotted time (just like this sentence). Even our verbally generous speakers today would be hard pressed to maintain the long sentences of the past, although there are some modern speakers who need to learn the value of concise language. Shorter is better. It is certainly better for the text of the delivery manuscript.

Third, use only two-thirds of the page. Every part of every page is not equal. The top is better than the bottom. With each line that gets closer to the end of the page the speaker sacrifices eye contact and lowers the face to better read the lines at the bottom. In order to maintain eye contact the speaker must avoid bobbing the head up and down. Also, the speaker has to breathe. Bobbing the head contributes to a cut-off of air-intake while speaking. So, many speakers only use the top two-thirds of a page. Good idea. This allows them to keep their head level and to better co-ordinate the reading of the manuscript with eye contact.

Fourth, end each page with a complete sentence. If the idea in preparing the manuscript is to increase the effectiveness of the speech, then the sentences must flow. If the sentence is interrupted by the. . . turn. . . of. . . a. . . page, and the continuity of thought is lost, then the speech starts to lose its effectiveness. Avoidance of such an interruption can be easily addressed, pre-empted, by making sure that each page ends with a complete sentence, not merely a fragment or a clause.

Fifth, place page numbers on the top right-hand corner. Amazingly, with page numbers at the bottom of the page, many speakers don't pay attention and then miss a page as they move on. Equally amazingly, the audience rarely realises this because the speeches are usually so muddled that clarity has been lost long before such a mistake. But if one really cares about the message and wants the audience to listen, then page numbers should be in a place of prominence (top better than bottom) and usefulness.

Sixth, underline or highlight the key words in each sentence. The underlining helps the speaker to remember to emphasise certain words. Such emphasis can assist to make the sentence livelier. A sentence without emphasis is sterile. Delivering a sentence with no emphasis on key words is reading, not speaking. One of the great gifts of Reverend Jesse Jackson in his prime was his tremendous ability to emphasise words, sometimes even adding syllables or stretching out the endings. Tony Blair has the ability to change rate, volume and emphasis from word to word, while most great speakers only do this sentence to sentence, and bad speakers use little or no emphasis at all. Underlining can help. It can work wonders for some speakers.

Here is an example with one possible interpretation from the 'Iron Curtain' speech by Winston Churchill in 1946:

The <u>Dark Ages</u> may <u>return</u>, the <u>Stone Age</u> may return on the gleaming wings of science, and what <u>might</u> now shower immeasurable material blessings upon mankind, <u>may</u> even <u>bring</u> <u>about</u> its <u>total</u> <u>destruction</u>. <u>Beware</u> I say; <u>time</u> is plenty <u>short</u>. Do not let us take the course of allowing events to drift along before it is <u>too late</u>.

That is just a sample of what one might do. The emphasis could be different for each speaker; idiosyncratic and personal. It could be placed on proper names, verbs or direct objects. Each choice dictates the way the audience hears the speech. Consistency might be helpful to forming patterns that construct listening habits for the audience. Underlining might also be helpful for difficult words or facts. Some speakers like to underline or highlight proper names or statistical facts. It helps them to get the words right during delivery.

Seventh, structure pauses in speech for better control of rate. In his Inaugural Address John Kennedy confronted a very tricky passage near the end. Successful delivery required great understanding of the text. Here are the words:

> Now the trumpet summons us again – not as a call to bear arms, though arms we need – not as a call to battle, though embattled we are – but a call to bear the burden of a long twilight struggle, year in and year out, 'rejoicing in hope, patient in tribulation' – a struggle against the common enemies of man: tyranny, poverty, disease, and war itself.

That passage requires some directions about how to pause in order to maintain the coherence of the idea. Remember, the audience does not have the text. So people in the audience need verbal cues to help guide their listening. Some speakers like to engineer the pausing in the speech, using a method called the 'Slash' or 'Diagonal' (it looks like this: /). They put the 'slash' in between words to help remind the speaker to pause. Typically the 'slash' is used in place of hyphens or at the end of sentences and paragraphs. But it can be used for more than pausing in those circumstances. The 'slash' can be used to indicate pausing anywhere it would be effective for the listening audience: commas, prepositional phrases, using the conjunction 'and' or the disjunction 'or', giving a list of reasons or names, or for emphasis to allow an audience a few seconds to think about what has been said. Using the 'slash' method, the passage might look like this on the delivery manuscript:

> Now the trumpet summons us again // not as a call to bear arms / though arms we need // not as a call to battle / though embattled we are // but a call to bear the burden of a long twilight struggle / year in and year out / 'rejoicing in hope, patient in tribulation' // a struggle against the common enemies of man // tyranny / poverty / disease / and war itself. ///

Try giving that passage out loud without pausing, guided by the hyphens and the punctuation. It would be incoherent. But it can be understood with guidance from the 'slashing.' The important thing is to know when to pause and for how long. Each 'slash' is one unit of pausing, for example one second for some speakers. Once a speaker becomes used to the 'slash' method of pausing, the speech itself becomes composed of words and pausing, or, in my mind, words and silence. The pausing is built into the speech.

By the way, this method is better than actual stage directions, which often confuse the speaker or sometimes are even said inadvertently, such as the speaker saying, 'In conclusion, pause two seconds, I would like to remind the good people of London that. . .' Disaster!

Anticipate problems and prevent them. The extra effort to prepare the manuscript is worth it. One bad speech is more than momentary failure; it can cost a job, end a career, or stop a policy from being adopted. A poorly prepared manuscript just might be the difference between success or failure at the ballot box on polling day.

Years ago, an American cabinet member was giving a speech at Mt Vernon, the home of George Washington. The speech was outdoors and it started to rain. Drop by drop, the water started to wash away the ink on his manuscript. Soon, rivulets of black flowed down the paper; the speech washed away, the soggy pages blank.

Murphy's Law: if it can go wrong, it will. Plastic covers and a binder could have saved the speech. A good speaker is always thinking ahead, using imagination to anticipate problems, and then acting to avoid them. Over time, speakers confront the unexpected in a speech. But prepared speakers prevent problems.

Effective speechwriting

Most political speeches are instantly forgettable. They are the equivalent of sound and fury, signifying absolutely nothing at all. They fill the air with words and take up space and time. Yet, they move no one, only demanding the patience and loyalty of party.

But some speeches transcend the moment, remain in the memory, becoming part of history. They may be given in a great hall or a humble classroom, heard by millions around the world or by an audience counted in single digits. They do something.

Every great political speech fulfils the task of persuasion. In fact, that is how a political speech may be judged, by its persuasive effectiveness. Did it convince the audience to vote in a certain way, or to adopt a new attitude on taxes or government services? Did it make an audience support a piece of legislation or initiate an action? A great political speech must do more than energise the base or reinforce previous beliefs. A great political speech changes the audience; it changes the world.

So a great political speech is more than an essay or collection of words. It is language in action, language as action. It shows that the speaker is a leader and an authority on the subject. It also advances the debate on the issues discussed. And a great political speech unites an audience around a point of collective agreement.

It does this by presenting a persuasive argument, making a case for a person, belief, philosophy or action. As an argument, it requires proof and reasoning, leading to a conclusion. So it does not conform to the standard plot of a speech learned in communication courses: tell them what you will say, say it, and then tell them what you said, winning virtue with circularity. Rather, it is more direct and economical, starting the persuasive enterprise with the first sentences, stating a thesis, developing that thesis as an argument, and then inspiring the audience with a conclusion that demands immediate results. The goal is to channel the thinking of the listening audience to a point of agreement with the action steps proposed later in the speech. The speech development increasingly narrows the scope of thinking to the point of the action steps.

A great political speech starts quickly with few acknowledgements and restrained appreciation. By using principle, historical context, great thoughts or a statement of purpose, a political speech wastes no time. It gets right to the point. It has to do this because an audience wants content and involvement right away, not the slow and crunching list of thanks and names that takes away momentum and interest.

In fact, the best political speeches in our time are front loaded. Studies show that audiences make quick decisions about the character, likeability and credibility of a speaker within seconds. And some studies show that audiences lose interest within seconds. So a smart strategy is to give the audience a reason to listen for thirty seconds, and then give them another reason thirty seconds later, and keep up that pace of measuring audience interest throughout the speech. Perhaps the best way to approach a speech is to ask this question: what do I have to say that will interest an audience, measured in thirty-second increments?

A great political speech is always audience centred. The audience is sitting there thinking 'What's in it for me?' The speech has to answer that question. It cannot be about posturing for the speaker or self-absorbed comments about the speaker's life or pleasures. The speech must be about the audience, showing a concern for each member of the audience that demonstrates respect, regard and concern, without pandering or begging. A political speech starts to become effective and successful by framing the content in terms of the audience. A political speech is always, always, always about the audience. Therefore, audience analysis is vital. The speech will be constructed based on information about the demographics, beliefs and needs of the audience.

So, before anything else takes place, find out everything possible about the audience. That is 'Job One.' What does the audience want?

How can the speech meet their expectations? Those questions must be answered. Understanding the 'psychology' of the audience is vital to the persuasive element of the speech. In fact, persuasion cannot take place without some knowledge of the way the audience thinks.

Once key information is obtained about the audience the speechwriting process can begin.

Here is a progressive checklist that can be used to construct the speech.

First, the speaker should acknowledge key people and the sponsors. Limit this list. If a number of people need to be mentioned, generalise if possible.

Second, the speaker should tell the audience the purpose of the speech. This should happen at the start of the speech, within the first 30 seconds. This thesis statement is the thread running through the speech, enabling the audience to understand the speech, even if something is missed or the audience periodically loses interest. The thesis statement should be a clear, short, memorable declarative sentence, usually no more than six or seven words, such as 'We must lower taxes' or 'The National Health System must be fixed'.

The thesis statement is indispensable. Many speakers are so wrapped up in themselves that they forget the power of simplicity for an audience, the people who are trying to follow along without a script, for whom the speech is a new experience, revealed at that moment, sentence by sentence. A short thesis statement vastly increases the ability of the audience to understand and follow the speech as it unfolds. This must happen at the start of the speech.

The thesis statement then frames the speech, which now will flow out of it. That's right. . . a great political speech flows like a river out of the thesis statement, gaining point and purpose as the words and ideas spread out, channelled and directed by the development of the argument proving the thesis.

So, third, the speech should be developed as a persuasive argument. This gives point and purpose to every paragraph, every sentence, and even every word. Each paragraph further develops the argument of the speech. That is why the paragraph is there, to do that very thing. Each new paragraph takes the argument further, expands and extends the original thesis statement. Such an approach gives unity and cohesion to a speech, linking paragraphs together and moving ideas forward. Such an approach also allows for an expedient decision rule: if the paragraph doesn't develop the argument, cut it. If the sentence within the paragraph doesn't help develop the argument, cut it. If the word is not doing a job that helps persuasively to develop the argument, cut it.

In the development of the argument, let simplicity govern the construction. The speech should contain short, clear sentences, usually with one-syllable words. A quick look at the most famous speeches, such as Jesus' Sermon on the Mount, Abraham Lincoln's Gettysburg Address, or Churchill's 'Blood, Toil, Tears and Sweat' remarks, would show simple speeches, with short sentences or short phrases, and simple, one- or two-syllable words. John Kennedy's masterful, compelling and quotable speeches are models of the strength of simplicity. His Inaugural Address shows this: 70 per cent of the words are one syllable. Yet that speech is one of the most complex and inspiring arguments ever made.

The word choices in a speech demand special attention, especially the pronouns. Great political speeches unite and heal, they don't tear apart. That means there must be use of inclusive language, such as the pronouns 'we' and 'us'. This unifying language is how the speaker becomes the voice of collective assent, joining with the audience, making the speech an act of union. Divisive language, especially language divisive along the lines of nationality, gender, race, class or income, polarises, creating an 'us v. them' environment, which is dangerous in an election and deadly for governance after an election. Great political speeches are language in action, and should be used to bring people together, not drive them apart.

Word choices can do more than develop an argument; they can capture it. Great political speeches have organic sound bites, places where the message is condensed and stated in a way that compresses the entire speech. Kwame Nkrumah spoke of Ghana's liberation as 'the motion of destiny'. John Kennedy's *Ich bin ein Berliner* is a fantastic display of one sentence expressing the whole point of the speech. Earl Spencer's comment about Princess Diana as 'the most hunted person of the modern age' abbreviates the speech in a haunting sentence.

Examples help. They humanise the abstract. Use of a good example becomes a way of telling a story or offering an instance that proves a point. Audiences relate well to examples, often thinking 'Oh, I know someone who did that' or 'There, but for the grace of God, go I'.

Also, great speeches almost always have a vision of the future. They compare a known present with a possible future. Those that persuasively articulate a better future help people visualise, then actualise, change. One of the most famous examples is Ronald Reagan's constant reference to the 'Shining City on the Hill', a future where America remains a beacon of hope for the world. Dr Martin Luther King, Jr had a dream he shared with others: 'With this faith we will be able to transform the jangling discords of our nation into a beautiful symphony of brotherhood.' Margaret Thatcher said: 'Let me give you my vision: a man's right to work as he will, to spend what he earns, to own property, to have the state as servant and not as master – these are the British inheritance.' When George Herbert Walker Bush was criticised for not having a vision, the 'vision thing' became more than an issue. Its absence was fatal. Vision is more than platitudes. It gives the audience hope and a way to a better future.

Fourth, after developing the argument of the speech, after the audience has been brought to a point of collective agreement that something should be done, then the speaker must explain the solution in clear, workable steps. The speaker must outline the action that must take place, explaining what each member of the audience must do, what the audience must do together. The speaker should show why these action steps or attitude changes are practical, advantageous and desirable.

Fifth, the conclusion should follow right away. It answers the question 'When should we do all this?' The answer: right now, immediately, urgently. Delay is fatal. The conclusion is the place to ramp up the enthusiasm, providing a powerful, inspiring, motivational ending to the speech.

What should be the length of a political speech? Be brief – shorter is a lot better. Time is valuable. Audiences have short attention spans. This is another set of reasons for a political speech as argument, a condensed and simple message that flows, rather than a ponderous and puffy speech that is fattened prose. A speech is not a movie or a concert, although some politicians want to make speeches into 'events', like a hippie happening. A serious and credible political speech should be no more than 10–15 minutes, 20 on the outside. Then open it up for questions. Don't ever keep an audience for more than an hour. Again, shorter is better, so a speaker should not waste time. Keep the event moving. It is better for the audience to want more and be a bit unsatisfied than for them to be sitting there hoping the speaker will shut up.

A great political speech should be bold, within reason. Qualifications, hedging and hesitancy all take the life out of speech prose. They kill a speech, draining it of its life force. A speech must be bold to change the world!

A great political speech is more than an essay. It is writing for oral delivery. One expert has said that speechwriting is 'for the mind's ear'. The evaluation of speechwriting is how the words will sound with the voice, not necessarily how they look to the eye. That is why speechwriting is a unique form of writing, judged by its own standards. A successful political speech must be effective. It must be persuasive. It must unify. A great political speech must demonstrate leadership and vision. And if it can do all this, then a political speech can make a difference, become part of the current discussion of issues, and become a part of history. A great speech moves the audience and stays with them, achieving a kind of immortality.

Effective delivery

Cicero said that an orator's power depended on three things: delivery, delivery, delivery. And that thought has been endlessly reworked and ripped off ('education, education, education'). But Cicero's view was based on a lifetime of excellence in masterful rhetorical ability. He knew that delivery could shape circumstances, create a new reality, channel thinking, touch the heart and remake the world. For him, delivery was the key element in a persuasive speech. As a student of rhetoric, he understood that the act of persuasion was a very human interaction between speaker and listener, a very personal exchange of information and trust. In turn, an audience listens to good delivery with more interest and enthusiasm.

But delivery is not just standing up and talking or, worse yet, standing up and reading. Delivery is a sharing of the self, using both the voice and non-verbals, an understanding of the mission and message of a speech, a utilisation of the power of words, and a strategic enterprise that persuades an audience, bringing them to a point of collective agreement, uniting with the speaker, using language to heal division and to create unity in a community. Good delivery is an act of good faith, evidence of preparation, proof that the audience matters.

Delivery is also not acting, although elements of an actor's trade are involved. A typical criticism of Ronald Reagan or Tony Blair was to attack their background in acting. But such an attack entirely missed the point. Both learned key skills from acting: understanding the meaning and use of every word, developing a pleasant and clear voice for projection of language, recognising the power of pausing and the profound impact of the sound of silence, interpreting a writer's words so they become natural and conversational, learning the ability to make a text written by someone else your own, and using delivery to reach out to an audience and become one with them. These are all skills needed by any speaker. Reagan and Blair should be praised for having them, not condemned. The 'acting' criticism somehow suggests insincerity, a masking of self through verbal ability, a practised deception. But an acting background can give a valuable appreciation of language, or, as the actor Richard Burton once said, 'a love of language'.

So good delivery is important, and should be essential, in public life. Sadly, there is often a low bar for delivery, especially in the United States, where good delivery is viewed suspiciously as a trick or an invitation to deception. A few years ago, a British historian wrote an article about rhetoric in the 'Age of the Osbournes', suggesting that Ozzy and Sharon, Austin Powers, and *South Park*'s

Eric Cartman were the real rhetorical models of America. I can think of no sadder commentary. (I'm sure Ozzy would put it more expressively.) I know some speakers who have said they don't want to have good delivery, because it is not 'authentic', 'not who they are'. They proudly embrace verbal mediocrity. However, as Barack Obama has most recently demonstrated with such effectiveness, good delivery can be a powerful, profound tool in the right hands. In my view, speakers with bad delivery are lazy, insecure, frightened or arrogant. Possibly all are true at once. Their frailties are obvious every time they speak, which may explain why fear or some other failing trumps the search for quality.

However, if one wants to be a good speaker, there are five cardinal rules in delivery.

First, a speech is an oral activity. So communication depends, in part, on the quality of voice, clarity, emphasis and richness of timbre.

Second, a speech is both verbal and non-verbal. There are some studies that indicate audiences are more suggestive to the non-verbal, so appearance, clothes, backdrop, and gestures matter. . .perhaps a great deal. They may be the message. Again, delivery includes both verbal and non-verbal messages. That is why the speech begins *when the speaker enters the room*. Already non-verbal messages have begun. Is the speaker confident? Does the speaker's appearance inspire hope and faith? Does the speaker look like a leader? Is the speaker a person of good character? The answers to these questions and more are being transmitted immediately, creating a deep first impression with the audience. The audience is immediately determining likeability, personability, warmth, sincerity, transparency and, most important, trustability. Numerous studies show that, in a conflict between the verbal and non-verbal, the audience will give presumption to the non-verbal. That is why the spoken words and non-verbals must be consistently harmonious. If they are not, the speaker becomes his or her own self-contradiction, resolved by the audience through belief in the non-verbal.

Third, every speech is a persuasive activity. The voice is being used to try to persuade an audience to adopt an attitude, change a belief, undertake an action or make a decision. The voice is a vital element in that persuasion. There is no such thing as a purely informative speech.

Fourth, every voice is different. A great speaker recognises the strengths and limitations of his or her own voice, and works to balance the presentation with complimentary elements, such as good writing or expressive non-verbals. Every speaker has a unique rhetorical persona. Great speakers find the right mix of variables to make a lasting, singular impression. Dr Martin Luther King, Jr had a unique, defining voice. So did Winston Churchill. When you hear the voice you know the speaker. That is the end result of the creation of a unique rhetorical persona.

Fifth, delivery makes a speaking event human. The voice is the thing. It creates emotion, empathy, sadness, joy, love, hate, even hope. Especially hope. The words are important for sharing meaning. But the voice makes the words work, makes the interaction human. Think about listening to an electronic voice in a communication network, not a human voice recorded, but an electronic voice simulating a human voice. It seems alien and makes us angry that we aren't talking 'to a human'.

Of course, the words of a speech set up the delivery. But the delivery makes the words come alive, instantly making a speech three dimensional, an event with shades of grey, depths of meaning and vastly more levels of communication. Without delivery, the speech text remains two dimensional. A wonderful Greek rhetorician named Dionysius once made that point in a very revealing way. He compared Isocrates and Demosthenes and wrote:

> When I read a speech of Isocrates, I become sober and serious, as if I were listening to solemn music; but when I take up a speech of Demosthenes, I am beside myself, I am led this way and that, I am moved by one passion after another: suspicion, distress, fear, contempt, hate, pity, kindliness, anger, envy – passing successively through all the passions which can obtain a mastery over the human mind . . . and I have sometimes thought to myself, what must have been the impression on those who were fortunate enough to hear him?

Indeed, the delivery could have made the speech livelier, vastly more effective. A great speaker knows how to create the right impression at the right moment with word choice and delivery, never sliding into farce, never seeming to act or manipulate. The speaker is letting the words do their job.

Given the importance of deliver, good speaking is a necessary part of political training. Those who excel at it, like former British Prime Minister Tony Blair, Shadow minister William Hague, Israeli Knesset member Natan Sharansky, French President Nicolas Sarkozy, Russian Duma deputy Aleksandr Lebedev, Colorado Representative Diana DeGette or New York Senator Chuck Schumer, are exciting to hear and observe, masterful in their ability. They are persuasive, educational, entertaining, relaxed and congenial. They have likeability, in large measure, because of their communication skills.

So what are the elements of good delivery? Here is a partial list.

First, every political speaker must 'find their voice' – they must know who they are and what they represent. Each politician is symbolically representative of certain messages. In political 'self-help' language, a politician must not try to be all things to all people. But they should not try to polarise audiences either. A political leader become the voice of the audience, giving voice to their hopes, aspirations, dreams, fears, worries and troubles. A good politician will try to unite the audience in common purpose. Personally, I don't think a speaker should pander to an audience. I also don't think a speaker should use wedge politics to polarise and divide an audience. Rather, a political speaker should let the audience see that the speaker is comfortable with message and position.

Second, the speaker should dress appropriately. In other words, dress for success. The speaker will be judged by appearances, everything from tattoos to toe-nail polish, bling to belt. I suggest dressing a bit better than the audience, but don't go over the top.

Third, good posture is important. Credibility is often correlated with posture in the minds of the audience. But a speaker shouldn't be 'stiff assed' either. Comfortable good posture is best. Good posture also sets up a more intimate gesture, leaning forward to show engagement and earnestness.

Fourth, the speaker should maintain eye contact. The audience is watching the speaker's eyes throughout the speech. Real eye contact creates a moment of connection with the audience. I suggest a speaker should try to have three to five seconds of eye contact with each member of the audience (although audience size will ultimately determine whether this ideal can be achieved). In my view, eye contact is the most important non-verbal because of the power of such a connection.

Fifth, the speaker should vary rate and volume. This helps the listening audience stay interested. The changes should be strategic, giving the most impact to the words and ideas in the speech. A speaker should know the point and purpose of every word, and every pause, in a speech. That is how a speaker displays the intelligence behind the words.

Sixth, the speaker should use appropriate gestures. The point of a gesture is to highlight or enhance a message, not overwhelm it. Repetitive or unnecessary gestures create confusion and actually diminish the power of a speech. Gestures should be used with economy to enhance the message.

Seventh, the speaker should employ some limited physical movement. Step away from the podium on occasion. Turn and look at different sections of the audience. Shift your torso. Even take a step closer to the audience. This variety helps with active listening for the audience and helps create a more intimate, dynamic delivery. It also helps everybody stay awake.

Eighth, the speaker should enunciate clearly. A missed word can change the entire message of a speech, causing the audience to hear a different speech than the one given by the speaker. The goal should be complete shared meaning. Imagine the disaster for the message if the 'not' is not clearly heard in the following: 'We must not raise taxes.' The speaker should also project to make sure everyone can hear.

Ninth, the speaker should adopt an appropriate demeanour at the beginning of the speech to signal how the audience should listen. A speaker should set the tone and create the atmosphere for the speech. A joyful face sends one message; a perplexed face another; a sad face yet another. The audience will take cues from the speaker's face, initiating a process of listening. The speaker must make sure the audience is listening in the right way.

Finally, the speaker should stay confident and in control. The audience likes measured confidence. By staying in control the speaker becomes the master of the event.

Cicero was right about the importance of delivery. Good speakers are students of delivery, always thinking and watching, learning and maturing. Good speakers are constantly working on their craft. This has a tendency to create a much more developed appreciation of the human condition, a deeper insight into the lives of others, and a more developed understanding of the self. Far from being a tool of propaganda or a device of deception, good delivery should lead us to a more authentic and aware rhetorical persona. This is why Aristotle and others stressed the importance of character in public speaking. Good character is essential for public trust. Audiences determine character from what they see and hear. The speaker must earn trust and faith through the human interaction of a speech.

Dr John Shosky is a Washington speechwriter

30

Mastering debates

John Shosky

Given their importance, mastering debating skills is a necessary part of political training. Those who excel at it, like Neil Kinnock or William Hague, race ahead of their opponents and marshal arguments that support their viewpoints. Whether in a parliamentary setting or as part of political campaigns, debates can be persuasive, educational, entertaining. . . even decisive. They are also memorable. Many years ago, sitting in the public gallery of Commons, I watched Harold Wilson and Margaret Thatcher go at each other in one of the most exciting exchanges in my experience. It was intense, breathtaking and electric. I thought you could see the sparks. In more recent memory, millions of people around the world have witnessed the outstanding exchanges between Tony Blair and David Cameron. Debates can cut to the core of an issue and expose difference, leading to clarity and understanding. That is why debate is an essential check against tyranny and injustice. It is a powerful weapon for free thought and democratic choice, which is why the free speech of debate is feared, and outlawed, in many countries.

Strangely, few politicians are actually good at debate. For most, it is unnatural, difficult to understand, a source of anxiety and dread. They lack the persuasive ability to carry an audience. Most politicians do not have a good turn of phrase or the ability to condense difficult issues into a comprehensible sentence. Many of them treat debates as nothing more than events for prepared mini-speeches, totally missing the cut and thrust of a direct clash of ideas. Sadly, many are clueless about how to prepare for a debate; others over-prepare and find themselves lost in the details. And some arrogantly, and wrongly, believe that all they have to do is show up, that preparation is unnecessary because their personality and presence will carry them to victory. Because of these problems, and others, many politicians find themselves ill-suited to the format and cautious to engage in the debate.

But these worries can be overcome with a sound strategy of preparation and skilful participation. The following list may be helpful.

First, know the format. Start by finding out everything you can about the event. Be comprehensive. Details are vital. What is the format? What do you know about the room and the podium? What kind of microphone will be used? What do you know about the lighting and the acoustics? Who are the other debaters? What do you know about them? What are their positions on current issues? Who will moderate? What do you know about the moderator? Does the moderator have a favourite? Does the moderator favour one party over another? What media will be present? Where will the television cameras be? Who will be in the audience? Where will your supporters sit? Can the audience participate? Will they be able to ask questions too? These are not trivial or idle questions. The answers are powerful determinants of your success.

Second, prepare thoroughly and comprehensively. You want to be prepared. And good preparation must be comprehensive. There is a right way and a wrong way to prepare. The wrong way is to get too caught up in the small details and lose sight of the big vision. Too much detail is worse than none at all.

Here is a sequence to follow with each argument.

A good debate answer starts with a general statement of your policy proposal, such as 'I am committed to lowering taxes for the middle class'. You start that way because you want the audience to think about an issue along certain pre-determined lines of thought. This first statement of position narrows their thinking right away, enabling you to channel thought towards your desired conclusion. If you don't do this, then the audience's thinking may become confused or derailed. Help the audience by showing them the direction you want to go.

You follow the general statement with a small collection of facts that support your view, maybe two or three factoids. Then you offer up your proposal and show why it will work. Give an example of a real person who will benefit from your plan. Finally, compare your plan to your opponent's, showing how that same person would not benefit, and that this person is typical of those who will be affected by your opponent's plan.

Since most debate answers are limited by time, you should look at your answer as a two-to-three-minute speech that must condense some difficult problems and proposals into understandable, concise and memorable statements. That is part of the trick to debate: finding a way to turn complex discussions into comments that are clear and persuasive.

Now, how to prepare? Begin by writing out every possible question that could come up in the debate, from policy-making to personal preferences. I know some debaters who will put each question on a single page of paper and then index them and file them in a binder for easy reference. Then, as you craft every answer, start with a clear, concise statement of your view.

After the question, write out the answer following the format suggested already. Edit, rework, condense and memorise your answers. But most importantly, memorise your initial statement of your position. That is the most important sentence of your answer.

If you have to ask a question, there is a three-step format: identify the issue, state your opponent's position and then ask the question. Here is an example: 'On climate change, you advocate a higher carbon tax for Edinburgh. Would this have an impact on profitability for local businesses?'

And whether you are asking or answering questions, watch out for loaded or leading questions, such as 'Why would you advocate such a dangerous and provocative response to Islamic fundamentalism?' That question is actually a statement. You need to reword such questions to remove or address such embedded statements. Then answer the question along the lines most favourable to your position.

Third, debate strategically. Don't become obsessed by your opponent or what that person says. Stay on your point. Develop your argument. Keep talking about the debate from your perspective. Don't be led away to debate on your opponent's ground. That is an old trick. . . baiting someone into talking about an issue from another perspective, one that is stronger for an opponent than for yourself. There is a saying in debate, 'If you shift to your opponent's ground, you will lose the debate. If you stay on your own point, you will win.' I believe that is true. . . when you shift away from your own rhetorical ground you will lose.

Think about this from a strategic standpoint. You should choose the strongest rhetorical ground for your position; 'strongest' is defined as that ground which places your opponent on weak ground if the opponent makes the direct opposite argument. Here is an example. You say: 'Air pollution is dangerous to public health.' The direct opposite argument is to deny it, which would be unbelievable to an audience, or to claim that air pollution is good, which is also hard to believe. So, the opponent would probably shift the argument, to claim that you don't know what you are talking about, or that the pollution really comes from France or Ireland, or blustery politicians ('ha ha ha. . .'). Don't be led off your point. Rather, come back to it again and again, and show how your opponent is non-responsive, that you are the serious one who will cut pollution and help the citizens of London breathe better air.

Also, a point once made by Aristotle should be kept in mind: don't debate common ground. In other words, don't debate everything that is said. You and your opponent probably share considerable common ground. So only debate the points in contention and agree on anything that you share in common. This helps keep the focus on the points of contention and helps the audience see your position more clearly with less confusion. Here is an example: 'Yes, we both agree that the situation in Iran is serious. Where we disagree is whether or not to pursue diplomacy through the European Union or the United Nations.'

Fourth, control your non-verbals. This may be the real message of a debate. Some studies indicate that an audience obtains more information about you from your non-verbals than from anything you say. So, establish good and direct eye contact with the audience. If there is a television camera, periodically look directly at it to create the impression of direct eye contact with those watching at home or the office. The audience will be looking at your eyes and mouth, so use the full range of facial gestures (as appropriate): smiles, frowns, surprise or perplexity. Stand upright, relaxed, with good posture to convey confidence and credibility. Use your hands for an occasional gesture to highlight a point. Don't over-gesture because that will become a distraction. Don't grip the podium. I would also recommend that you put considerable thought into the way you look: competent, understated, elegant, successful and tidy.

The audience will look at you to watch your reactions to the other speakers. Remember to keep control of your non-verbal responses. Don't do anything that can be used against you. Don't make any gesture or facial expression that undercut your credibility or likeability. I am convinced that former United States Vice President Al Gore lost to George W. Bush in 2000 because of his arrogant, self-defeating non-verbals in their presidential debates. The Vice President rolled his eyes, loudly sighed during Bush's answers, showed impatience, and was extremely condescending with his head shakes and facial grimaces. It was obvious that Gore couldn't believe Bush was a viable candidate or that his answers were plausible. The cameras caught it all. That means the American people saw it. Gore's attitude was widely debated in the press. And enough Americans were offended by it that those non-verbals surely cost him the election. So don't do anything rude or foolish. Stay focused. Stay on guard. Keep a serious, respectful demeanour when the other debaters are speaking. Your success may depend on it.

Fifth, never lose your cool. Debates are a test of temperament. There is a lot of pressure on the debaters. Aristotle also said that people come to see a speech to assess the character of the speaker. If you are hot headed, easily offended or pushed to anger, unable to remain calm and rational, people will probably think that you lack the temperament for high office. As well, if you say or do anything offensive, the audience will be put off, determined to vote against you. Be polite. . . always. Remain cool and collected. Let your opponent feel the pressure and lose control. My watchwords for debates are these: 'ease and elegance'. Never let them see you sweat or get angry. Show the audience that nothing will get under your skin. You cannot be flustered. And that is why they should vote for you. You can handle the pressure.

Sixth, don't do anything stupid. Many debates are lost because of stupidity. By this I mean that the debater tries to become funny or cute or condescending or randy. When you do this, you take unnecessary, dangerous risks. Sometimes less is more. Avoid unnecessary risks.

Seventh, capitalise on mistakes. When an opponent makes a mistake, seize the moment. Go directly to the mistake and blow it up. Direct the audience's attention to it. Hold your opponent to what he said. Make the mistake an issue. Go for the jugular vein. Clamp on it. And don't let go.

Eighth, spin the debate. Stay confident throughout the debate. Smile often. No matter how disappointed or defeated you feel, never show it. You may think that you only performed at about 30 per cent of your capability. But to the audience you may be doing extremely well. Don't signal to the audience that you are failing in the debate or that you could have done better. If you send a negative signal, the audience may start doubting because your non-verbals signalled to them to do so. Stay confident.

After the debate is over, the media will be looking for commentary and assessment. Your supporters will spin the debate your way by pointing out your virtues and the promise of your proposals. It is vital that you stay confident long after the debate is over, because the spin after the debate may actually determine how it is reported the next day. I have a saying: 'There are two debates – the one before the audience and the one after with the journalists. No matter how you performed in the first debate, you can win the first by winning the second.'

Ninth, lead, don't follow. A debate is an exciting format.

Everything happens quickly. It is easy to become distracted and side-tracked. Mastery of debate requires sound strategy, solid and clear thinking, comprehensive preparation, disciplined presentation, and a good understanding of the arguments as they unfold. You must know where you want the debate to progress, and then lead the audience to that pre-determined end. Don't be led elsewhere. One of the best compliments I've heard from one debater to another is this: 'You were always five seconds ahead of me.' In other words, one debater led the debate and the other followed. Lead the debate to the place you want it to go, persuading the audience that you have the vision, ability and leadership skills to get the job done.

A good debate performance may not win an election by itself, although that has happened. But it can get you closer to a successful election. A bad debate performance has often, more often than not, doomed a candidate. So don't underestimate the format or the results.

Dr John Shosky is a Washington speechwriter

31

Surviving in the studio

Shane Greer

Let's be honest, if you want to be a politician you're almost certainly someone who likes attention. Good news: as a politician or political candidate you're going to get it. Sometimes it'll come from voters asking you questions on the street, sometimes from a journalist who's putting together a piece for the local paper, sometimes from a speech to local residents, and sometimes it'll come in the form of a television or radio interview. For some people, broadcast interviews are like a drug; they simply can't get enough of them. For others, they're a source of fear, nervousness and discomfort. But as a political candidate it doesn't matter whether you fall into the former or latter category; you simply have to accept that you will, on many occasions, find yourself in a radio studio or in front of a television camera.

I'll never forget the first time I found myself in front of a television camera. It was in 2007 and I was taking part in an online political show. The nature of the channel was such that there couldn't have been more than a few hundred viewers (if that), and a fair few of those were most likely made up of my family! Nevertheless, as I sat waiting for the show to go live my nerves were rattling. My heart was beating so fast that I could literally see my tie moving ever so slightly when I looked down. It was terrifying. Thankfully it's not like that any more!

But let's be clear about something: your performance on television or radio could very well make or break your political chances. Get it right and you could win big. Get it wrong and you could find yourself out for the count. Scared? You probably should be, a little. But make no mistake, there are things you can do to improve your chances of success. Let's take a look at some of them.

What to do when a journalist calls

Nine times out of ten your mobile will start ringing (or you'll receive an email) and it will be a journalist on the other end asking you to come on air to discuss X, Y or Z. This is your first opportunity to lay the foundations for a successful appearance. How? By asking the right questions:

1. *What is their name, email address and contact number?* When you get a call on your mobile it will inevitably be from a withheld number. Not very useful from your point of view. By getting their name and contact details you ensure a number of things: (a) if you end up running late for the interview, have to cancel or have any supplemental questions, you'll know who to contact and how to contact them, (b) if you're not happy with how you were treated during the interview (let's say you feel you've been misrepresented) you'll have a point of contact for making a complaint, (c) you now have the details of a useful contact in the world of broadcast media (and in politics, relationships are everything).

2. *Is there a general phone number?* Getting the phone number and email address for your individual contact is great, but the nature of broadcast media is such that they'll often be away from their desk. And if you need to get hold of someone on the show urgently, that can be a real problem. Accordingly, you should also ask for a general phone number.

3. *Where and when?* The last thing you want to do is arrive late or turn up at the wrong studio. Knowing the time and place of your interview is crucial. Time waits for no man, and in most cases neither does broadcast media.

4. *Will it be live or pre-recorded?* If it's live you don't have to worry about being edited; if it's pre-recorded, though, you do. What's more you'll avoid the worst mistake of all: taking part in a live show when you think it's being pre-recorded and then asking if you can start again when you make a mistake during the broadcast – something John Prescott is all too familiar with!

5. *What station and show do they want you to appear on?* Knowing the station is tremendously important. Appearing on BBC News is very different to appearing on Press TV (believe me!): forewarned is forearmed. Knowing what show you'll be appearing on is also important. Different shows have different formats, different audiences etc. The approach you should take on a daytime chat show like *The Alan Titchmarsh Show* is very different from the approach you should take on *Newsnight*. Also, once you know what show it is, you can take the time to watch some previous editions (if possible) in order to get a feel for what it will be like.

6. *Who is/are the presenter(s)?* The importance of this cannot be overstated. Different presenters have radically different styles: some are very easy going and some are hard as nails, some are confrontational and some are very passive. Don't get caught by surprise. As above, once you know the presenter you can take the time to review their style by listening to recent interviews they have conducted.

7. *Who will you be appearing with?* More often than not you'll be interviewed alongside other people and that means you'll be engaging in some form of debate. You need to know your enemy. Always, always, always ask this question. There are two reasons for this:

   a. *On finding out your opponent's identity you may not wish to appear.* An acquaintance of mine was once asked to appear on radio to debate General Pinochet's record. My acquaintance was a supporter of Pinochet and was delighted at the opportunity to defend him. Sensibly though, he asked who his opponent would be and was told it was a woman who had been tortured by the Pinochet regime. He knew immediately that there was no way he could win the debate and declined the invitation to take part.

b. *On finding out your opponent's identity you may be able to uncover information about them which will aid you in the discussion.* If, for example, your opponent is a sitting politician you may find that they've said something in the past which directly contradicts what they're going to say during their discussion with you. You should always research your opponents, you never know what will crop up!

8. *Where will you be during the interview?* Don't assume you'll be in the same studio as the presenter or indeed the other guests. On radio you'll often find that you're sitting in a studio on your own (with the presenter and other guests in various other locations). And on TV you'll find that in many cases you're sitting alone in a small room staring directly into a camera. I always prefer being face to face with the presenter and my opponents, but if that's not the case I like to know in advance; it ensures I'm not surprised when I arrive at the studio.

9. *How long will the interview last?* This is such an important piece of information. I learned this the hard way. One of my first appearances on Radio 5 was on the Richard Bacon show. I'd been asked on to discuss the privatisation of British Rail with renowned transport journalist Christian Wolmar. I, stupidly, assumed that it was just going to be a quick five-minute segment. Imagine my horror when I arrived and was told I would be on with Wolmar for an entire hour! Needless to say I wasn't nearly prepared enough and my performance suffered as a result. Don't make the same mistake I did.

10. *What line do they want you to take?* When a given show is setting up a discussion/debate they naturally want to ensure that their guests will disagree to some extent. For that reason you should make sure that the show's understanding of what you are likely to say tallies with what you actually think about the subject. The last thing you want to do is give the journalist who called you the impression that you misled them. And if your view differs from the view they're looking for, simply turn down the invitation.

11. *What is the format?* Is it a debate, a straight interview with the presenter asking the questions and you answering them, a phone-in discussion, or something completely off the wall? You need to know. Again, forewarned is forearmed.

12. *Will a makeup artist be provided?* Obviously this doesn't matter on radio, but on TV it's crucial. If you'll be appearing from the main studio then chances are a makeup artist will be on hand to get you ready for your appearance (but not always). If you're appearing from a satellite studio (4 Millbank in Westminster for example) though, odds are there won't be a makeup artist. If you discover that a makeup artist won't be provided then you should bring your own makeup. And if you don't know what to bring I suggest doing what I did; have a chat to the makeup artists you do meet to see what they suggest for your skin.

13. *Confirm how you'll be captioned.* Always check that the show has the spelling of your name right and your correct job title. The last thing you want is for the wrong name to appear on the screen (especially as a political candidate!). And job titles can be a nightmare. For example, I'm the 'executive editor' of *Total Politics*, but I often get introduced as the 'editor' of *Total Politics*. Needless to say, there's no way of correcting this mistake live on air without looking like an ass.

14. *Do you have access requirements?* A while ago I was at Sky News and one of the guests appearing after me was an older lady who had some difficulty moving about (a slight problem when the studio, at that time, was up a flight of steps). Thankfully, Sky knew in advance and made arrangements to get the lady to the studio much earlier than normal, thus preventing an embarrassing situation where they couldn't get the guest on air in time. Equally, if you're disabled (perhaps in a wheelchair) make sure to tell the show as they may need to make some additional arrangements to accommodate you.

15. *What are the travel arrangements?* Almost every time the station which has invited you to appear will arrange for a car to bring you to and from the interview. But if a car is provided you should always make sure to check that a return car is also booked; on

more than a couple of occasions I've found myself stranded at Television Centre at 1 a.m. because I hadn't bothered to ensure a return car was booked. And if transport isn't provided you'll want to find out the best way to get to the studio.

Preparing for your interview

Okay, so you've said yes to appearing on the show. Now what do you do? Well, you prepare. But be warned, you won't always have a lot of time between the call asking you to appear on the show and appearance itself. Recently, for example, I received a call from the Stephen Nolan Show on Radio Ulster asking me to take part in a discussion then and there; as soon as I said yes I was literally patched through to the studio, live on air! But don't worry, this doesn't often happen (and when it does, you're usually being invited on to discuss a subject you know very well). In most cases you'll at least have a few hours to prepare. Use this time well. As Abraham Lincoln famously said: 'Give me six hours to chop down a tree and I will spend the first four sharpening the axe.' These are words to live by.

First, as suggested above, make sure you're familiar with the show you'll be appearing on and the presenter who will be interviewing you. That might mean heading to the BBC iPlayer to listen to some recent broadcasts, or perhaps hitting YouTube for half an hour. But you should also take the time to pick the brains of anyone you know who's been on the show previously and/or had run-ins with the presenter. You might learn for example that the presenter in question tends to ask very superficial questions and avoids confrontation. If so, they'll quite likely be open to suggestions on your part for questions they might ask (which will help you shape and frame the discussion!). On the other hand you might learn that the presenter in question thrives on confrontation and engages in deep preparation for each interview they conduct. If that's the case then you know you're in for a fight and can prepare accordingly. And don't forget, impartial though journalists are supposed to be, everyone has prejudices. You may learn for example that the presenter has a friendly relationship with an individual you'll be debating or that they have a record of opposition to precisely what it is you happen to be proposing. Information like this is vital and can make the difference between success and failure in the studio.

Second, once you know who your opponent is, take some time to do some background research. In many ways this is even more important than the point above. As with researching the presenter, make sure to review past appearances by your opponent. Are they aggressive, are they passive, are they prone to fumbling and mumbling, or are they a master in the arena of presentation? For example, if you're debating someone who's particularly passive, you'll want to avoid being overly aggressive as it will likely give the audience the impression that you are little more than a bully. But just because the person you're up against is incredibly aggressive doesn't mean that you should meet them with equal amounts of aggression. If you do that you risk leaving the audience thinking that 'they're both as bad as each other'. Instead you'll want to deliver a firm but reasoned performance. They'll come across as angry, you'll come across as 'in control'.

Then there's the substance. You need to delve into your opponent's past. What have they said previously on the subject? Where have they worked previously? Have they ever been embroiled in a scandal that raises questions about their trustworthiness? A firm grasp of this kind of information can deliver victory into your hands. An example evidences the point. When Sir Digby Jones said that Whitehall could be run with half as many civil servants I was invited onto the Richard Bacon show on Radio 5 to debate Sir Digby's point with the general secretary of one of the trade unions. I didn't agree with Sir Digby that as many as half could be fired without service being affected, but I did think that there was a case with trimming some of the fat. What's more I knew that public sentiment would be on my side. If I kept the debate focused on staffing reductions in Whitehall I knew I would win the debate. Equally though, I knew my opponent would want to move the debate away from Whitehall and suggest that Sir Digby was talking about the civil service as a whole. In particular, I knew my opponent would try to suggest that Sir Digby was calling for as many as half of the UK's frontline civil servants being cut.

Clearly, if the debate moved to this area my chances of winning would be dramatically reduced. Having conducted some research I learned that my opponent's entire career in the civil service had been at the front line in Jobcentres (which meant that my opponent was likely to use this example of the front line to make his point). What's more though, I learned that my opponent's last position in the Jobcentre was part time and that his wage was, as a result, about half that of most frontline Jobcentre workers. Great news! Why? Because if my opponent tried to play the sympathy card about how little frontline workers earn, and used himself as an example, I could immediately point out that he was misleading listeners and that he therefore couldn't be trusted. And that's exactly what my opponent did. End result, he was left spluttering while I shifted discussion back to Whitehall and planted the seed in the mind of listeners that everything my opponent said had to be taken with a pinch of salt. Obviously it's for others to decide whether I won the debate, but for what it's worth I'm certain that I did. The lesson is clear, to beat your enemy you need to know your enemy.

Third, whatever subject you're going on to talk about, make sure you understand it thoroughly. This might sound obvious, but it's astonishing how many times I've locked horns with somebody who clearly didn't have a firm grasp of the subject we were discussing. Don't be that person. If you don't know the subject thoroughly you're much more likely to get caught out. Additionally, a deep subject knowledge enables you to spot weaknesses in your opponent's position and equips you to exploit them. Thankfully, conducting research is easy in the age of the internet. As a candidate your first port of call will likely be your party's policy papers and speeches. These are a wealth of information and statistics that will support your position. But it won't hurt to go further, particularly as a political candidate. Let's say you've been invited onto your local radio station to debate your party's latest proposal on the economy. For sure, party policy papers will help you make your case but they will only do so in an abstract way. They'll talk about national statistics, about the billions which will be saved and the thousands (or maybe millions) of people who will benefit. To really strike a chord with the audience you need to humanise the abstract, and that means expanding the scope of your research. For example, let's say your policy is designed to benefit single mothers. If that's the case you should start speaking to single mothers in the area about your policy, and find one who supports it and who's happy to do so publicly. During your appearance you should draw attention to that individual, tell the audience about her circumstances, about how she's struggling, about the specific difference your policy will make to her and, crucially, why she supports the policy. Do this and victory will come much more easily.

One source of information that I've always found tremendously useful when preparing for discussions on television and radio is think tanks. Indeed it was thanks to a think tank, the Adam Smith Institute, that my debate with Christian Wolmar on Radio 5, highlighted above, wasn't a complete disaster. Their briefing on the subject of the privatisation of British Rail was worth its weight in gold. As a candidate, think tanks (or rather those think tanks that are more in tune with your party) have a vested interest in currying favour with you. Don't forget, their objective is to see their ideas given life through government policy. So the next time you need a little extra information on a subject outside your area of expertise, give the wonks a call. You'll be surprised how helpful they can be!

Fourth, condense the message. Just because you've taken the time to develop a thorough understanding of the subject under discussion doesn't mean you should simply regurgitate everything you know as soon as you go on air. Verbal diarrhoea does not impress an audience. In the studio, less is more. People can only absorb so much information at one time, and the more information you attempt to squeeze in, the more people are likely to forget. And don't forget, time is also against you; most media appearances are no longer than a couple of minutes. You need to decide what it is you want the audience to take away from your appearance. Is it that your opponent has been dishonest and can't be trusted? Is it that your party's new policy on tax credits will support young families? Is it that only your party can be trusted to deal with knife crime? You need to have a very specific goal in mind when appearing on television or radio. And once you have settled on a goal, you need to identify the two or three points you need to make to achieve your goal (these are the points you want the audience to remember). During your appearance you state these points and repeat them. And then you should repeat them some more. And don't ever be tempted to make more than three points; you'll simply set yourself on the path to defeat. The audience can only take in so much. Let me say it again, less is more.

Fifth, craft a killer sound bite. This is tremendously important. A well-honed sound bite will stick in people's minds for years to come:

> 'Ask not what your country can do for you, but what you can do for your country.'
> 'Education, education, education.'
> 'It's the economy, stupid.'

But your sound bite should be more than just memorable; it should also encapsulate the totality of your argument. The power of an effective sound bite cannot be overstated.

Sixth, a good set of notes will make your life a lot easier. More often than not, when it comes to television appearances you have to cope without the assistance of notes. That means taking the time to memorise statistics, quotes from key figures etc. But radio is a different beast altogether. On radio you can bring in some carefully prepared 'cheat sheets'. But be careful, don't overload yourself with paper; you're only asking for trouble. I recommend no more than two pieces of A4. These pages should include the key points you want to make, statistics you need to be aware of, quotes that support your argument and, crucially, important facts about your opponent.

Seventh, don't leave your travel arrangements to chance. Most times the station on which you're appearing will provide a car to take you to the studio. If that's the case you should always err on the side of caution when indicating what time you will need to be collected. For example, my apartment is about fifteen minutes away from Television Centre, but I always allow at least thirty minutes' travelling time. Better to arrive early than late. And if a car isn't provided you should take the time to familiarise yourself with the route you must take and, once again, err on the side of caution when allotting time to reach your destination.

Eighth, you should never leave your physical appearance to chance. Dressing for radio is easy: most of the time I'll turn up in jeans or shorts (and a T-shirt too, obviously!). But always think ahead. For example, if you've been invited to appear on Radio 5 to discuss a developing story and will be at the studio in Television Centre, there's always a chance that you'll be called to appear on the BBC News channel as well. And something tells me you'd rather not appear on national television in a pair of Levi's and a Hollister shirt! So, if you think there's even the slightest chance you'll be invited to move from the radio studio to the television studio, make sure to dress appropriately.

Thankfully, dressing appropriately for television is very simple. If you're a male candidate it will almost certainly mean wearing a suit. Avoid ones that are solid black, a they absorb light and simply don't look as good on camera. Generally, I wear either a dark blue or grey suit. Whatever you do, though, don't choose a suit with tight patterns (such as a very narrow pin-stripe) as these will strobe and distract the viewer. When it comes to your shirt, you should avoid white, as it can bloom on camera. Instead, opt for a solid colour. As for ties, again I strongly suggest opting for a solid colour or thick stripes. Anything patterned runs a real risk of strobing. But be warned, ties aren't always appropriate. For example, if you find yourself invited to appear on a daytime chat show such as *Alan Titchmarsh*, it's often best to go with an open-collared shirt. As with all things in politics, your dress should reflect your environment (and that might mean ditching the suit altogether!). Regardless of the environment, though, you should never wear anything that could distract the viewer. A classic example is lapel pins; if you're the President of the United States you can get away with it, but for the rest of us it's simply not an option. Why? Because viewers will end up focusing their attention on the badge, trying to figure out what it is. And if they're doing that, they're not paying attention to you. Similarly, be careful when choosing watches and cufflinks. For example, one of my favourite sets of cufflinks comprises a number of crystals. Needless to say, they catch the light (and the eye) a lot. As a result, I never wear them on television.

If you're a female candidate your options when it comes to dressing for television are much wider, but many of the same ground rules apply. Avoid blacks and whites, avoid patterns which will either distract the viewer (floral dresses for example) or which are so tight that they'll strobe on camera. Additionally, though, you should avoid low-cut tops and short skirts, for obvious reasons. And if your outfit doesn't include a jacket or blouse, you must be careful not to wear a top which restricts the ability of studio staff to attach a microphone to you (turtle necks are a big 'no-no'). When it comes to makeup you should go for an understated look. That means no bright lipstick or bright eye shadow, and using a base which is slightly warmer than your skin tone (the orange look is not a winner!).

Candidates, whether male or female, should take care to maintain a tidy hairstyle. Messy hair, even if it is in fashion, will distract the viewer and undermine your performance. Likewise, candidates should take care to remove any traces of dandruff from their person. And if you wear glasses, I strongly suggest investing in a pair of anti-glare lenses. Finally, I always recommend wearing something that compliments your eye colour as it does wonders on camera; your eyes will look much brighter!

It's Game Time

So you've done your preparation and it's time to head to the studio. Are you nervous? Are you worried you're about to make a fool of yourself in front of thousands (or millions) of people? Don't be. There's a lot more you can do to make sure appearance is a complete success.

1. *Arrive at the studio early.* Whether you'll be travelling to the studio via public transport or in a car provided by the station, make sure you leave plenty of time to get there. The last thing you want to do is arrive late or sweating and out of breath

(or both). Aside from anything else, if you're out of breath you aren't going to put in a top class performance; you'll appear shifty and out of control. And if you appear on television with sweat pouring down your face, as Bill Rammell MP did not so long ago, people will question your honesty.

2. *Double-check your name and title.* When you arrive at the studio, make sure to check with the producer that they have your name and title correct, and if you're appearing on television that they've spelt it correctly. The last thing you want if you're a candidate called Shane Greer is to be captioned throughout your appearance as Sean Grear! Moreover, correcting the presenter on air if they get your name or title wrong can prove problematic. As highlighted above, I'm the executive editor of *Total Politics* and often get captioned as the editor. I could correct it on air, but if I did I'd simply look pretentious and vainglorious (at best). When it comes to your name and title, as with so many other things in life, prevention is better than cure.

3. *Dealing with nerves.* I'll be honest, I don't have a silver bullet for dealing with nerves. And if you're new to television and radio the odds are that you will be a bag of nerves. For sure it will get easier with time, but that doesn't help you in the here and now, does it? Nevertheless, here are a few tips. Number one, take time to familiarise yourself with the studio layout and where you'll be sitting. Number two, try to ignore the cameras and microphones, focus instead on the other guest(s) and the presenter. Number three, make sure you've done your preparation thoroughly and know your points like the back of your hand; if you've done this you'll feel a lot more confident. Number four (and I found this was tremendously useful when I started doing media), where possible sit with both hands overlapped in front of you and with the backs of your hands facing forward. When you feel nervous during the appearance simply start to rub the thumb on the hand furthest from you into the palm of the other hand. This might sound silly, but for whatever reason it really does help settle you down.

4. *Most of what you communicate isn't verbal.* A Princeton

University study found that what people take most of their cues from are non-verbals (55 per cent is visual, 38 per cent is vocal and 7 per cent is verbal). What that means is that, in many ways, how you say something and how you move when you're saying it is more important, in terms of winning over an audience, than what you actually say. With that in mind you should exaggerate your movements slightly (by up to 25 per cent), emphasise points with movements of your head, lean forward into discussion (never slouch), smile almost all the time (even if you're being attacked), maintain eye contact with the presenter and other guests (if you're in the same studio), avoiding looking upwards (it communicates dishonesty), gesture with your hands (but make sure to use the hand furthest from the camera as it avoids the possibility of covering your face)... the list goes on. Think about the television presenters and pundits you most enjoy watching and learn lessons from the way they move on camera.

5. *Control your voice.* Work to eliminate 'um' and 'er' from your vocabulary; it sounds terrible and distracts the audience. You should also slow your rate of speech (slower than your normal rate of speech in conversation) to ensure clarity and proper enunciation. And don't forget the power of a pause. Just as in public speaking, a well-timed pause can really help hammer home a point you've just made. Make sure to vary your tone, moving up and down through sentences; you'll sound a lot more interesting and will hold the audience's attention more easily.

6. *Smile on radio.* No, really. Strange though it may sound, if you smile while you're on the radio your voice will sound a lot more positive and upbeat. You'll also find that some performers will hold a smile before they 'go on' as it helps create an internal feeling of positivity that carries through to their performance. Give it a go!

7. *Choose your words carefully.* One of the first people to coach me on media presentation said the following: when you appear on television or radio you have zero per cent control over the questions you are asked and 100 per cent control over the answers you give. Too true. Remember, just because you're

asked a question doesn't mean you have to answer it. Broadcast appearances are battles in which each party (presenter and guests) has an agenda. If you want to win you have to ensure that it's your agenda that dominates. And to do that you need to think carefully about what you say and the words you choose. For example, if you don't like a question you've been asked you shouldn't feel obliged to answer it. Instead, you should transition by using a 'transition line' like 'The real issue here is. . .' or 'What voters really care about is. . .'. That doesn't mean you should ignore every question that comes your way, rather that you should only accept the premise of a question when you are happy with it. Equally, you shouldn't allow your opponent to steer you off course. Just because they level an accusation or ask a question, doesn't mean you have to waste your valuable airtime by addressing it. Instead, brush it to one side and make the points you went there to make. And keep your sentences short. Long sentences, especially ones with sub-clauses, will lose the audience and make your appearance less punchy. And remember: repeat, repeat, repeat. As indicated above, you need to decide which two or three points you want to make during your appearance, then during your appearance you need to repeat them over and over again. If you don't repeat your points you won't cement them in the mind of the audience. But that doesn't mean repeating the same exact sentence over and over again; mix it up, but keep the central message consistent.

8. *Use statistics and humanise the abstract.* As Arthur Christiansen said: 'Always, always, always tell the story through people.' As indicated above, that means humanising the abstract by incorporating real-life examples that support your point. That might mean drawing attention to a local business that faces bankruptcy, or quoting a single mother who supports your new policy. Whatever way you do it, though, always relate the issue you're discussing back to the real world and real (individual) people. But don't shy away from quoting statistics and polls. People love them, particularly if they reflect what they already believe.

9. *Always assume the microphone and/or camera are on.* Far too many politicians have said more than they should when a microphone was on them and they assumed it wasn't recording or wasn't being broadcast. Perhaps the most memorable example in history was when President Ronald Reagan said, while preparing for a radio address, 'My fellow Americans, I'm pleased to tell you today that I've signed legislation that will outlaw Russia forever. We begin bombing in five minutes.' The Soviet Far East Army was placed on alert after a recording of the statement leaked out. Truly, a gaffe of presidential proportions. So, if there's a mic anywhere near you (or you think there's a mic anywhere near you) don't say anything you wouldn't be prepared to say on air. Equally, you should always assume the camera is on, and that extends to always assuming that the camera is always on *you* during your appearance. Just because you think the only person on the viewers' screens at the moment is your opponent doesn't mean you should relax your posture, start to frown or look bored. Remember what was pointed out above. The majority of what you communicate is non-verbal, so for the duration of your appearance make sure you tightly control those non-verbals.

10. *Know when to look into the camera.* If you're sitting in the studio with the presenter then you should maintain eye contact with the presenter and, when appropriate, other guests. But if you're doing a 'straight to camera' interview – where you're sitting in a separate studio from everyone else and have a camera directly in front of you – you should pretend the camera lens is the presenter's eyes and maintain eye contact with it at all times. You may find this difficult at first, and in particular you may find it difficult to maintain a friendly composure on camera, but practice will make perfect. One trick which will help you maintain eye contact and appropriate facial expressions is to pretend that the camera lens is a friend's face. It might sound silly, but it will improve your performance immensely.

11. *Control the setting with Skype.* You may find yourself asked to appear on television via Skype. That will mean sitting in front

of your computer with a webcam and microphone broadcasting your appearance and utterances to the world. If this happens, make sure to pay particular attention to what's behind you. For example, on the wall behind the chair in my office is a massive portrait of Lady Thatcher (yes, I'm a Tory!). Usually there's no problem with that (although my Labour colleagues tend to raise an eyebrow), but when Sky News asked me to appear on a show via Skype I made a point of moving the portrait out of the way. Had I left it in place it's fair to say that the audience would have spent more time considering the portrait than considering what I was saying!

Shane Greer is the executive editor of Total Politics

32

Effective networking

Jonathan Sheppard

It has often been said that 'getting on' in politics is more about who you know, and less about what you know. While you shouldn't completely subscribe to that school of thought, it is indeed a truism that having a good set of contacts and being able to network effectively is an invaluable skill that can only serve to help you in your political career.

If you want to become a councillor, you need to know the people who not only can help you get selected, but then will help you get elected. If you have an ambition to become a Member of Parliament, the same is also true. Even if you are already a Member of Parliament, good networking skills are essential. If your ambition is to lead a political party, do not think for one moment that it could be possible without building political alliances, which can only come through networking.

There are many different aspects involved in networking, from how to 'work a room' at an event to how to engage in small talk. While there are no hard and fast rules, this chapter will provide some advice that will help you to build relationships that will stand the test of time.

Why network?
Networking is part of life. It is just another form of communication

although slightly more formalised and sometimes with an end game in mind. There is nothing wrong with that, but you have to be careful not to make people think you only want to know them because you want something. Building relationships is a two-way process and if you don't bring anything to the table, as with any relationship, it will be doomed to failure.

Personal contacts are very important in all walks of life. How many jobs never get advertised because people hire someone they know, or through a personal recommendation from someone they trust? We have all seen it when a football manager leaves one club and, once in situ in his new club, buys some of his former players. Is that because they are the best players in the world? No. It's more than likely because the manager rates and trusts them. And why does he rate and trust them? Because he knows them. They are personal contacts.

When faced with the known or the unknown, human nature will more often choose the known. Therefore if there is a job on offer, or a contract to be awarded, having that personal contact is highly valuable. Networking is the way to make yourself known and to develop that worthwhile relationship for your future.

Networking at an event

In the world of politics, perhaps one of the most likely places where you will put your networking skills to use is at some sort of event. There are literally hundreds of events, receptions and dinners every year, many of them attended by the great and the good. If you are a prospective parliamentary candidate (PPC) you will no doubt attend events in the area you want to represent. At such events you may well be the star turn. People will proactively come up to you to talk, as they want to know your views. Networking in a situation such as this is easier, as people know you and often you won't even need to make an introduction. But what happens when you aren't the big fish in the small pond? Then you may really need to put some work into your networking activities to get something out of them.

As a PPC you will undoubtedly have been invited to various events at Party Conference. Here you are just one of hundreds of

PPCs. If your objective is to secure the visit of a high-profile MP to come and talk at an association event then you will have to make the first move. You know them. You know what you want. But they may have no clue as to who you are.

One of the biggest fears people give about attending an event is 'I won't know anyone'. The easiest solution is to take someone with you. If you take a friend you'll have someone to talk to and won't feel so self-conscious, but don't spend the whole evening talking to them!

Approaching a group

When you are going to an event there is always the dilemma of when to arrive. Turn up early and you could feel awkward, as you will be the first one there. But arriving fashionably late often means groups have already formed, and it can feel really daunting trying to approach people already deep in conversation. If you are nervous at approaching pre-formed groups you may be advised to turn up to an event early. Then if you are one of the first there the onus may well be on others to approach you to start a conversation. Of course that is not always possible, so you will have to prepare for what you will do if people are already in conversation in groups.

When groups have already formed, part of the skill of networking is judging body language. If the group is closed and very much in deep conversation, steer clear. If a member of the group makes eye contact or smiles, then go and introduce yourself. There is no substitute for shaking hands and doing some basic introductions. The person you have just said hello to will very likely do all the hard work for you and introduce you to the rest of the group. Suddenly you have become part of the group. If you know someone that is part of a large group then even better. Go and say hello to them and the natural course of events will mean they will introduce you to others in the group. Having someone make introductions for you is particularly useful. They may well know someone else at the event who could be chatting to someone elsewhere and you could ask them to make a further introduction to a new group.

Where groups are concerned it is essential that you put your inhibitions to one side. Yes, it can seem intimidating, but the worst thing that can happen is that the conversation does not flow. If you are confident in how you present yourself, breaking into a group can be extremely easy.

Breaking into conversation

Breaking into a conversation always seems hard to do the first time you do it. Initially you could consider approaching a couple rather than a big group to start with. Approaching an individual can be hard if the conversation doesn't flow. When two people are already chatting it should be less daunting to go over and say hello, and if you suddenly dry up, they will keep the conversation going. There are always some easy things you can talk about. Go over and tell people who you are. It could go along the lines of 'Hello, I'm ——, I work at ——'. Then ask them to reciprocate. Ask them their name. What do they do? Why are they here? Have they been to one of these events before? Asking questions is a good way of getting a conversation going. Why not have three or four topical news stories in your head so that if the conversation slows you can say 'Did you see so and so?' or 'What do you think about that story?'. Not only will it keep the conversation going, but it will show you are up to date with what is happening in the world. So make sure you go prepared!

Don't worry if the talk doesn't flow the first time you attempt to break into a conversation. This is one instance where practice really does make perfect. Of course you may find yourself talking to someone who actually isn't that interesting so, no matter how good you are at breaking into a conversation, nothing much is said. What better excuse to try breaking into another conversation somewhere else in the room and to try to refine your technique? You must have been to an event and seen someone seemingly effortlessly glide from one group to another being able to break into conversations at the drop of a hat. What did they do that seemed to work? Try to emulate it. The biggest asset you have is your confidence. If you have the confidence to go up to someone then there is nothing stopping you. Why not practise making introductions with a friend? At first it will seem strange but by trying different ways to approach someone and say hello you will eventually find a form of words or tactic that you're are comfortable with.

Working a room

When you are networking you often have a limited amount of time. If you are at a selection meeting and need to meet all the people who are eligible to vote it is imperative that you are able to work the room. This means not only making sure you talk to everyone but having the confidence to end one conversation and move on to the next. If you aren't able to do this you could end up not speaking to all the people you really need to, which could be detrimental to your objective of getting selected. Always be polite, but don't be afraid to say something like 'It's been lovely talking to you but I must speak to Mr Jones' or 'I know Councillor Smith wanted a word', as that's the art of good networking.

If you are at a selection meeting and your partner, husband or wife is there, why not split up? You can each go round the room from a different direction and cover twice the number of people in the same time. They should be your greatest advocate, and if they meet someone who needs to speak to you directly they can beckon you over. Another piece of advice is to make sure you don't reject a possible contact too soon. I've lost count of the times I have started a conversation I didn't think would result in a useful contact, only to discover a mutual business or political interest after a few minutes.

That person who you thought would be irrelevant to your political campaign may be lined up to be the next association chairman, or may know someone who might want to donate to the campaign. Make sure you don't dismiss people out of hand too soon, as it could well be to your detriment.

The worlds of politics and business can often be very similar. In both it isn't just about who you know, although knowing the right people can often be helpful. If you can learn to enjoy networking it can help you socially, politically and even in business. Instead of looking for excuses as to why you can't network or why you don't want to, give it a go!

There are some helpful dos and don'ts that will make your networking activity both fun and ultimately rewarding.

Dos and don'ts

› Don't hide in the corner of a room and expect people to come to you. Do be prepared to introduce yourself. Remember – many people will be just as nervous as you.
› Don't fall into the trap of believing that successful networking is all about how many contacts you get at an event. A quality conversation with a few people can be far more valuable than exchanging business cards but little else with everyone in the room.
› If there is a political 'big name' at an event, don't just focus your efforts on them. They will undoubtedly meet lots of people and may not remember you. Instead make sure you have a target list of other people you also want to meet.
› When you are actively networking, try to make an introduction to a select bunch of people. Don't just talk about what you do, ask them open questions, so that they can tell you all about themselves. They will feel you took a real interest, and are likely to want to build up the initial contact.
› Remember that everyone you speak to could well be an important contact. Don't ignore certain people because you don't think they would be a good contact. You never know what or who they know, and how useful they could be.

At the end of the day everyone has their own style of networking and there are no hard and fast rules. It should come naturally and not feel forced. But one thing that you cannot do without is preparation and groundwork. Plan exactly who you want to meet and what you want to get out of a networking event. That way you get the most out of what is often a limited amount of time. If it is essential to meet as many people as possible in a room then some tips on 'working a room' will come in handy.

Finally you should never forget that even if you have a specific objective with regard to networking, be it to make a new business contact or to get to know someone, networking should be fun. It is all about communicating in a social setting, so go out and enjoy yourself. Happy networking!

Jonathan Sheppard is a political advisor

33

Your first six months

Your first six months as a councillor

Louisa Thomson

I was elected in a by-election in Hackney in January 2009. I had previously worked at the Local Government Association so came to the role with some prior knowledge of local government. I also live in the ward I represent. Naively, I thought that this would help me in the first six months of being a councillor – but no matter how prepared you think you are, it has a massive impact on your life, and you quickly realise that one of the biggest myths circulated by people who are trying to get you to stand as a candidate is 'it only involves one meeting a month'.

A year later – do I know how to make a difference as a local ward councillor? What did I learn from those first six months?

Get an induction at the town hall
I got elected at the peak of a snowstorm and in the middle of an electoral cycle. As a result, I never had a proper induction, and very basic things like a council laptop were a frustratingly long time coming. It would have helped me in those first few months to know or have access to: meetings with directors of council departments; what work was already underway or planned in my ward; and different scenarios where you might need information and support

from officers and how to go about requesting this. If you're lucky, these things will be automatic. You don't want an information overload about the inner workings of the Local Strategic Partnership – just a few key tools at the beginning to get started.

Love your ward

Following an election campaign, you will have talked to a lot of residents and picked up many local issues. Now you've been elected you can start delivering on the pledges you made. Being a councillor involves a community, council and political role and the emphasis you put on each will vary at different times. But your ward should remind you of why you wanted to make a difference. You should be obsessive about monitoring and spotting what is happening locally and being accessible to residents (I find my favourite red coat helps, but draw the line at answering my mobile at weekends).

It's a balancing act

I got elected and knew that I would face another election within fifteen months so have found juggling full-time work, the demands of the council and keeping some semblance of a social life one of the hardest things to achieve. You can quickly find evening meetings filling the weeknights, and weekends disappear following up on all the issues that were raised. Be strategic, and recognise that just because you're not at every single meeting you're invited to, the world (or ward) won't come to an end.

Ask for help from political colleagues

I wouldn't have got through the first six months without endless conversations over coffee where I had lists of questions for more experienced comrades. For example, what do you do when you've written countless letters to the council asking for an unsightly bin to be removed. . . only for it to reappear again? Do you give up, or do you call the head of Waste? These conversations taught me always to challenge where you think there's a problem and to be persistent. Change takes time where the bureaucratic beasts of councils are concerned.

Remember you're slightly odd for wanting to do this in the first place
Being a councillor can feel overwhelming, especially in the first six months. It changes your relationship with your neighbourhood – sometimes, I want to just walk down my street without getting angry about dumped rubbish, or be able to come home late at night without an underlying fear that I might bump into the local Safer Neighbourhood Police Team. Be patient, make lists, prioritise. But most importantly, remember to keep the conversations about recycling bins and the new Local Development Framework for council colleagues rather than your normal friends!

Louisa Thomson is a Labour councillor in the London Borough of Hackney

Your first six months as an MLA

John McCallister

The decision to stand as an Ulster Unionist in the 2007 Assembly elections was not one I took lightly. Being 'blooded' two years earlier for a council seat meant that I knew what I was signing myself up to, especially since that baptism of fire coincided with Westminster elections which saw the UUP lose all but one of its MPs. Having made my pitch to my local association, I secured the nomination for the South Down constituency on 18 January, leaving me just seven weeks to run a winning campaign.

Having already faced the electorate with the party at such low ebb taught me many lessons, not least the need for policies that had broad appeal. So I jumped at the chance to join the party's agriculture and rural development policy group. One highly successful initiative was the party's now annual presence at the Balmoral Show, Northern Ireland's premier agricultural showcase. I felt that this provided a unique platform for the party to reconnect with the public. Politicians cannot expect to hide away from voters and a willingness to engage with people on the ground is essential for successful electioneering.

Given the political dynamic at the time of the campaign, one huge obstacle to overcome was the media's reluctance to take our campaign seriously. This meant that the election team had to work especially hard to get our message across on the doorsteps or via telephone canvassing, with the latter allowing us to contact several thousand households in the constituency who might not otherwise have been reached.

In addition to all of this was the small matter of running the family dairy farm, plus the fact that I was scheduled to play the lead in an amateur dramatics production of Sam Cree's *The Mating Season* mid-campaign! Obviously these commitments meant that planning was crucial to ensure the best use of individuals' time; so a good election agent, coupled with advice from experienced party stalwarts, ensured that the operation ran smoothly.

After a successful campaign covering every corner of the constituency and the elation of being elected came the surreal experience of driving up to Stormont for my first day at 'the office'. To say that the first six months working as an MLA is a steep learning curve is an understatement. Striking the right balance between constituency work, making contributions to debates in the chamber, and performing an important scrutiny role on committees is something of an art form. And here too the need for teamwork and planning is a recurring theme. Seeking advice from more experienced colleagues is an invaluable resource and one which I have drawn upon frequently. Ultimately, however, it is best to take time to draw your own conclusions and identify what best suits your own constituency's needs.

With regard to the nuts and bolts of an effective constituency presence, the consideration given to establishing good administrative practices – such as managing a contact database – will pay dividends. I cannot emphasise enough the importance of employing capable staff; quite simply they are worth their weight in gold and knowing that my constituents are in good hands is essential for allowing me to perform my duties.

I strongly believe that no one should regard their particular skills or background as something that disqualifies them from seeking office, since broadening the range of people who seek and hold such positions benefits society as a whole. To be honest, I never really imagined that I would one day sit in Northern Ireland's legislature! However, I have found that my experience gained through my work in the Young Farmers' Clubs of Ulster and my involvement with amateur dramatics, has equipped me with several transferable skills – including the ability to chair meetings and make contributions in the chamber. My own background, though not typical for most politicians, has in fact provided me with much to draw upon and helped me find my feet in those first few months when everything was new.

Life as an elected representative is unique on many fronts. There is no training manual or induction, yet the responsibility placed on your shoulders can be heavy. The job description is non-existent, yet constituents' expectations are high. The demands placed on your time and family life can be challenging but the rewards, in terms of job satisfaction, are substantial. At the end of the day, no matter how frustrating politics can be, we do the job by choice and the sense of satisfaction that can come from helping to improve the life of a constituent makes it all worthwhile.

John McCallister is the Ulster Unionist MLA for South Down

Your first six months as an AM

Eleanor Burnham

As with many other elected positions there is no job description for an Assembly Member, so successful applicants come to Cardiff with a wide variety of backgrounds, skills and attributes.

Very little can prepare a new AM for arriving at the National Assembly for Wales and the huge task ahead: a budget of £16 billion, responsibility for effectively scrutinising government decisions, holding the government to account in committees and plenary, and a whole host of other issues not least of which is finding your way around the building!

New AMs need to quickly establish an office in the Assembly and in their constituency or region. My own North Wales regional office is in Wrexham, close to my home. I hold AM surgeries there (and elsewhere across the region) and it is this office local residents contact when they have problems. The North Wales region stretches from Anglesey to the Cheshire border and incorporates nine constituencies and six local authorities, so the office is always exceptionally busy. Finding trustworthy and efficient staff to run the office on your behalf and often in your absence is therefore a major priority.

As an AM representing a region more than three hours away by train I also recognise the importance of finding a suitable place to live while I am in Cardiff. Assembly business is conducted mostly on Tuesdays, Wednesdays and Thursdays, but anyone expecting a straightforward nine-to-five with an hour-long lunch will be very much mistaken! Some committees start around 8 a.m. and the main plenary sessions can go on until after 7.30 p.m. It is then typical that AMs attend one or more of the events put on by lobby groups and charitable organisations in the Assembly. The information gleaned at these events informs the decision-making process at government level and the scrutiny and questioning process for opposition AMs. Later, it's back to the Cardiff flat to catch up with committee papers and the day's news and current affairs on *Newsnight*. From an equalities perspective these are hardly child-friendly working conditions!

Campaigning, living and working in an area gives a prospective AM the opportunity to meet with local 'movers and shakers' and to establish a network of contacts in a variety of organisations. Keeping in touch with the chief executives and leaders of the local authorities is very important.

Communications skills are paramount in elected office because building and maintaining relationships with individuals and groups from all walks of life is a key element of any AM's work. My experience as a magistrate and a manager within social services helped me enormously here when first elected.

As a Welsh speaker I am often asked to appear on Welsh-language television and radio current affairs programmes. One of the most recent programmes was examining how various AMs engage with the voters and what innovative means they are using to keep in touch. I don't have the time to blog, but I have a website, I've started to Twitter and have a Facebook profile. I have also just made a CD, which I am pleased to say has been very well received. The profits will go to Marie Curie Cancer Care and it was very exciting being asked to sing on the radio and television in the run-up to Christmas 2009.

Combining the different demands of Assembly member work in the region and in the Assembly is a delicate balancing act. While I am in the Assembly I make every effort to ask pertinent and searching questions at every opportunity – I like to speak plainly and ask the sort of questions the people I represent would ask if they were here themselves. It's important that people in my region know what I'm doing when I'm down in Cardiff, so I put out regular press releases and have a weekly slot in a North Wales newspaper. I also send letters to the press when an issue is particularly important to my region.

In North Wales I try to accept as many invitations as possible to events and meetings taking account of the size of the region and the time I have there from Thursday night to Monday afternoon. I also put out an annual report in the region to let people know what I have been doing throughout the year.

The first six months are centred around protocols, prioritisation and procedures, but with sound preparation a new AM can quickly establish him or herself as an effective political force.

Eleanor Burnham is a Liberal Democrat AM for North Wales

Your first six months as an MSP

John Lamont

A politician's best ability is their availability.

Congratulations – you have just been elected as a Member of the Scottish Parliament! The campaign is over and the endless hours spent canvassing, delivering leaflets, visiting local organisations, writing literature and making speeches have come to an end. Or so you thought. . .

The exhilaration I felt on being elected as the MSP for Roxburgh & Berwickshire in 2007 soon turned to a realisation that the hard work was only just beginning. Having stood as a candidate in the 2005 general election, I was familiar with the rigours of a political campaign but in my first few months as an elected politician I learned that the campaign never really stops.

After my election it became clear that most of my time would be spent looking after the 48,000 constituents in my vast rural constituency. Contact with voters had been key to my election victory during the campaign (I had personally knocked on 22,000 doors in the twelve months prior to the election) and it seemed to make sense for me to make it as easy as possible for constituents to contact me, whether by telephone, email, post or in person. As well as a special surgery tour in the summer break, I held sixteen surgeries every month, across every town and village in the constituency. I was surprised by the number of people who came to see me – over 2,000 in the first year. People want an MSP who is available to listen to their problems and, more importantly, to take action on their behalf. I have a standing invitation to any constituent who wishes to visit me in the Scottish Parliament, where I am happy to show them round the building. Despite all the modern ways of communicating with voters, people still like to know and meet the candidates who are asking for their vote – and not just at election time.

As well as engaging with constituents on an individual level, I made a deliberate effort to get involved in local organisations and community groups. I offered to visit every single community council in my constituency during my first year as an MSP. Although I didn't quite get round them all, it was a tremendously valuable exercise in building relationships and getting a feel for the main issues in each of the individual communities I represent. I have also taken time to visit many of the local schools, helping with modern studies classes and taking question-and-answer sessions. I made it a priority to meet local voluntary groups, charities and the main employers in my area, again with a view to building productive relationships and hearing about how I could assist them as their local MSP. Building up good relations with local media outlets was also a key part of building a strong local profile. My constituency also demands the added responsibilities of attending the many summer festivals and common ridings which are the highlight of the calendar in many local communities. To be honest, this is more like a perk of the job!

My constituency responsibilities also extend to my parliamentary duties. Whether it be representing the views of constituents during debates and question times, liaising with ministers about issues affecting my constituency or speaking on justice issues in my role as Shadow Minister for Community Safety, a local MSP can make a real difference in bringing important issues to the fore.

If my experience as a new MSP has taught me anything, it is the importance of keeping a campaign going and building a strong local reputation as someone who is willing to work hard for the people they represent. Good luck!

John Lamont is the Conservative MSP for Roxburgh & Berwickshire

Your first six months as an MEP

Mary Honeyball

We've been called a Tower of Babel spouting Eurobabble, though I think of life in the European Parliament as more of a magical mystery tour. Ours is truly international politics, from the Arctic Circle to the shores of the Middle East, from agricultural Ireland to Germany's industrial might, twenty-seven countries and nearly as many languages.

So how does the new MEP get to grips with all of this? Since my own debut was out of the ordinary, I had to learn the hard way. I did not start the 1999–2004 mandate at the beginning, but became an MEP after Dame Pauline Green resigned on 1 January 2000, having the dubious distinction of being the first British Euro candidate to come into the Parliament after the European elections via the list system. Neither was it an expected elevation. Placed at seven on the list with four Labour MEPs elected, no one was more surprised than me when, following Pauline's departure, the two higher candidates decided the European Parliament was not for them.

Given I was caught by surprise, I was not as well prepared as I might have been. My strong advice therefore is get yourself up to speed with the lifestyle before you stand. Visit Brussels, and possibly Strasbourg, before the election, look at the blogs and the websites and read the books on the European Parliament. Above all, pick the brains of MEPs past and present. The European Parliament set-up and its procedures are a million miles away from Westminster and the relationship between the three European institutions, Commission, Council and Parliament, takes some deciphering.

So now you've now arrived. You will need to do four things very quickly: get stuck into your national delegation, make your mark in committee, appoint staff and sort out your personal living and other arrangements.

National delegations and political groups

Your national delegation (the group I belong to, for example, is the European Parliamentary Labour Party) is the bedrock of your parliamentary activities. At the beginning you will probably feel more comfortable with your national delegation than anywhere else. They do, after all, speak the same language as you, both literally and metaphorically. The political parties in the European Parliament come together to form political groups and your national delegation will therefore be in one of these groups.

Committees

Preparation will help enormously in choosing your committees. I use the word 'choosing' loosely, as available places depend on a number of factors, but it's obviously a good idea to know what you want. You can be on two committees, one as a full member and the other as a substitute. Since there is a high turnover in the European Parliament, with over half of the MEPs in the 2009–2014 mandate being first-timers, there is huge scope, and you should be able to become a rapporteur (the person who takes a report through the Parliament) or shadow rapporteur relatively quickly.

Staff

You will need staff in Brussels/Strasbourg. This is absolutely vital and a good team around you can make all the difference. I advise making this a priority, and would suggest you include staff appointments in your preparatory work, and that you also get an idea of the way the European Parliament deals with finance for MEPs' staff.

Personal

As a British MEP you will have to stay in Brussels and Strasbourg during the week when the Parliament is sitting, and you will obviously need accommodation from day one. If you do eventually decide to take an apartment in Brussels, you should factor in the time required to deal with Belgian bureaucracy.

You will inevitably be out of the office much of the time. It is therefore wise to maximise your use of technology; a Blackberry or equivalent is essential.

And finally: the monthly trip to Strasbourg is universally disliked by the Brits. There is not much any of us can do to beat the Strasbourg blues, but a good hotel may help. Both Strasbourg and Brussels are one hour ahead of the UK, so the clocks change every week and this takes time to get used to. It is also responsible for adding to the general feeling of fatigue because, although it is just one hour's difference, your body clock is all over the place. Losing one hour here and gaining another there takes some time to get used to, and I'm not convinced the body ever recovers fully from this. You will adjust to this, but in the meantime, as with so many things, forewarned is forearmed.

Mary Honeyball is a Labour MEP for London

Your first six months as an MP

Douglas Carswell

What is the most important thing to do in your first six months as a new MP? Show some humility. Whether you won by a crushing landslide, or squeaked in by the slenderest margin, a new MP needs humility.

As the returning officer reads out your name at the count, your supporters will no doubt cheer loudly. But don't raise your arms aloft in triumph. Remember instead that most folk in your new constituency did not vote for you. Indeed, four out of every ten adults you will be meeting probably didn't even vote at all. It is going to take quite something to win them over.

Sitting for the first time on the green benches, you will soon be tempted to see politics from the perspective of those in SW1. Clever-dick questions. Ha-ha answers. Tactical positioning.

But never, ever forget how it all looks to the increasingly anti-politics people who put you there. They do not care if you're party spokesman for widgets if you are not on the case defending the local school or hospital.

Political capital cannot be banked. So spend it. In the immediate aftermath of your election success, organise yourself in the constituency the way you want without delay. Make certain you have an efficient and accessible office where local people can reach you. Arrange lots of advice surgeries in community centres, supermarkets and church halls, not just party offices. Within six months you ought to have a reputation for holding regular, well-attended surgeries, and for responding quickly to letters and emails.

As a new MP in 2005, I calculated which colleague elected at the previous election had achieved the greatest incumbency swing. And then asked him for advice on everything from diary management to newsletters. I am still learning from him.

Accept every invitation going – in your constituency, but not in Westminster. Ignore the hordes of lobbyists wanting to make you see why their clients need more public money. Instead show an interest in all the local charities and community groups, who will be wanting to get to know you. I wrote to every community group I could think of, and went to see them. Indeed, I ended up spending part of my first recess doing voluntary work for a local charity that helps drug and alcohol abusers. I learned more doing that than from any number of speeches in the Commons.

Talking of Commons speeches, I did not rush to make my maiden speech. Listen to others first – there's no shortage of talkers in SW1. It could even give you some tips on what you ought not to say.

As a new MP, the sun shines on you. But inevitably there will be some horrid days ahead. Expect to take the rough with the smooth. Or, as a colleague put it, 'remember that nothing in life is ever quite as good or as bad as it might at first seem'.

And what about climbing the greasy pole in Westminster? It's for you to decide if you are to latch onto any particular frontbench team, or curry favour with the whips in the hope of becoming one. Only you can decide if you are in Westminster principally to be a part of the legislature or to become part of the executive. But I would just say this: today many MPs answer inward to Westminster, rather than outward to the voters. Safe seat or marginal constituency, this is going to change. Even without open primaries or recall ballots, the internet and rise of anti-politics mean that your share price as an MP will be determined by far more than those in SW1. Once upon a time, an MP's standing outside Westminster reflected how far they had progressed up the greasy pole in Westminster. Soon, I suspect, it may be the other way round.

A note of caution; remember what you cannot do, and manage people's expectations of you. You cannot be in two places at once (I know, I tried). When it comes to constituency casework, avoid second-guessing professionals, or taking sides when faced with a contractual dispute between two private parties. And, whether you happen to be a localist like me or not, remember that local councillors were elected to make local planning decisions, not you.

By all means have a view on major planning issues. But make it clear that ultimately – and quite rightly – it is not your call.

And finally, don't forget to thank everyone who helped get you elected. You cannot ever thank people enough.

Douglas Carswell is the Conservative MP for Harwich & Clacton

So you still want to be a politician

Shane Greer

OK, so you've read the book. You're hopefully more confident about the process of getting selected, and if you've already been selected you've got a much better idea about how to run an effective campaign. But remember, much though this book focuses on the mechanics of getting into office, politics is more than just campaigning; if you get elected, that's when the work really begins.

Thankfully, though, the skills and techniques required to secure public office lend themselves as much to the effective execution of that office as they do to the delivery of a robust campaign. After all, the individuals you think of as 'voters' today will, you hope, be your 'constituents' tomorrow.

Far too often people think of political campaigning as a cynical enterprise which sacrifices substance at the altar of political expediency, as something that's somehow dishonest. For sure, there are times when campaigns indulge the 'black arts' a little too much, when the facts are pushed out of the way by spin, and when victory is sought with an 'ends justify the means' approach. But more often campaigns are the product of a dedicated band of activists, firm in the belief that their candidate has what it takes to deliver real and positive change in the lives of those people the candidate hopes to represent. Far from being cynical enterprises, campaigns are noble endeavours designed to bring large numbers of people together for a common purpose.

And it's in their ability to bring people together that an elected politician will prove their worth. Are your constituents angry that their local hospital is under threat of closure? It's your job to fight their corner, and the communication skills you developed during the campaign will ensure that in the media and at the lectern you're able to channel their frustrations and drive the debate in the right direction. To achieve the best outcome for your constituents, you'll need to build alliances with other politicians and persuade them to support you (even when at times it's not in their best interest). Again, the skills and techniques discussed in this book will prove vital in this endeavour.

However, in recognising the inherent power of these skills and techniques, be sure not to become too enamoured with them. They are after all mere tools. And like any tool their value is determined by the end product they make. You use a trowel to lay bricks in a new house, you use a screwdriver to construct a set of shelves, and you use campaign skills to win an election so that you can advance a particular set of policies designed to improve the lives of those you hope to represent.

Politics and politicians have been the subject of much derision recently, and there are many with aspirations for political office who are thinking twice about their career choice. Is it really worth it? Do I want to put myself through all that? But for those who genuinely want to deliver a better and brighter future for the United Kingdom, there is no other arena in which so much can be achieved.

It is worth returning to the words of Tony Blair, quoted in Chapter 1 of this book, which he uttered during his last Prime Minister's Questions:

> Some may belittle politics. But we know, who are engaged in it, that it is where people stand tall. And, although I know it has its many harsh contentions, it is still the arena that sets the heart beating a little faster. And if it is, on occasions, the place of low skulduggery, it is more often the place for the pursuit of noble causes.

totalpolitics

Britain's leading monthly magazine
for politicians and political insiders

AGENDA-SETTING INTERVIEWS
•
HARD-HITTING DEBATES
•
THOUGHT-PROVOKING FEATURES
•
THE LATEST CAMPAIGN TECHNIQUES
AND TECHNOLOGIES
•
POLITICAL LIFESTYLE, HISTORY AND CULTURE